I0521057

THE 7PILLARS

A GUIDE TO TRANSFORMING YOUR LIFE

NATHAN MORIS

PUBLISHING

Copyright © 2025 Nathan Moris

All rights reserved. No part of this book may be reproduced, stored in a retrieval system, or transmitted in any form or by any means—electronic, mechanical, photocopying, recording, or otherwise—without prior written permission from the publisher, except in the case of brief quotations used in critical articles or reviews.

Published by NM Publishing, an imprint of The 7 Pillars System LLC

New York | www.the7pillars.com

ISBN: 979-8-9939038-0-4

Manufactured in the United States and internationally

A Word of Caution

I need to say this, though it should go without saying. I'm not your therapist or your doctor. I'm not a lawyer or a financial advisor. This book is my story and what I've learned from living it. Before you make any big decisions about your health, your money, your legal situation, or your career, speak with qualified professionals who can actually help you. You're responsible for your own choices. I can't guarantee outcomes; I can only share what I've lived through and what it taught me.

TABLE OF CONTENTS

THE EDGE OF IT ALL

I had it all, or at least it looked that way on paper. The executive title, properties in three countries, ski trips to the Alps. A family. My three children attended good schools. Success. That's what it seemed like from the outside. But I was standing on the edge, staring at the emptiness. Or maybe it was staring back at me. I don't know.

I stood at the cliff alone, watching everything I'd spent years building start to come apart. The real collapse, though, was happening inside. Quiet and invisible. The wind kept pushing at me, steady, like it was waiting to see what I'd do. Whether I'd stay or just let go. Below me, the sea folded in on itself, breathing almost, pulling at the rocks and, somehow, at me.

I felt numb, as if my body were no longer mine. My hands trembled, but I couldn't feel them. My breath came in shallow bursts, sharp and uneven. And then, just a few words spoken. Ordinary, almost, but unmistakably final. They tore through everything. My future, the one I had built, sacrificed for, poured myself into brick by brick, was gone, swept away in an instant of brutal knowing. The picture-perfect plan. The framed photos on the mantel of who we used to be. That life had vanished.

How did all that effort lead me to this point? The life I had spent decades creating had disappeared in an instant, and in its place was this. This chasm stretching out before me.

I had followed the script we're all handed from the day we step into the world: work hard, climb higher, secure the future. Play by the rules, and you'll be rewarded with a sense of meaning. Or so we're told. But no one tells you what to do when you reach the top and feel something fundamental is missing, nor what to do when it all falls apart. As I stood there, staring into the void, it hit me: I had done everything I was supposed to do, yet here I was, clutching at memories like shadows, the life I had built dissolving in the darkness.

I had been running for so long. I kept wanting, chasing, reaching for the next rung. But in that moment, there was nothing left to pursue. No clear next step, no system to repair what had cracked. No lifeline to pull me back from the edge. Just me, and the silence. Standing in the ruins of a life I once called mine.

The Crisis We Can't Ignore

At first, I assumed that my breakdown was personal. That I was the problem. I had made the wrong decisions and failed in ways others hadn't. Maybe I had been overly ambitious. Maybe this was just the consequence of not getting life "right."

But the deeper I looked, the more I saw it wasn't just me. Beneath the polished smiles was the same unspoken despair. The exhaustion, the Sunday-night dread, the dull ache that won't leave: an emptiness spreading through us like a slow poison. Researchers call it a societal breakdown at epidemic levels.[1,2] But beneath the labels, it was the same silent question: Is this all there is? We were all playing the same game, following the same script. And yet, the more we achieved, the more lost we became.

Psychologists, neuroscientists, even the U.S. Surgeon General had been sounding the alarms for years.[3] But most people weren't listening. Depression was at record highs. Teen suicides were skyrocketing.[4] Loneliness and isolation were surging. The modern world, always on, always chasing, was driving people to burnout. And the worst part? We blamed ourselves for not being happy. For feeling unfulfilled. For thinking we had done something wrong.

The Illusion Shattered

With my life unraveling before my eyes, I did the only thing I could think of. I tore apart, piece by piece, the building blocks of the models we're taught to live by. I spent years searching for answers, to uncover the hidden code underneath it all: the symbols we missed, the facts buried in plain sight. Books and science joined with time-tested wisdom and modern psychology. Anything to explain why so many of us feel that same lingering ache. That elusive, unshakable knowing: life must be more than this.

And what I found shocked me. There is a flaw at the core of the systems we live by. And it's been there all along. Once you see it for yourself, everything will shift. When you finally realize you've been misled, that the life you're living was never designed to bring fulfillment, you're left with the real question: What now?

I understand if you're skeptical; I would be too. But this is more than just a feeling. I'll show you the scientifically proven truths I uncovered. Troves of research, data, and evidence confirmed what I had only sensed: something is broken. Not just around us, but within us.

We're living with an outdated internal wiring system, built for survival in a world that no longer exists. Our emotional, mental, and physiological responses, sculpted millions of years ago, are now misfiring in today's always-on, hyperstimulated reality. There are no saber-toothed tigers to outrun. Just inboxes, traffic, and breaking news piling on, hour after hour, until our nervous systems fray.

But here's what most people miss.

This primordial circuitry isn't just running in the background. It's actively driving your choices, fueling your anxieties, and distorting your deepest needs—and you're not even aware that this is happening. To understand how and why, I'll introduce you to the Foundation, where the hidden forces finally come into view. The neural systems influencing your daily behavior. The invisible architecture of your decisions.

But the Foundation was only part of the answer. Breaking free required something more: a complete framework that would rewire how I thought, how I chose, how I moved through the world.

The Journey

I nearly lost my way as I ventured further on this journey. Each time I thought I'd arrived, I realized I was only scratching the surface. But ultimately, I had two choices: continue down the same road, pretending I didn't see the truth, or throw it all out again, and go even deeper. So, I chose depth over comfort.

At the time, I had no idea what I was walking into. What started as a search for answers unraveled all that I thought I knew. I didn't just question my life. I had to deconstruct it. Layer by layer. A years-long descent within, hacking away at old patterns, tearing down inner walls, rebuilding from the foundation up.

What I found wasn't comfortable. It required dismantling every assumption I'd made about success, meaning, and who I thought I was supposed to be. I was forced to face the illusions we take for reality. The ones shaping so many of us. And finally, then, confront the deepest questions we carry. What actually makes life worth living? And what do we do when the answers we've relied on stop working?

Over the next decade, I immersed myself in the science of change: cognitive behavioral therapy, mindfulness-based approaches, and the latest research on well-being, neuroscience, and how purpose takes shape in the human mind. But I didn't just study them, I lived them. I ran experiments in real time: in my work, my relationships, my daily rituals. Some failed. Some undid me. Others rewired me from the inside.

Slowly, a structure began to form, etched into the bedrock of the life I was trying to build. It appeared in brief moments of clarity. Not gentle answers, but raw truths I hadn't been ready to see.

This Book Is Your Invitation

This isn't just my story. It's yours. If you've ever followed the rules or built the life you were supposed to, only to feel something missing, you already know. The old map leads nowhere. At least, not to the life you long for. As the poet Rumi once asked, "And you? When will you begin that long journey into yourself?"[5]

What follows is drawn from the real events in my life, and the inner transformation that shaped what came next. Some names have been changed to protect privacy, and certain scenes have been condensed for clarity. Yet the core experience is intact, grounded in lived truth. It's not fiction. It's a real descent. And what I discovered at the bottom wasn't a theory.

It was a series of Shifts, each one dislodging an old belief and bringing a new awareness. They didn't arrive all at once. They came when I could no longer avoid them, when something broke open. And yet, each Shift demanded more. That I go further, dive deeper. But what I didn't expect was what came next. Taken together, they revealed a system, one that didn't just help me rebuild; it changed the way I live.

If you choose to walk down this path, you won't just witness these Shifts, you'll feel the unlock within you as they reorganize how you see yourself and what matters. Those lessons and tools are woven into the story itself, emerging through lived moments, failures, and the structures shaping my life.

One word of caution before we start. This book won't give quick fixes or comforting answers. There is no shortcut. The only way out is through. To understand how the elements come together, walk with me on this journey. Not to revisit the past, but to move through it step by step. And when you do, it will awaken new ways of seeing, thinking, and engaging with the world.

That's how the 7 Pillars were born. Not as ideals or theory, but as a practical system for navigating life. One designed to help you make sense of your patterns, decide when clarity is gone, and rebuild without pretending life is simple.

This is not a one-size-fits-all approach. It won't give you premade answers. Instead, it equips you with a new map, one you can use in moments of darkness to rebuild with purpose. And when you do, something remarkable starts to happen. You don't just find direction. You transform.

This won't be comfortable. You'll have to look at things you've been avoiding. And if you do, you might discover what I found: a way through.

This is what saved me when nothing else worked: a guide, a system.

It will change how you understand yourself, and how you build the life that comes next.

Let's begin.

Part 1
THE COLLAPSE

CHAPTER 1
The Cliff

The Call That Changed Everything

The call came, and with it, my world shattered. I still clung to hope, desperate, naïve, but then, two words cut through it all: "It's over."

Silence. A pause so heavy it swallowed everything. I begged and pleaded, grasping at anything that might undo the inevitable. But deep down, I already knew. It was no longer an argument; it was something I could no longer fix. It was the turning point, where my life, as I had known it, ended.

For years, I built what I thought was the perfect life. A successful career. A beautiful family. We lived in a large house with a private gated driveway. Mornings were filled with familiar voices, and we enjoyed holidays in our chalet in Switzerland or our house in Provence. Stability and achievement.

Then, in an instant, the future I had planned for and envisioned was gone. The pain hit like nothing I'd felt before. I had been so focused on work, on climbing higher, that I failed to see what mattered most was coming undone.

The Pull of the Void

I hung up. The weight in my chest was suffocating. A fine tremor moved through me, as if the body understood before the mind did. Everything around me seemed to pull back.

I stood there, unmoving, the limestone cliffs of Corsica dropping away just ahead of me. The wind beat into me with a force that made it hard to stay balanced, as waves crashed hundreds of feet below. Then, without thinking, my feet moved even closer toward the edge. Toward the void. For the first time in my life, I felt something unfamiliar: the depths calling me. There was no drama in it, no self-pity. Only quiet. A single sharp moment where I questioned if there was anything left of me that could go on.

I stumbled aimlessly along the rugged coastline, a heavy, burning weight pressed against my chest. I had come to Corsica to try to piece together what now lay in ruins. To understand where it all went wrong. To find a way forward, or at least, to try.

At some point, we all face a crisis that pushes us to a breaking point. You end up at the edge of your own cliff, unsure of how to overcome the challenges before you and which path to take. Whether it's illness, divorce, the loss of a loved one, the collapse of a dream, or simply realizing you're not living the life you want, these reckonings strike with such power that you're left shaken and disoriented.

As I stood on that windy ledge in Corsica, my world unraveled. The foundation I had built, the life I had carefully crafted, was crumbling beneath me. Images were spinning in my mind, one after the other. My children, the joys of my life, waving goodbye. My family, my sense of identity, the version of me I thought was real, all dissolving into a blur of uncertainty. I didn't just lose them. I lost the world I thought I belonged to. Numbness. That was all that remained.

It is strange how, in moments like these, the day-to-day worries that once consumed us suddenly vanish. My sense of self-importance, so long tethered to professional success and the illusion of control, evaporated. I had climbed to the upper echelons of a multinational company, yet none of it mattered now. I felt small. Alone. And in that loneliness, I saw, with stark clarity, what actually mattered. The unhurried hours we shared as a family. The simple, unremarkable joy of spending time with my children, a presence I had once taken for granted. Suddenly, everything felt ephemeral, like morning mist. It could all be gone in an instant.

No one prepares you for this, or teaches you how to navigate the turning point when the life you built ceases to be your own. And yet, there I was, standing at the threshold of a life I no longer recognized.

My mind filled with worst-case scenarios, a relentless spiral of fears I couldn't suppress. I looked toward the vast open space before me, realizing I had no idea where to go or how to begin again. The waves rose, shattering into white spray against the stone walls below. The wind howled, its force tugging at me, urging me forward. I moved closer to where the world fell away.

I wandered in a daze, my thoughts circling in endless loops. Eventually, I came across a narrow path winding down into a small canyon. Ruins lay scattered along the way, old stone houses, built generations ago, their walls weathered but standing. Step by step, I descended toward the sea, the scent of wild flora thick in the air. My body moved instinctively, yet my mind remained distant, consumed by grief and disbelief.

Finally, I reached the final drop-off. The precipice. The end of the path.

The Promise

The wind tore through the rock face, ricocheting up from the ledges like a force refusing to settle. I planted my feet firmly, resisting the pull. Below me, the sea hurled itself against the rocks in a steady rhythm. I stood silent, unmoving. The weight of it all pressed against my chest.

I closed my eyes.

I focused on my breath, on the pulse of the air around me, on the warmth of the sun battling against the cold gusts rising from the sea. I had nowhere to go. Nothing to do. No more plans, no more strategies, no more battles to fight. My chest heaved, but I had no tears left. And in that emptiness, I finally stopped resisting. Stopped fighting against reality. I wasn't just at the edge of the cliff. I was inside a collapse, something vast and hollow having opened within me. And for the first time, I let myself feel all of it. The weight of it. The uncertainty that pressed in. The truth I could no longer avoid.

This was the end of my previous life.

At first, there was only pain. But then, an undercurrent. The wind roared, the sea exploded into foam below, and yet… a calm settled inside me. The frantic noise in my mind began to quiet. I stopped feeling consumed by sorrow and the swirl of what I lost. I accepted the reality that I was facing. Slowly, but surely, silence enveloped me. I leaned into the wind, with my arms rising up and spreading wide. In that stillness, as I lifted my head and heart to the sky, a force stirred, subtle but undeniable. It wasn't a revelation. It was simply a sense that I could no longer stay where I was. That moving forward was the only choice, even if I didn't know where it would lead. Somehow, I felt I needed to make a commitment, a promise: to what or who, exactly, I couldn't say right then.

I looked up and said out loud: "I promise." I wasn't speaking to anyone. Or maybe I was speaking to it all. To the sea, to the sky, to a presence beyond myself.

This is the beginning. The life I have known is over. But this moment, this storm, will not be my undoing. I will rebuild. I will find my way back. Not to who I was, but to who I was meant to be. From this day forward, I promise to reconnect to my authentic and true inner self.

I drew in a slow, trembling breath.

Forgive me. For all the ways I abandoned myself. For the choices that led me here. For the years I spent chasing what never truly mattered. Give me the strength to stand again. To search. To listen to what I have ignored for too

long. To re-embark on a new path of discovery and rebuild my life. I ask for
support as I start along this new journey.

A steady resolve settled in me. There was no clarity or relief left in me,
only a choice taking shape. A decision to stand, to move forward, because
the only alternative was to keep slipping into numbness. I stood there for
a long time, letting the weight of it all sink in. A moment before I had
been trapped between two forces: one pulling me toward despair, the
other toward the unknown. And yet, as I spoke that promise into the open
expanse before me, a third possibility emerged.

Neither escape nor collapse. But transformation.

I closed my eyes and exhaled, releasing a weight I had carried for years:
the illusion that I was in control. The pressure, the expectations, the stories I had told myself about success, security, and stability had already
crumbled. I sensed that the path would be rough, to say the least. I did
not realize the depths I would fall to, and how much further I would still
have to descend. There would be significant pain, many times where I
would lose my way, when what I was doing no longer felt meaningful,
while confronting parts of myself I didn't yet know were there.

For the first time in years, I wasn't clinging to an identity. I wasn't trying
to fix things. I wasn't trying to make sense of the past or map out the future.
I was just… there. Present, standing at the edge of my old life.

But somewhere within that pause was an almost imperceptible current. A
spark. It was faint, but unmistakable. A single ember glowing in the darkness. It wasn't hope. Not yet. Hope still felt distant, abstract, a luxury for
people who weren't standing in ruins. But this? This was deeper. Something primal. More essential.

A pull, a pulse of life still stirring beneath the weight of what had been lost.
It wasn't strong enough to erase the grief, the regret, the sheer magnitude
of what had been torn apart. But it was there. A trace of possibility.

I opened my eyes. The wind still howled and the sea raged. Nothing outside
had changed. Within me, however, something had broken free. What I didn't

know, what I couldn't yet see, was that this single collapse would unravel far more than a relationship. It would peel back the entire blueprint I had built my life on. And in its ruins, I would find a truth I never expected.

I turned away from the ledge. Not because I had answers or knew where to go. But because staying meant decay, the slow fading of a self I could no longer hold together. I took a step forward. That step didn't come from clarity or courage. It came from something deeper. A tension I had long ignored. Old forces I had tried to suppress were surfacing. And soon, they would collide. Psychologist James Hillman once wrote that "sooner or later something seems to call us onto a particular path... This is what I must do, this is what I've got to have. This is who I am."[6]

I didn't yet recognize it that day on the cliff.

But that deeper pull, the one that refuses to be ignored, had already taken hold.

CHAPTER 2
Two Voices, One Mind

The Seeds of Conflict

We all feel it, even if most of us can't explain what it is. One voice pulls you toward safety. Get the job. Stick to the plan. Don't mess it up. The other insists that there's more to feel, more to live, more to become. For years, I thought this tension was just mine. A flaw in my wiring. Always one foot on the gas, the other on the brakes.

What I later discovered, and science eventually confirmed, is that this inner struggle isn't just personal. It's ancient. It's universal. And it's wired deep into our brains. I didn't realize, until the day I stood at the edge of all that I had built, just how much of my life had been shaped by this silent war.

I once believed my collapse came from the pressures outside me, from the job, the choices, the divorce. But the rupture began long before that, when I blindly followed one voice and betrayed the other, slowly stripping away the very foundation beneath me, until nothing was left to hold me.

This is not just about my breakdown; it's also about the conflict within you. If you've ever felt torn between what's logical and what feels alive, then you've already met them, too. And what might surprise you is that these aren't poetic ideas. They're primal. Built-in. As real as fear or hunger. Modern neuroscience has uncovered systems in our brain responsible for these exact tensions. And, without you knowing, they shape many of the decisions you make in life.

But who are they? Long before I knew the research, I had already given these two forces names.

The Seeker and the Analyst

For as long as I can remember, these forces have shaped my choices. The first, the Seeker, urged me toward adventure, compelling me to step outside my comfort zone, to experience life in its rawest form. It pushed me to travel across continents, dive into other cultures, seek love with abandon, and challenge the world's status quo. It was never satisfied with a surface-level existence. It was hungry for intensity, for meaning, for the draw of the unknown.

The Analyst, in contrast, craved structure. It was logical, meticulous. It studied cause and effect, sought out patterns, and warned against chaos. It saw the world through a lens of probabilities, calculations, and carefully measured decisions. It sought knowledge, order, and strategy. If the Seeker was wildfire, restless and untamed, the Analyst was a fortress, disciplined, and determined to stay safe. One burned with possibility, but could be fickle. The other stood steadfast, ready to weather the storms, but missed out on what lay just beyond its walls.

Even as a child, I was tuned to both. While other kids played, I filled notebooks, studying people, mapping out theories. This relentless curiosity I share with my father, a professor of sociology and anthropology. His walls were lined with books; he had amassed 30,000 over his lifetime, and his conversations were filled with questions about human nature and societal structures. I was drawn to patterns, always trying to understand how the world worked beneath the surface, trying to uncover the invisible rules that governed everything around me. In some ways, I inherited his hunger for understanding. By the time I was a teenager, I had built countless models that helped me make sense of the world around me. I became known in school as "the kid with the theories," always observing, always deconstructing, always looking for meaning in the structure of things.

But knowing wasn't enough. The Seeker wanted to feel it firsthand. As a boy, I had a poster on my bedroom wall of a man diving off the cliffs of Acapulco, suspended between sky and sea. Beneath him, a single line: "You only live once, but if you live right, once is enough."[7] That line stuck with me. Freedom. Aliveness. No safety net. But I didn't understand its weight. Not really. And so I chased what I believed was the answer.

As Antoine de Saint-Exupéry wrote in *The Little Prince*, "It is only with the heart that one can see rightly; what is essential is invisible to the eye."[8] Back then, I didn't yet grasp the truth of those words. I was still convinced the answers were out there, in the world, in the experiences I could collect, rather than within.

At 19, armed with little more than the idealism of youth and an insatiable hunger to explore, I took on whatever jobs I could to finance my travels, including working in a wastewater treatment plant, a job that paid well, but left the stench of ammonia clinging to my clothes long after I clocked out. The work was grueling, but the reward was freedom. With that money, I traveled across Asia, Europe, and the United States, embarking on a six-month journey around the world.

The Seeker came alive in uncertainty. I jumped out of planes to confront my fear of heights, hiked alone in grizzly bear territory, scrambled up the sides of volcanoes, and crawled into slot canyons miles away from anyone, just to capture their beauty on camera. I chased experiences that made my heart race, moments that made me feel utterly present and alive.

Yet even in those wild, exhilarating years, the Analyst never disappeared. My journals weren't stories; they were labs. Experiments in meaning. Every wild chapter was deconstructed, mapped, and studied. I wasn't just living. I was analyzing my own life as I went. The Analyst reminded me that, in the end, life was about being responsible. Eventually, the trip ended, and it was time to come home.

For a while, I thought I'd found a strange equilibrium. The Seeker chased wild experiences; the Analyst recorded and made sense of them. One pulled me forward, the other kept me grounded. I believed I could live in both realms, adventure and structure, instinct and logic.

Torn Between Two Worlds

But I couldn't. Because these weren't just traits, they were competing, opposing forces. When the Seeker led, life came alive until it spun out of control. When the Analyst took over, I felt safe, but life lost its luster. And so, I spent years swinging between them. And somewhere along the way, I started to split. I didn't realize that unless I found a way to reckon with both, my life would never be whole. You've felt this too. Between craving freedom and fearing instability, between dreaming big and playing safe.

Psychologists have studied and explained the Analyst in detail, the part of us that plans, predicts, and controls. It maps onto the prefrontal cortex, the brain's hub for logic and decision-making. But the Seeker? That's no metaphor. Neuroscientist Jaak Panksepp discovered the SEEKING system[9] in the brain, a primal drive for exploration and meaning. Our seeking mechanism originated as a foraging behavior, a constant search for resources such as food, shelter, or a mate. It was essential to our survival. So the voice inside that longs for something more is not just a whim or wanderlust. It's one of the primal emotional systems in the brain, hardwired into the fabric of who we are. It's not about reaching goals; it's about the quest itself, the act of seeking that makes us feel alive.

The Timeless Search

Suddenly, it all made sense. Throughout history, human societies and spiritual traditions have sought to understand not just themselves, but what lies beyond, something deeper than survival. A hunger not for more, but for meaning.

And in the process, they left behind more than monuments; they left behind maps. In the jungles of Guatemala, the ancient pyramids of Tikal lie buried in green silence, cathedrals of stone swallowed by time. In England, Stonehenge stands in alignment with the stars. No one knows exactly why. But these weren't random. They were attempts to answer the deeper questions.

Long before science gave us formulas, we were etching patterns into stone, seeing stories in the stars. Searching for some kind of compass, not only to navigate the terrain, but life itself.

At some point, we all hear them, those aching questions that press through when the noise dies down. The questions we asked as children, before the world trained us to forget. Before we were blindfolded by systems, rules, and expectations.

At the time, I knew nothing of this. I just felt it in my bones, that persistent longing. What I was about to uncover wasn't advice or theory, but a different kind of knowing. Patterns and keys that revealed what had long been forgotten, drawn from ancient texts, modern science, and human experience. When a key turned, a shift occurred. An assumption broke. What I thought I understood no longer held.

The Silent Split

These voices shaped me, but never more than at the subtle crossroads. The moments that seemed ordinary and harmless. Small decisions. Until one day you look back and realize they changed the course of your life.

We rarely notice the slide. Just tiny compromises. Little rationalizations. Until one day, we look up… and don't recognize the life we built. And that's the danger: it doesn't feel like a fall, until it's too late. Adulthood requires compromise. But the slow erosion I'm talking about is different. It's the kind that happens when we tell ourselves we're being "responsible" or "adventurous," when in truth, we're starving a part of ourselves.

I know, because I did it. Twice. Once I buried the Analyst and let the Seeker take over. Another time it was the other way around. Both times, I paid the price, in ways I couldn't see until much later. And you've probably done it too. Maybe unconsciously. But somewhere along the way, you made the same choice. The safe road, or the wild one. Don Miguel Ruiz wrote that there is always something inside us that longs to be free: "This is not who I really am. This is not what I really want."[10] Yet most of us don't hear it, or we silence it, because we're trapped by images of who we think we should be.

I learned the hard way what happens when you blindly follow one voice too far. And the consequences can be dramatic. One path led me to counting my last minutes looking down the barrel of a gun, the other left me surrounded by everything I thought I wanted, but waking up feeling empty.

What comes next is the true story of those forces at play, and the danger of not seeing them. Of how they fractured the foundation of the life I was trying to build. To understand how I got there, and what most of us don't notice at first, we have to go back. Not to the collapse, but to the quiet, invisible decisions that seemed harmless... until they weren't. The small cracks, the doubts you silence, the slow drift from what matters most.

Hidden within those moments are the truths I uncovered. Each one unlocked a new phase in my transformation. And each one can unlock something in you.

So let's rewind to the choice that set everything in motion.

The moment that would ultimately lead me, years later, to that windswept cliff in Corsica.

CHAPTER 3
Which Road to Take?

Standing at a Crossroads

It was a bright summer morning by Lake Geneva. A college degree in hand, mountains in the distance, the world spread out before me. But instead of feeling limitless, I felt the weight of expectations closing in, my parents urging me to "get serious," to "find a good job," to "build a stable life." From their point of view, there was only one path, clear, linear, leading to a certain future.

The world was telling me, "You should feel proud," yet I felt a part of me slipping away. There was this subtle ache that freedom, and the last trace of innocence, were about to be packed away. Like dreams of boyhood stuffed into suitcases and put aside. I sensed the tension growing in my chest. This was supposed to be when I finally grew up. And yet, I dreaded it.

Looking back, I see it clearly now, this was the first real fork in the road. The world was pointing me down one narrow track, toward the star we're told to chase. The real journey, the one with multiple unseen shifts, wasn't on any map yet. Just a restlessness inside me. A knowing that something didn't fit. I was at the first crossroads, where I had to choose between the two voices inside me: one that longed for freedom, for discovery, for the unknown… and the other that craved control, security, and approval. Until then, they were just part of life. And I had found a way to juggle between them. Study hard and play hard. Go with the rules and break them. But now, in that moment, the world seemed to point to only one option. And the choice I made, without even realizing it, would shape the course of my life.

To most people around me, the path was obvious: finish college, land a respectable job, climb the ladder. A no-brainer. And eventually, I attempted to do precisely that. I applied to large organizations, banks, and prominent firms. After several denials, one offer finally came through. An entry-level position at a multinational firm in the United States. My golden ticket. The safe bet. "We're proud of you, son," my parents said. I nodded, smiled. The sliding door opened, and I stepped onto the escalator. Just like that, I was off. A new chapter. Not the one I expected.

The Truth I Ignored

First stop: St. Louis, Missouri. A city somewhere out there, a dot in the middle of the American continent. I moved into a cramped, bare-bones apartment that I shared with my roommate, Alex, a sharp, wide-eyed grad from one of Brazil's top business schools. The flat had nothing fancy. A futon, a few mismatched dishes, and a single lamp casting uneven light across bare walls. We were two newcomers trying to find our footing, but we had our youth, hunger, ambition. For me, it felt like the beginning of something grand.

One cool October night, Alex and I sat on the curb outside, wrapped in hoodies, cheap red wine in hand, watching the city buzz around us. We talked about dreams. Opportunities. Making it big.

Then Alex looked at me in the dim glow of the streetlight and said: "I met them all, you know, the CEOs, even the billionaires. When I was the president of the student association back in Brazil, they were always around. Jets. Mansions. Power. And yet…" He paused. Looked down the street as if scanning for an answer only he could see. "Most of them weren't happy. Not even close." Alex leaned forward, elbows on his knees, the shadows carving sharp lines across his face. Then he said: "Addicted. Divorced. Numb. They'd built castles with no windows. It all looked perfect on the outside. But inside... it was cold."

I stayed silent. That kind of truth cuts deeper when you're still chasing the dream. "Money's not the enemy," he said. "But it doesn't fix the emptiness. The happiest people I met weren't the richest. They were just... aligned. Doing what felt meaningful to them. Something that felt real." I nodded. Pretended to agree. But deep down, I still believed I could outrun the trap, that I could climb the ladder and stay whole, that I could have it all, without losing myself.

I didn't realize it then, but that belief would cost me more than I imagined. It would impact my health, my relationships, and one day, my role as a father. I remembered his words years later, after the burnout, after the stress, after I'd lost myself chasing someone else's idea of success. Truth can be spoken too early. You hear it, but don't let it in. That night, Alex handed me a glimpse of what lay at the end of the path I was sprinting down. He offered me a mirror, and I looked away.

In those early days, St. Louis carried a sense of forward energy. A new city, a new rhythm, a new version of me waiting to emerge. Everything felt open, unwritten. The routines of Geneva were a distant memory. Now, every corner was full of new streets, neon signs, strange accents, and the thrill of what could happen. It wasn't a beginning. It was a new life.

Even though St. Louis lacked the alpine peaks I loved, no mountain trails to disappear into, I made it work. I found joy in the little things: smoky jazz bars tucked into basements, nights that stretched long with conversation and possibility. On weekends, I chased nature, camping in wooded valleys, building fires under constellations I could only recognize by shape, standing beneath freezing waterfalls, the shock of it reminding me that I was alive. The newness, the movement, the sense that anything was still possible.

That winter, I flew back to Geneva for the holidays. One night, I slipped into the old bar I used to haunt as a student, the one with the uncomfortable stools and sticky wooden floor. I ran into an old acquaintance. We chatted by the counter, just like we had many times before. Halfway through the conversation, it hit me that he had no idea I had moved. Six months had passed. My life had changed completely. But his? The same bar, the same beer, the same old jokes.

And that's when I saw what transformation isn't. It doesn't happen while you're standing still. You have to step off the path. Risk the unknown. Otherwise, time just loops, and you're still exactly where you were, only older.

That night, as I walked through the streets of Geneva, I felt it in my chest how much I had changed. St. Louis wasn't perfect, but it was movement. I told myself I could be fulfilled anywhere, as long as I kept learning. Kept breaking routine. I didn't know then that I was hardwiring an addiction, not to place, but to motion itself. Sometimes movement looks like freedom, when it's really a disguised way to run.

As I settled into my job, the novelty of living in a new city started to wear off, and a silent rumbling rose from within. At first, I thought it was just a phase, a passing unease. But as the months stretched on, the daily grind felt mechanical. The spark I once had dimmed.

Each morning, I followed the same ritual: shower, coffee, the drive to work. I should have felt grateful. I worked for a respectable firm. My family was proud. But instead, I felt dread: the weight of habit resting on my shoulders like an iron cage.

I was living a monochromatic life. One dimension. Mostly focused on my career. Emotionally, spiritually, I was starting to feel empty. That real unlock would come much later, after I uncovered the 7 Pillars and began to see what I'd been missing all along.

During meetings in St. Louis, my mind wandered, imagining places I'd rather be. At first, I wrote it off as normal restlessness. But the feeling only grew. The Seeker was no longer a background presence. It was screaming.

It felt trapped. But how could I justify walking away from the path I had spent years preparing for? Everyone around me thought I was doing well. That I was on the rise. But inside, I was starting to fracture. And it's always the cracks you don't acknowledge that come back to break you open.

I was about to confront a question that would haunt me for years: Would happiness come from following the blueprint I'd been handed... or from daring to break it? I didn't know it then, but that question resurfaces. Not just in periods of doubt, but in the biggest decisions of our lives. And one day, it demands an answer we can't ignore.

I was drifting toward a life I never consciously chose. And the scariest part? I was getting good at it. Competent. Comfortable. On paper, everything looked fine. But inside, I was disappearing. Ten months in, the pull became unbearable. One afternoon, an email arrived: I'd be working on Saturday. Another weekend gone. I stared at the screen, heart pounding, throat tight. Something snapped.

And I quit. Walked away from the certainty of a corporate ladder I had barely begun to climb. Packed my bags and set off for Central America. As the plane took off, I looked out the window at the grid of highways fading below me. I had no plan, just an unshakable sense that a different kind of life waited out there. Something I couldn't find in a cubicle.

Officially, I told people I wanted to become fluent in Spanish. That it would open up better career opportunities. But that was just a cover story. The one I sold to my parents, who reluctantly agreed, "Well, you're a grown man now. We hope you know what you're doing." But I had no clue.

The truth? I was running. Running from the polished mask I was already wearing. Running toward something wild, something unknown. Chasing freedom. I had saved enough to take a few months off. But the moment the plane cut through the clouds, a voice rose from deep within: "This matters. Don't waste it." And for the first time in a long time, I heard the Seeker stir.

It reminded me of a line from Edward Abbey, an author my father once pressed into my hands when I was young, telling me I'd understand one day: "May your trails be crooked, winding, lonesome, dangerous, leading to the most amazing view. May your mountains rise into and above the clouds."[11]

Guatemala: Stepping Off the Grid

The bus rumbled into Antigua just past dawn, its brakes hissing, its engine coughing like an old smoker. I stepped out onto uneven cobblestones, my feet landing in a city that felt paused in time: Spanish Baroque arches, mustard-yellow walls streaked with vines, and crumbling colonial ruins that spoke of centuries past. Volcán de Agua rose in the distance, steady and watchful, as if it was waiting for me. There was something about this place, as though the land itself remembered truths modern life had forgotten. Antigua didn't move at the speed of ambition. Time stretched into the streets, unhurried.

It felt like a different world. A jarring contrast to the corporate grind I'd left behind. My short escape stretched into a period that would profoundly reshape my view of life. But what was meant to be a temporary detour took an unexpected turn. It wasn't just a pause. It was a rupture, a line drawn between two lives I was about to live. One with almost nothing, another with everything, two extremes pulling at me. Both appealing. And for reasons I couldn't yet see, both were unsustainable.

In that moment, I had just taken my first leap. I took a deep breath, and for the first time in years, felt free. At least, for a while. In the months that followed, I experienced a level of inner peace and connection that I have often sought since. I was young, time was on my side, and I could pause my life while contemplating the options that lay ahead. But beneath the serenity, I would uncover a darker undercurrent I hadn't yet sensed, one that was waiting to surface.

"What Should I Do with My Life?"

It was one of those chance encounters that seem to happen in remote places. I was having breakfast at a little guesthouse called Arco de Noé. I welcomed the sun's warmth on my skin, easing the early-morning chill. On one of my weekend escapes from Antigua, I had discovered this small haven of peace on the shores of Lake Atitlán.

That morning, I sat in silence, taking in the view. The near-perfect reflection of Volcán Atitlán on the deep blue lake began to blur as the morning breeze picked up, drawing ripples over the surface of the water. Santa Cruz was a small village, perched on verdant hills, nothing but footpaths and silence.

I barely noticed Elsa, a travel acquaintance from Sweden, until she pulled out the chair next to me. We'd only met the day before. There was something about her presence; her short reddish-brown hair, her worn jean overalls, the way she carried herself. She had an easygoing air, but behind it, her pale blue eyes held an intensity that pulled you in.

"I have an hour," she said, leaning back, stirring her coffee with slow, deliberate movements. "Tell me what I should do with my life."

I blinked, caught off guard. Of all the things she could've asked, she'd cut straight to the heart of what had been gnawing at me. I had asked myself the same thing, first in Geneva, then again in St. Louis. And finally, I chose freedom and said yes to the road less traveled. That choice would come back to test me, not in theory but in blood and bone, through a series of events I could never have predicted. It wasn't just a passing doubt; it was the deeper question that reshapes you, waiting at every turning point. The one that reveals just how much hinges on how we answer it. And how often do we choose wrong?

I looked at Elsa. I saw it in her eyes, that same fork in the road, the one only you can feel deep in your chest. One path was the safe one her parents expected her to take: find a traditional job back home and lead a "normal" life. The other offered freedom, but uncertainty.

One option I proposed would be to take odd jobs, earning enough to travel intermittently for a few years. To taste life for a while. She countered, "But that wouldn't be fulfilling. I need something that creates a sense of meaning. I can't just work to travel." In those days, internet access was limited, and jobs from remote locations were rare, so living the life of a "digital nomad" was not an option. The work available to travelers tended to be manual labor and, as Elsa put it bluntly, "I did not spend all those years studying to end up picking berries on a farm in Australia."

She was conscious that her next choice would have a profound impact on her life. "Each choice will take me down a different route, which worries me, because I saw my parents get stuck in work that sapped the life out of them. I really don't know which path to take."

But she didn't want to be safe. She wanted real. Something she could call her own. She stood there, uncertain, caught between two voices. She didn't have a name for them, but I knew them well. That invisible pull I had spent years trying to understand, feeling it, resisting it, never quite able to reconcile the two.

As she stepped onto the boat back to Panajachel, I sat in silence, watching the wake trailing behind her. And I thought about how many others I'd met, drifting through mountain villages, lakefront docks, rooftop bars. All asking the same unspoken question: Is this it? The job, the grind, the life everyone expects.

So many of us have followed the script: Go to school. Get a job. Be responsible. And yet, there we were, half a world away, aching for more. Travel had peeled away the layers; it had awakened the Seeker, but I hadn't yet grasped that the Seeker offered no clear path. Only a hunger.

And that longing came with a cost: low pay, hard work, and a future that made no promises. Idealistic on paper, but brutal in reality. So, what do you choose? The path they hand you, or the one that pulls at your soul, even if it leads into the unknown? Most of us aren't prepared to answer that. Our families, schools, and society hand us maps drawn decades ago. And if you stray too far, the judgment is quick: He's wasting his life. But what if the real danger is staying on the path that slowly kills your spirit?

That conversation wasn't just a travel memory. It was a spark. The moment I glimpsed a question that would echo through every stage of my life. But back then, by the shores of Lake Atitlán, I couldn't see it. I was too high on freedom to grasp what had just passed between us. As far as I was concerned, my clock had stopped. I'd been handed a window of time to live and not worry, and I wasn't going to fumble it away.

Freedom or Illusion?

After completing the three-month program of Spanish lessons, I found a reason to extend my stay. I met the founder of a small startup who was hiring young international professionals. Although extremely low paying, the work allowed me to prolong the dream I mistook for freedom. Each morning, I took the one-hour ride from Antigua to Guatemala City on one of the colorful "chicken buses," crammed with people, sacks of grain, and every so often, a live chicken clucking beneath someone's seat.

Compared to the hustle of the capital, Antigua was a small enclave of peace. With no distractions, no television, no movie theaters, and just a few hours at the internet café each week, I suddenly had the greatest resource of all: *time*. Antigua moved at its own rhythm, the cobbled streets resting beneath the hush, as if the earth itself had chosen stillness, and the modern world softened to a murmur.

During my time there, I felt the pull to go inward. I read for hours in quiet courtyards and wandered through unfamiliar towns without a plan. Along the way, I met people in cafés and on long bus rides, strangers drawn together by a shared hunger for something more. I turned to books, philosophers, poets, truth-tellers. Their words struck a chord, pulling something deeper into focus.

The Seeker was given full rein during this period. Disconnected from worldly pressures, I embraced this simple way of living and felt a growing sense of connection and confidence in myself. This was a different kind of achievement, one measured not by paychecks or progress, but by the energy that flowed from within.

The urgency to "get my act together" suddenly felt very distant. I had found a place of peace. But underneath the serenity, the calm, I could sense a growing tension.

Are We Just Running Away?

I was enjoying happy hour at a small bar in Antigua, two drinks for 7 Quetzales, about a dollar back then, when François appeared out of nowhere. With his shiny hazel eyes and mischievous dimples, he had a way of pulling you in. I liked François. Everyone did. He reminded me of something Robert Louis Stevenson once wrote: "We are all travelers in the wilderness of this world, and the best we can find in our travels is an honest friend."[12] We'd met a few weeks earlier and immediately connected. He was halfway through a year-long trip across Latin America, and he carried stories like souvenirs, each one vibrant, a little wild, and full of heart.

The mood was festive that evening. Upbeat Latin music spilled through the speakers as the bar filled with laughter, clinking glasses, and the rising chorus of a familiar song. The space pulsed with movement, people swaying, leaning in closer, shouting over the noise to be heard. It was a night wrapped in rhythm and just enough rum to dull the weight of the day.

Then I noticed François's face shift. The smile had faded. He lowered his glass, eyes shifting toward the ground. His expression had gone inward, haunted, maybe, like he was watching something only he could see. His gaze then locked onto mine, steady, distant, as if the room had gone silent and some darker thread of thought had taken hold. A tension hung in the air between us, subtle but unmistakable. And then, over the hum of music, leaning forward slightly, he asked: "Do you think we might simply be in denial? Think about it. Are we really living... or just running away from the next phase in our lives?"

His question completely threw me off. I paused, processing his words, and then countered, somewhat defensively, that I was an example of someone who seized life, who took control. I was a modern-day warrior, braving the world by traveling alone on a shoestring. Armed only with a giant appetite to see the world's colors and taste its flavors, I was living proof that one could be happy with little. With my meager $400-a-month salary, I could still live a simple yet fulfilling life. In fact, I argued, I had never been happier.

François let me finish, then leaned in even closer. "You really think this is it?" His voice dropped. "Be honest. Are you actually living... or just avoiding what comes next?" The question hung there, quiet, cutting through the noise with the precision of a blade. I blinked, trying to absorb it. "What do you mean?" He didn't flinch. "Traveling is easy. It gives you movement. Something to chase. It can keep you from asking the harder questions. Like... what does your life mean? What are you building? What do you actually want?" It hit closer than I wanted to admit, and so I pushed back, instinctively, too quickly. I told him he was wrong. I was doing what most people never dared to do: living with presence, not stuck in some corporate treadmill chasing a future that may never come.

"Isn't that what the Buddha taught?" I shot back. "To be here. In the now?" He smiled faintly but didn't respond. Just raised his glass, took a slow sip, and let the pause linger between us. The music swelled. Glasses were raised. Someone nearby let out a loud cheer. But at our small table, the air was still. He didn't push. He didn't have to. The question was already doing its work. I shifted in my seat, suddenly aware of how loud the bar felt. How muted I had become. And then, maybe out of discomfort, or maybe because I wasn't ready to go there, I laughed. "Come on," I said, "not everything has to be so serious. Let's have some fun. Enjoy life a little." He clinked his glass against mine. Said nothing. And the evening slipped back into motion, as if the moment had never happened.

But it had. We never spoke of it again. But something had shifted. A thread pulled loose. A tension that didn't just fill the space; it stayed with me. I began to wonder if what I called freedom was just restlessness, well-disguised noise. What if real freedom required something else entirely? A deeper sense of meaning. Of building. Of belonging.

Much later, as the Framework took shape, the Pillars, the tools, the clarity, I would see it for what it was: the first crack in the illusion I'd been living. The misguided belief that the Seeker alone could sustain me. That adventure was enough. Long after the music faded and the night settled, his words still echoed in me. Had I really found freedom, or just distraction? Had I avoided reality in the name of living in the now? What about the longer term? If I ever wanted to have a family, to build a future, I would need to confront these questions.

The vagabond path had its poetry, but it wasn't a map. It was motion without a destination. And maybe I was just postponing confronting the real decision. The day I'd truly grow up and get serious. I didn't have the answer then. In those days, life felt like a choice between two extremes: stability or adventure, responsibility or freedom. It was the duality between the Analyst and the Seeker. But I could already sense that this binary approach wasn't the whole story.

Years later, after going through even greater trials, I finally glimpsed the full picture. I used to think the battle was only in my mind. But the truth was more complex. There were layers beneath the surface, forces shaping my everyday life without my knowing: the rhythms of my energy and the patterns of my thought, the people I held close and those I kept at a distance. Even the roles I played in the world. Each one pulling at the shape of my life. And at the center, woven through it all, something else. The silver thread I hadn't yet traced.

I had tasted freedom. But I didn't yet know how to live with it. And soon, life would show me just how steep that lesson could be. This wasn't just about one restless young man. It was about the quiet war we all carry, torn between the life we're handed and the one that keeps calling, the thrill of possibility pulling against the gravity of responsibility. I couldn't see it then. But that question, that ache, it was already working its way toward an answer. And life, patient yet ruthless, was about to provide one.

The next morning, my head splitting, I went searching for what I knew was a surefire cure: *arroz y frijoles* (rice and beans). On the edge of town, hidden at the back of a small bookstore, the quaint little Rainbow Café was my secret hideaway. I often went there to read and sample the cheap yet delightfully tasty items on their menu. That Sunday morning, as I browsed through the used books section, my eyes landed on *The Road Less Traveled* by Scott Peck.

As it happened, François had mentioned this book during one of our spirited conversations. Was it a coincidence, or something more? I bought the worn paperback and walked to the Parque Central, the historic heart of the city. I sat down in the shade of the large Jacaranda trees, surrounded by the sounds of children, hawkers selling their wares, and the water splashing from The Fountain of the Sirens. It was the perfect setting to get immersed in a new book.

Life Is Difficult

The book's opening three words, "Life is difficult,"[13] were more sobering than the rice and beans. They cut through the morning calm, a truth laid bare without adornment. It was such a stark contrast to the insulated bubble I had been living in. The author suggested that much of our unhappiness resulted from our attempts to avoid the pain that is required to face and ultimately solve life's problems.

Was I just running away, escaping to this quiet refuge, trying to forget what lay ahead: the need to take responsibility for my life, my desire to build a family, the urge to accomplish something?

I struggled with the book's core idea, that a better life, and even real love, required discipline. It clashed with everything I was embracing: spontaneity, going with the flow, seizing the moment. Wasn't that what made life feel alive? I lifted my head from the pages, lost in thought. For months, I had let the Seeker take control, drowning out the Analyst's careful reasoning. I had chased experience, avoided structure. But as I read Peck's stories of people searching for meaning, a creeping discomfort settled in.

Maybe I had been avoiding something. Maybe there was truth in what he was saying. Discipline wasn't just rules; it was ownership. The choice to plant the seeds, then tend to them. To put in the work and build what you don't yet see. And that realization was harder to ignore than I expected. I thought I was chasing freedom, but maybe it had always required effort, discipline, even. As travel writer Rolf Potts would later write in *Vagabonding*, "The idea that freedom is tied to labor might seem a bit depressing. It shouldn't be... The 'meaningful' part of travel always starts at home, with a personal investment in the wonders to come."[14]

At the time, Scott Peck's approach felt rigid, too structured, too absolute. But I couldn't ignore the uncomfortable truth: it made sense. Even in my Seeker's idyll, I had been practicing a form of discipline. This journey hadn't been entirely impulsive; I had saved, planned, and made sacrifices to make it happen. Perhaps, without realizing it, the Analyst had been guiding me all along, ensuring I had a foundation beneath my wandering feet.

And now, that same voice was growing louder. Whispering that I wasn't just stretching my freedom, but risking something more important. What if I wasn't just drifting, but slowly sliding off course? What if I were trading my future for some fleeting experiences?

I thought I could outrun the questions. That I still had time to figure things out.

But time doesn't wait.

And sometimes, it answers you with an unexpected turn, a moment that bends your life in an entirely new direction.

CHAPTER 4
When the Road Ends

A Brutal Wake-Up Call

Scott Peck's book, and François's incisive questions, had stirred something I could no longer ignore. A flicker of doubt. Was I really living... or just skillfully avoiding the next chapter?

I wasn't ready to leave. Not this life. Not yet.

Guatemala had become a kind of suspended reality. My days were filled with purpose, connection, and the rhythm of a language I was just starting to master. I told myself the tradeoff was worth it: the low pay, the chaotic city commutes, the hints of instability. That's what made it real. Alive. And just when I'd convinced myself it was enough, life decided otherwise.

One afternoon, I was at my desk in Guatemala City, staring at a spreadsheet, the hum of fans spinning above me. Nothing unusual. The clatter of keys, muted voices, and a radio murmuring from across the room. The doorbell rang. I didn't think. I just stood, crossed the room, opened the door. And stared into the barrel of a gun. *Silencio o los matamos* (Silence, or we kill you). The voice was steady, chilling in its lack of emotion. A simple order that left no room for doubt.

Four men. No yelling. Just calm, calculated force: crisp, unhurried, no wasted steps. No need for theatrics. One of them motioned with the barrel of his gun. We didn't resist. They herded us into the back room, a windowless cell of a space. The walls were a sickly off-white, smeared with fingerprints, and a single fluorescent tube buzzed overhead, flickering unevenly in the stale air.

¡Al suelo! (Get on the floor). We obeyed. They bound our wrists and ankles and then covered our mouths with duct tape. Rough. Final. My pulse thundered. The air was suddenly too thick. My thoughts ricocheted, sharp and panicked, slamming into each other with nowhere to go.

This isn't real. This can't be happening. But it was.

I lay face down on the cold tile, cheek pressed flat against the floor, heart pounding against my ribs. Around me, my colleagues were frozen. Eyes wide. No one moved. No one dared. Was this it? I had heard the stories, everyone had. Men shot over a cellphone. A woman killed for her purse. Sometimes they didn't even need a reason. In Guatemala, they said, life was cheap.

And then ... silence.

The kind that presses against your ears. Were they gone, or just waiting? My ears strained for a sound, any sound. My pulse hammered, and every shift of air felt like something was about to happen. The tension stretched like a taut wire... one more second, and it might snap. The quiet was unbearable.

Finally, after a long, suspended moment, we heard the main door slam close. They were gone.

We scrambled to free ourselves, our hands fumbling with the tape, numb and shaking. Nobody spoke. The stillness in the room was suffocating. We just sat there, staring at each other, the reality settling in. They had taken our computers, our wallets, anything of value. But what they stole ran deeper: the quiet belief that you could walk into work whole and walk out the same.

I stepped out of the building into the bright afternoon light. The world outside was unchanged: street vendors shouting, the scent of grilled meat hanging in the air, the honk of impatient drivers, as if nothing had happened. As if my world had not just tilted on its axis.

But inside, I felt it.

That night, I lay awake beneath the pale ceiling, my body still buzzing with leftover adrenaline. Every noise outside the window felt like a footstep. I kept replaying the scene when the gun was raised, the cold detachment in the man's voice. "Silence, or we kill you." My mind refused to let it go.

I'd spent years chasing the thrill of uncertainty, telling myself that was the price of feeling life in its rawest form. And yet, here I was, faced with the kind of brutal, unfiltered reality that could end a life, not enrich it. The thought needled at me. Had I crossed some invisible line where adventure had turned into recklessness? Had I mistaken living on the edge for flirting with danger?

And yet, despite it all, I told myself it was just a blip—a hazard of life in Guatemala. A story to tell later, a one-time thing. I just had to move on. Or at least, I tried to.

And then, three months later, life reminded me, again, that some wake-up calls don't come gently.

Hurtling Toward Reality

I was sitting on a packed chicken bus, the kind that rattled down winding roads with reckless abandon. Brightly painted, wildly decorated, and driven like a getaway car. The air inside was heavy, bodies pressed too close. We were packed to the brim.

I barely noticed when we approached the curve at full speed. I'd grown used to near misses. But this time felt different.

The tires screeched. Passengers shifted uneasily. I gripped the metal bar in front of me, my book slipping from my hands. The bus lurched. The world tilted. People screamed. For an instant, we hung there, suspended. And then the world exploded.

Gravity slammed us onto our side. A deafening shriek tore through the air: metal grinding against asphalt, sharp and excruciating, like steel ripping itself apart. Sparks burst from beneath us in a trail of orange fire. People shouted. The hot air filled with smoke and panic. My chest collapsed under the sudden weight of bodies. Limbs entangled, a backpack slammed into my ribs, my arms pinned—I couldn't breathe. Pain bloomed, immediate and searing, spreading like fire through my side. My worst fear came alive. I would suffocate. I tried to stay calm, but my mind was frantic. Smoke. Shouting. Someone trying to force open a window. I focused on one thing: staying conscious.

Finally, the pressure eased. Bodies shifted. People scrambled toward an opening. I pulled myself through a shattered window, legs shaking, and stumbled onto solid ground. I pressed a hand to my ribs, sharp pain flaring. Hopefully just a fracture. Others weren't so lucky. A man staggered past me, his arm torn open, muscle dangling like cloth. Blood was splattered on the dusty road. People sat dazed, clutching injuries, shock dulling their expressions.

I should have felt relief. I had survived. Again. But it never came. Instead, something else coiled inside me, slow and insidious.

Doubt.

The Point of No Return

For a year, I had romanticized the Seeker's path as soaking in life. But now I saw it clearly: this wasn't courage. It was a roulette wheel. And I'd been spinning it blindly. I had chosen to live in one of the most violent cities in Latin America. I had boarded rickety buses on cliffside roads where accidents were routine. I told myself I was fearless—but maybe I had just been reckless. Maybe I hadn't found my way; maybe I'd lost it.

François's voice echoed in my mind: "Are we really living, or just running away?"[15] Had I been chasing experiences, or avoiding responsibility? Had

I mistaken momentum for meaning, risk for depth? I had always believed that rejecting structure meant choosing freedom. But now, I saw the illusion. And perhaps, I had just traded one prison for another.

The real question surfaced again: Could I build a life I didn't need to run from? I didn't know. I saw where the Seeker's call had led me. There had to be another way, another path, a way to reconcile the opposites. But to be honest, I wasn't sure.

Still, my time had come. A chapter was closing, unfinished, uncertain, but closing all the same. So, I left. The peace I'd found was gone now. A persistent unease had moved in that I couldn't shake.

As the plane lifted, Guatemala dissolved beneath me, its beauty and danger intertwined. I didn't know if I was heading toward a safer future… or surrendering to the very system I had once slipped out of. I had tasted something here: a unique kind of aliveness.

Just before I crossed into that new life, I hesitated.

What if the path I was about to choose would bury the person I'd only just begun to uncover?

Part 2
THE RECKONING

CHAPTER 5
Entering the System

The Slow Surrender

The fall was almost imperceptible
at the time, a drift so subtle that
when it finally hit me, it felt as if
the scaffolding gave way and collapsed all at once. And yet, it was
all right in front of me. The world
around me was full of signals—
instructions for a different operating system, with tools for navigating a life like this. I just didn't
know how to listen to them yet.

The system I would eventually uncover wasn't even a half-formed idea.

Until that point, I had followed the Seeker, lost in the thrill of the pursuit,
immersing myself in different ways of living. But after Guatemala, after
duct tape and gun barrels, something inside had broken. When I arrived
back in the United States, I told myself it was time to truly grow up. To
build something solid: a life with real direction and roots.

So, I let the Analyst take the driver's seat. No questions. No resistance.
Just a quiet nod to the rules of the game: optimize, outperform, outearn.
Like so many others, I chose the path that promised both safety and abun-
dance.

The corporate world welcomed me with open arms. And I didn't just survive; I thrived. The promotions came fast. The achievements stacked up. With the money I earned, I bought my first place: a sunlit apartment with stunning views over the city skyline.

I remember one night, coming home from work, barefoot on the cold tiles, holding a glass of wine. A sultry jazz melody played low through the speakers, Norah Jones, her voice drifting across the room. A gentle breeze moved through the open balcony doors. I recall thinking that this was it, that I had made it. It felt like I had cracked life's code, and for a moment, I believed I had.

I tried to convince myself I could have both. Career and curiosity. Stability and spontaneity. I squeezed in adventure on the weekends, optimized my holidays, and called it "balance." I told myself I was still the same person, the one who climbed volcanoes and chased sunrises far from home.

But slowly, as months slipped into years, the edges of my life started to dull. Little by little, the compromises stacked up. Days filled with the blue-white glare of office lights. Conference rooms where the air felt heavy, and meetings where people nodded, trying to convince themselves that somehow it truly mattered. The adventure trips got postponed, then canceled. I said to myself, just a little longer. One more promotion. One more raise. One more year. And then I'd live fully again.

I was playing a game where the rules kept changing, every win leading to the next requirement, the next sacrifice. And all the while, something inside me grew restless. But I wasn't ready to listen. Not yet.

I was on a business trip in Europe, somewhere in the French countryside, as the train slipped past wheat fields and winding farm roads. My laptop open, typing fast, I was deep in yet another presentation. The sky outside had dulled into a soft, metallic gray. I glanced out the window and caught a glimpse of a dirt road that led to a small stone house tucked beneath bare trees. A chimney curled smoke into the windless air. And for a moment, I wondered: What if that was my life? Who would I become if I stopped striving and just… was? A part of me reacted to the gentle rhythm it invited. Somehow it felt alive, at peace. But then the train jerked forward. My laptop chimed, a calendar alert for the next meeting. Just like that, the image vanished: the dirt road, the smoke, the stillness, swallowed by speed and signal.

I enjoyed my work, solving hard problems, shaping strategy, working with people I respected. But I couldn't keep it contained. The hours stretched. Sunday nights filled with emails. The urge to check my work followed me into vacations, into dinners, into bed.

And yet, when it came time to choose, I fell back on what I knew. I tried harder. I doubled down. At times, it even seemed to work. But something about it felt increasingly narrow, as if the path itself were closing in.

The Lies We Tell Ourselves

There's a point in our life when we stop questioning and begin to tell ourselves stories to smooth out the discomfort. I had created my own script for it. This is adulthood. Responsibility. Everyone feels this way sometimes. So be grateful. Look at what you have. I am part of the lucky ones, those who are succeeding. On paper, it explained the unease I felt and gave it a neat label.

We all do this. That's how it begins: we try to justify. But deep down, we know when the excitement has dulled, when the passion has faded, when our days have become predictable loops of obligation. And yet, we keep moving forward, as if momentum alone will lead us somewhere we want to be.

And step by step, we walk ourselves into a life that's nothing like the one we once imagined, not through force or failure, but through what felt right, familiar, and safe.

The Comfort Trap

When you've built the life everyone says you should want, the career, the income, the stability, it becomes harder to ask: Is this the life I am meant to build? Comfort isn't dangerous because it hurts; it's dangerous because it seduces. It keeps you still, numbs without wounding, and satisfies just enough to stop you from reaching. It tells you to settle. And the longer you stay in it, the harder it becomes to leave.

For a while, I believed I had made it. I was successful. I built a life that kept expanding. A beautiful and loving wife. Children who lit up my world. A life others admired. It gave me a real sense of meaning and justified the sacrifices I was making. And it worked, for a time.

But somehow, the more I embraced the system, the more something inside me began to dim. It happened quietly, depth not lost but redirected, poured into work, responsibility, and the visible rewards that followed. The cars got shinier. The houses got bigger. I chased the polished reflection, trading raw, simple moments for high-end dining, luxury resorts, curated escapes. They became my substitutes, but they carried none of the feeling, none of the fire. The wild, untamed wasn't in the picture anymore.

Sometimes I'd open the hallway closet and see it there, the old black duffel bag scarred from years of use. Inside was my climbing gear: ropes coiled tight, carabiners worn down by sandstone, a single belay device. I knew how it felt in my hands, fingers jammed into narrow cracks, my heart pounding as adrenaline surged. I had ventured into the mountains without a finish line, guided only by instinct, breath, and silence. I kept telling myself, "Next spring, next summer." But the bag stayed zipped.

Life had slipped into a lower gear. I no longer planned escapes to the peaks; I collapsed onto the couch instead. It wasn't just physical exhaustion. It was a subtle fading of spirit, one postponement at a time, until one day you realize: you're no longer choosing your life. You're just maintaining it.

And worst of all, I stopped doing what mattered most. I stopped sending my wife the midday texts, leaving small notes, and planning thoughtful surprises. The small things faded first, because I let them fade. And then, slowly, so did the deeper connection. My wife was beside me, but I was a ghost at my own table. I wasn't mean. I was just... gone, not in body, but in presence. She would tell me about her day, and I'd nod at the right times, but my mind was always elsewhere, chasing the next project, the next achievement, the next rung on the ladder.

I had followed the prescribed path. I had done what the world told me to do: build, achieve, provide. But in the process, something vital had gone missing. I wasn't the first to feel this slow erosion. Hermann Hesse captured it perfectly in Siddhartha: "Slowly, like moisture entering the dying tree trunk, slowly filling and rotting it, so did the world and inertia creep into Siddhartha's soul; it slowly filled his soul, made it heavy, made it tired, sent it to sleep."[16]

A French expression captures this perfectly: metro, boulot, dodo—commute, work, sleep,[17] a story of resignation in three beats. By the time the discomfort becomes unbearable, the system has done its job. You're too tethered by mortgages, expectations, and social pressure to make a real move.

I had seen it before. My parents, once full of life, slowly stopped doing the things they loved. They still could. They just... didn't. Increasingly, their time was spent in front of the TV. And that same quiet surrender was creeping into my life. I wasn't living with urgency. I was sleepwalking through routines, busy, tired, mildly content, but something vital had faded.

That kind of numbness doesn't last. Not forever. Eventually, something cracks. And when it did for me, I found myself standing at the edge itself. Literally. A line I'd once read from Paulo Coelho came back to me then, "If you think adventure is dangerous, try routine. It's lethal."[18]

Distractions: The Modern Escape

I remember scrolling one night, mindlessly, compulsively, the room lit by the cold blue glow of my phone. My wife was beside me, reading. The pages of her book turned with soft rustles. I didn't hear them. My thumb kept moving. Up... Up... Up... As if meaning might surface if I scrolled far enough. I had a rare window of stillness... and I couldn't sit with it. The feed kept refreshing with travel reels, house remodels, surfers gliding across glass waves. It all blurred together, only feeding my restlessness, and yet, I just kept scrolling.

Life is not just full of distractions; it is engineered for them. Our attention has become a currency, and the world is designed to keep us consuming and engaging. I used to believe these were harmless detours, light entertainment to soften the weight of a hard day. But they are something else entirely. They are the modern world's most effective way of keeping us from confronting reality.

Distractions are easy. A quick dopamine hit. Like sugar, they spike our sense of pleasure and leave us emptier than before. The problem seemed simple enough: time. If we just had more of it, everything else would fall into place. But beneath the scrolling sits a deeper hunger, something rawer. The words for it were not new. Hermann Hesse, in *Steppenwolf,* captured it this way: "A wild longing for strong emotions and sensations seethes in me, a rage against this toneless, flat, normal, and sterile life."[19]

With all the technology and conveniences we've created, you'd think we'd have more time. To do what matters, to feel alive. Instead, we have less. Not because life is harder, or because we have more to do. Centuries ago, Blaise Pascal put it starkly, "All of humanity's problems stem from man's inability to sit quietly in a room alone."[20] He was right. That, perhaps, is the real test, not how high we can climb, but whether we can sit still, with ourselves.

At some point, I had to face the uncomfortable truth: we fill our lives with distractions because, without them, we would have to ask ourselves the hardest questions. Is this the life I want? Does my life have meaning? What am I avoiding?

We'd rather stay busy, postponing our dreams to later. But later is a lie. The years slip by in a haze of work, entertainment, and routine, and then one day we wake up and wonder where it all went.

That night, as I closed the app on my phone and stared at the dark ceiling, I didn't feel relaxed. I felt hollow. Distractions don't just waste time; they dull the light inside us and blur what is true. Beneath the constant motion, there's always a voice trying to speak. But we scroll right past it. We mistake the noise for life itself. As Sadhguru writes in *Inner Engineering*:

"When most people say 'life,' they mean the accessories of life… The one thing they miss is life: the life process itself."[21]

Moments of Clarity

It wasn't until a trip to Brazil that the illusions finally broke. I had come to Camburi, a small town a few hours from São Paulo, hoping to step away for a while, to clear my head. My friend Alex had insisted, "Come to my beach house… you really need to disconnect."

The air was warm that afternoon, the waves steady, low clouds pressing down on the horizon. I walked down the beach toward some large boulders. My mind was this constant noise, thoughts tumbling over one another, never finding rest. To-do lists, projects, and future worries pushed out the silence I so desperately craved. Even here, in this place meant for peace, I felt the weight of all I carried.

I scrambled up the rough stone to a flat ledge overlooking the ocean. The waves kept coming, steady, unbothered, indifferent to the storm within me. I closed my eyes, inhaled deeply, and tried, to just be.

But my mind resisted.

The impulse was to reach for my phone, as if silence itself were something to escape. I was so trained now to be productive, to always be busy. Programmed to avoid pauses.

But as the minutes stretched into an hour, somewhere in that tension between motion and stillness, I began to surrender. My mind didn't quiet all at once; it fought, clawed for distraction. But eventually, it gave up. And in the quiet that followed, images began to surface.

My son reaching for me while I checked my phone. The way my wife's voice had dimmed over the years, her laughter rarer, our connection thinning, like breath in high altitude. The promises I'd made to myself, of weekends of adventure, slow mornings, guitar chords in the sun, quietly broken, then forgotten. But I had tried. Tried to balance the demands of work with being present at home. Telling myself the long hours were temporary, that I was building something for us, that this was what responsibility looked like. But somewhere in the constant juggling, I lost my way. Not because of one big decision, but a thousand small ones. A slow unraveling. A soul folding inward.

One thought cut through it all. This can't be it.

I didn't know what to do. I had no idea what came next. I only knew I couldn't go back to the life I'd been living unchanged. Sitting there above the ocean, I realized I didn't need another milestone. I needed a new compass. A way to navigate by a different set of rules.

For a long moment, I just sat there. Then I reached into my backpack and pulled out the small black Moleskine notebook I carried everywhere. On a blank page, I wrote three words: "Moments of Clarity."

In that instant, the shape of my life came into view. How far I'd drifted. But seeing is not enough. By then, the version of me that could act, that could change, was already slipping out of reach.

That moment on the beach in Brazil, clarity cut through the noise. But I didn't act. I let it fade. I went home and got back to work. For a while, I even convinced myself nothing had to change. Because motion feels easier than truth. But clarity, when ignored, always comes knocking. The signs were everywhere. But when you're sprinting in the wrong direction, you don't stop to check for cracks in the road. You just keep running. Until the life you've built suddenly collapses beneath you.

And that was how I found myself back at the beginning, standing on the cliff.

Where It Began

Corsica. The sea roaring beneath me, a living pulse shattering against the stone, while the life I knew came undone.

Two paths now lay in ruins. I had chased freedom, and nearly died. I had embraced the system, and nearly lost everything that mattered to me. In both cases, I had tried to build a life worth living, and I had failed.

Elsa's words, spoken years earlier in Guatemala, came back to me, sharper than ever: *What should I do with my life?* And now, standing there with the sea stretching out in front of me, there was no avoiding the question. No running from it.

I didn't know it then, but I had misread the moment. I thought I finally understood what had gone wrong—that I'd simply pushed too hard, could not balance the pressures of work and family, had chosen the wrong priorities. I believed that with the clarity I'd found, I could course-correct.

I was wrong.

What I was about to discover wasn't something I could fix with just more awareness of my mistakes or better choices. Something much deeper had been at work all along, subtle, structural, shaping the path beneath my feet.

CHAPTER 6
The Slow Collapse

The Life That Vanished

After Corsica, everything came apart, as if the seams of my life no longer held. The cliff wasn't an ending. It wasn't even the real collapse. It was the moment I saw what was coming and couldn't stop it. I stepped away from the edge, hoping to hold everything together. But it was too late. The marriage I had fought to save shattered. The family

I had tried to protect, fractured. I stood in the ruins of a life I once believed unbreakable: a tower I had built from ambition, success, and family. Now reduced to rubble.

And in the aftermath, I left. I relocated to Miami, taking a new job near where my children would live with their mother. In a way, it felt like forward motion, but in reality, the downward spiral had only just begun.

Miami greeted me with its neon warmth, bright skies, and humid air. But inside, I felt cold. I stepped off the plane with two suitcases and the feeling that I had arrived in a life that wasn't mine. The sun, the ocean, the palm trees, none of it mattered. My mind was spinning with anxious thoughts, playing worst-case scenarios.

Sunday drop-offs were the hardest. I'd return to my bare apartment, with no dining table, no chairs, just me sitting on the cold tile floor, eating dinner off a storage box. Despite Miami's heat, it felt like a prolonged winter had settled within me. It wasn't just the emptiness of the apartment. It was the silence. No sounds of my children playing in their rooms. No morning chaos of breakfast and backpacks.

Just stillness. I had been alone before, but never like this.

As my heart ached, my mind spiraled. The future I had imagined had collapsed. And the promise I'd made atop the cliff? Was it just a fantasy? I shook uncontrollably for hours, trapped in a whirlwind of doubts. How would I build my way out of this?

The Nights Were the Worst

The days were manageable. Work kept me functioning. I was fortunate to have a good job, a great boss, and to work at a reputable company. But as the sun set, the nights swallowed me whole. I didn't want to sit alone in my apartment with my thoughts. Outside, Miami pulsed with distractions, bars, flashing lights, strangers offering easy laughter. A world designed to numb.

In that initial period, a few too many glasses of wine seemed so innocent. They softened the edges. Quieted the voices in my head. For a second, the ache dulled. I told myself that it was harmless. That it wasn't affecting my work, my children, or my health. But deep down, I knew better. My sister, a doctor, had warned me. Addiction ran silently through our family, an old current that changed shape but never disappeared. My mother struggled with it, as did her mother. It moves through generations like a shadow, changing form but never leaving. Waiting. And once awakened, it doesn't let go easily.

Still, I kept telling myself: I'm fine. I'm in control. But I wasn't. Control had already started to slip, steadily, like sand through closed fists. And I was too proud to admit it, too ashamed to stop pretending. At first, it was just a drink or two. But slowly, the pull increased. The urge appeared the instant I walked through the door in the evening. Just one drink to calm down, to forget... And yet, the first sip always triggered something deeper, a slow, inevitable domino effect. A desperate attempt to push back what was brewing inside me, the weight of a reality I hadn't learned to carry. But trying to escape the feelings didn't mean they went away.

On those nights alone in the city, as the hours passed, I'd find myself opening up to strangers, spilling fragments of my story. You'd be surprised how many lonesome souls sit at bars at night, suitcases full of regrets, broken dreams, failed marriages. Some had lost family; others had lost themselves. I listened to their stories, nodded in recognition, knowing we were all searching for something.

And yet, despite the noise and the company, I felt utterly alone.

There were many beautiful-looking people, but somehow, at night, the smiles felt fake, the intent too shallow. Even the beat of the music felt too fast, too loud. I longed for something real, something pure. An honest conversation, a moment of authenticity. But I was at a carnival of distorted smiles, of people laughing, trying to cover the ache they carried inside.

Then, in the haze of late nights, I'd hear it, that quiet voice from deep within, cutting through the static. "What are you doing?" At first, I ignored it. The pull of forgetting, even for a few hours, was strong. Another voice, smoother, more persuasive, whispered back: "Relax. You deserve this." And so, I let myself slip further. Let the rhythm drown it out, the drink take the edge off.

Late at night, as I walked home alone, the reality I had been avoiding came crashing in, no longer blurred by wine or music. Just me, under the glare of streetlamps, with the last traces of the night's illusion already fading. And then morning came. Unforgiving. Light poured through cheap blinds, illuminating the silence. The empty bottle. The untouched pillow on the other side of the bed. The truth sat there, waiting, undeniable and sharp.

I was becoming a stranger in the life I had built. You don't always notice when you start to veer off course. One small deviation, then another. Before long, you're miles from where you're meant to be. That's what happened to me. In the pain I was carrying, I chased anything that offered relief. Something to shift how I felt, even for just a short while. Pleasure became an escape. A way to outrun the heaviness.

The first time I opened the app, it seemed harmless, just curiosity. A way not to feel alone. But the rhythm was addictive. Swipe. Match. A surge of electricity. It wasn't desire I was chasing, but the brief warmth of being seen and wanted. A stranger, somewhere, chose me. In a world where my sense of self was slipping away, that hit of validation was intoxicating.

At first, it felt like a real connection. A flicker of possibility. Someone to talk to at midnight. But slowly, almost imperceptibly, the longing shifted. It stopped being about intimacy. It became about the hunt. The chase. The illusion.

But deep down, I was just looking for a person to hold me in the dark and not let go. Someone who would see the imperfections and stay. But that isn't what I found. The faces changed; the emptiness did not. The nights all ended the same, me alone, staring at the ceiling. The high, fleeting; the emptiness, constant. I wasn't just lonely. I was lost. I was chasing hit after hit of alcohol, affirmation, distraction. Anything to outrun the ache. But the more I ran, the more it followed. I'd wake with the taste of regret on my tongue and the sinking feeling that I was becoming a person I wouldn't recognize, someone my children wouldn't either. Yet the pain wasn't visible. It was inside. And it wasn't going anywhere until I was ready to face it.

But at the time, I wasn't. I just kept going anyway. Yet somewhere beneath it all, I felt it. There had to be some other way. Something had to change before my life came apart completely. And so, I did what the Analyst in me always did when the ground crumbled: I started looking for answers. What I found didn't just explain my collapse. It revealed something far more unsettling—a pattern I'd been living inside without knowing it existed.

CHAPTER 7
Breaking the Spell

Storms Don't Arrive Overnight

One Sunday afternoon, I stood on my balcony in Miami Beach, staring at the ocean. A storm gathered on the horizon, massive clouds swelling upward, swallowing the sky, the wind rising, electricity crackling in the air. Minutes ago, the sky had been clear. Now, the atmosphere was tightening, charged with something inevitable. Storms don't arrive unannounced. They build. The air

shifts, the pressure mounts, the warnings are there, until suddenly, it's all around you.

Being at the cliff's edge in Corsica wasn't the breaking point. The pressure system had been gathering for years. I had spent my life believing I was in control, that I was deliberate, made conscious choices. But standing there, watching the storm roll in, I had to admit the truth. I had been blind. And I created my own downfall. Losing myself didn't happen overnight. It was a slow drift in priorities here, a compromise there, an erosion of what mattered. And now, I was left with the wreckage.

A song from my childhood echoed in my mind, Claude François's "Comme d'habitude."[22] As usual, we will just pretend. That's exactly what I had been doing. Pretending. Convincing myself that my life was special, when really, I had only settled. I had let the Analyst take over, allowing one part of me to dominate everything else, trading adventure for security, growth for predictability. And in doing so, I had shifted away from what once inspired me. I thought back to my younger self, the one who took risks, who was fueled by curiosity, who felt alive. Where had he gone?

But as I stood there, bare feet on the cold tile, eyes on the water, I couldn't shake the feeling that this storm wasn't only in my life. The clouds rolling in weren't just over Miami. They were everywhere. There was something going on.

I had followed every rule, marked every box, and still I was lost, staring into this dark pit. I began to wonder: If I ended up here, how many others had too? How many were smiling on the outside, yet barely holding it together inside? In a society that celebrates success, what if there were a broader pattern, a silent reality that was just not being spoken about?

For a long time, I thought that I had failed where others had succeeded. But then I started noticing the conversations that avoided what really mattered, glazed stares on morning commutes, the weariness behind curated smiles. The ache wasn't mine alone; it moved through everything around me. A low-grade hum beneath modern life. A shared fracture we'd all been taught to ignore.

The Hidden Epidemic

What I uncovered left me stunned. It wasn't one report, or one headline. The story showed up everywhere I looked. It began with one number: teen suicide, up nearly 60% in just a decade. Then the numbers kept coming, each one harder to ignore. Over 300 million people suffer from anxiety. Depression is now the leading cause of disability worldwide. Burnout is so widespread that the World Health Organization didn't just call it stress; they declared it a global workplace crisis.

I stopped reading for a moment. This wasn't just information anymore. It felt uncomfortably familiar. But the numbers only got heavier. What about engagement? Just 13% of employees worldwide say they feel connected to their work. That means 9 out of 10 are just surviving the day. Then comes loneliness: the U.S. Surgeon General called it an epidemic,[23] linking it to a 29% increased risk of heart disease, 32% for stroke, 50% for dementia. Even in the wealthiest nations, where all basic needs are met, life satisfaction is falling. A 2023 Gallup report confirmed it[24]: negative emotions, such as stress, sadness, and worry, have reached record highs. Not in one country. Everywhere.

I sat back, letting it sink in. The data show we aren't just tired. We are coming apart. But no one is talking about the deeper cause, not isolated symptoms, but the system itself. Modern life, the rules and aspirations we've been taught to follow, is making us sick. Progress soared: wealth, tech, convenience. But our inner lives? They are crumbling.

I didn't just see it in the data. I still see it in the faces around me, in a quiet ache that has become so common it barely registers. What I was living through wasn't unique; it was shared. Not my unraveling. Ours. And these aren't isolated symptoms, but fault lines running through the system itself. A silent epidemic, hiding behind high-speed internet and same-day delivery. Numbed by Netflix and mindless swipes and "productivity hacks." And the longer I paid attention, the more it all felt... normal. Accepted. How suffering has been rebranded as success. How burnout is seen as proof of ambition. How disconnection has become the default, and no one questions it.

It isn't just that people are tired. They are soul tired. Existentially exhausted. Running a race they never chose, toward a finish line that never arrives. And yet, we all keep going. Buying things we don't need. Dulling the discomfort with dopamine hits and distractions. Waiting for the weekend. Waiting for someday. Waiting for life to begin.

The Silencing of the Seeker

At first, I thought it was burnout, or the aftermath of collapse. But what if this wasn't just a cultural crisis? What if something deeper, older, was being starved?

The inner fire of curiosity, wonder, and desire that once pulled me forward had dimmed. I thought back to the animals I'd seen in zoos as a child. Beautiful creatures. Pacing in enclosures. They had food, water, and shelter, yet their eyes no longer searched. And then it hit me: maybe we weren't that different.

I remembered Jaak Panksepp's work on the Seeking System.[25] At the time, it struck me as insightful. Now, it felt urgent. Because what I was feeling, what so many of us feel, wasn't just exhaustion or depression. It was the dull ache of a life misaligned. A blueprint designed to dull the Seeker within us, the part wired not for survival, but for aliveness. That primal drive is wired to explore. To imagine. To move toward meaning.

When the Seeker is active, even the hardest day carries light. You feel momentum. The smallest steps feel charged. But when it's silenced, through routine and noise, you don't collapse all at once. You fade. Gradually. Like a door slowly closing.

I saw it one morning in the mirror. I was standing in the bathroom, half-shaved, steam forming on the glass. Then my eyes met my own. Something felt off, a slight dissonance, as if the reflection and I were out of tune. Like looking at an old photo and realizing you don't remember being there. The face staring back wasn't angry or sad. It was just... gone. Polished and presentable. Yes. But vacant. Like someone had filled in the lines, and in the process erased something essential.

I leaned in, looking for something familiar, but my eyes looked back at me like windows dimmed from the inside. That's what had happened to me. The Seeker hadn't vanished. It had been buried. Beneath responsibility, performance, and the pressure to hold it all together.

Because without the freedom to seek, something in us begins to decay. That's why even the most successful feel hollow. When I zoomed out, it became clear: We aren't just tired. We are starving ourselves. Of meaning. Of aliveness. The Seeking System has no room to breathe. Our lives are built for productivity, not fulfillment, curiosity, or wonder. We trade the joy of becoming for the illusion of arrival. And in doing so, we silence the part of us that is never meant to be still.

That realization split something open in me. If I had spent years suppressing the Seeker, maybe, just maybe, I could find a way to bring it back.

The deeper I looked, the more the truth revealed itself. I started seeing the cage, cleverly disguised as security. The reflection I once mistook for clarity now looked warped. A perfectly engineered loop—work, consume, compare, repeat—so polished it passes for purpose. We call it success. But it is eroding us from the inside. And still… we play along. We smile for photos. Check our likes. Hit our targets. All while a quieter question persists: Is this really it?

I had followed the script to the letter. Work hard. Build a career. Earn more. Be a provider. Be responsible. But the more I tried to hold it together, the more it came undone. And it wasn't just me. I started to see the fissures forming everywhere. People quitting well-paying jobs to live in vans. Becoming digital nomads. Moving to Bali, Portugal, and Mexico. Trading meeting rooms for coworking cafés, deadlines for surf breaks. It wasn't just rebellion; it was an escape. Not from hard work, but from meaninglessness. From a blueprint that promised so much and delivered so little.

And I realized: this was the choice before me too. To keep living someone else's story, or to write my own. As Rumi once urged: "Don't be satisfied with stories, how things have gone with others. Unfold your own myth."[26]

When the Blueprint Breaks

The full fracture came. The one that separated my life into Before and After. The rules from modern society, what we're encouraged to pursue, who we're told to become, were leading to our breakdown. This wasn't a personal failure or a short-term problem to solve. It was a broader collapse, societal, even global.

The blueprint was broken.

Once you see that, you can never go back. You can no longer walk the old roads and believe they lead somewhere. That's the 1st Shift.

It wasn't just my choices. It was the invisible architecture beneath them, the blueprint we inherit and obey. The curtain was lifted, and the world splintered open, forcing the question: What if life isn't supposed to feel this way? What if there's another way?

We're animals born to roam, wired for motion, for wildness, but instead we pace inside invisible enclosures. Routines. Screens. Roles. We're mostly overfed, overstimulated, yet starved for aliveness.

I sat there, still, trying to process it all. I saw the endless striving, the polished masks, the "look at me" posts that hid the emptiness inside. None of it made sense anymore. Everything I had been chasing, the titles, the images of success, felt like someone else's story. One I'd accidentally memorized and performed for years. The script we'd all been handed no longer made sense.

The realization cut through it all. And once the illusion broke, the bridge to the old way of being disappeared. The life I had built, full of metrics and milestones, suddenly felt empty. Artificial.

I sat in that stillness, letting the clarity sink in. That moment, quiet, yet brutal in force, was the 1st Shift. When the illusion finally broke.

Beyond the Pursuit of Happiness

I had woken up to a broken blueprint. But just because you see clearly doesn't mean you know what to do. I kept hearing the same advice, generic tips and positive platitudes: be present, live in the now. But what if the now feels hollow? Most people aren't avoiding the present because they're unfocused. They're avoiding it because it hurts.

Doubts swarmed around me. I wasn't just grieving the disintegration of my family; I was beginning to see the dissolution of the system I'd trusted, the promises I'd been handed. The pain was no longer just mine; it was woven into the world around me.

The hard truth: there is no manual for this. No clear path forward. Just a knowing that I had to keep moving, or risk being swallowed whole. I had spent my whole life constructing things: careers, plans, systems. But I had never truly understood why. I had followed blueprints drawn by others, walked the paths I was told were right. And where had that led me? To this moment, standing in the wreckage.

So, I began again. At first, I was just trying to survive. I had to function at work and stop the negative spirals because my kids depended on me. The pain and confusion still burned inside me, but for the first time, I didn't try to numb it. I let it pull me forward, toward answers I didn't yet have. And inside that pain, I felt the need to build something solid enough to stand on, some kind of system I could live by. That became my mission. I needed a lifeline when the darkness crept in.

I devoured every source I could find on depression, resilience, and the search for meaning. I set my course toward uncovering and organizing the works of some of the great thinkers. I read countless books, gathered scientific papers, listened to podcasts, and pulled old volumes from my library that had imprinted on me. I traced all the patterns and connections.

If I were going to climb out, I needed more than vague concepts. It had to be solid, grounded. And so, I dug deeper. Much deeper. Without realizing it, I started building the structure I'd one day live by.

I tackled the bigger question: What actually makes life worth living? And that's when I hit something that didn't make sense. Studies showed the more people seek to "feel happy," the less happy they become.[27] That couldn't be right. Everything I'd been taught, everything we're sold, said happiness was the goal. The thing to chase. And yet the research kept showing the opposite: direct pursuit of happiness backfires. I sat with that contradiction. What if we'd all been aiming at the wrong target?

I felt I was onto something, though I didn't know where the path would lead. Inside me, pieces reordered as the old story loosened its grip, and another way of seeing began to form.

The Hidden Patterns

Imagine waking up in a dream. Everything around you, the way you work, the concepts about life, the goals you chase, suddenly feels off. You see the illusion. That's the 1st Shift. It's powerful; it splinters the old lens. Shatters the model. Nothing feels true anymore. And in that rupture, something opens.

But what now?

You've lived so long inside that illusion, inside a blueprint you didn't design, you almost forget how to question it. But there's no going back. You pause, caught between the life you knew and the unknown ahead. You don't yet understand what's coming. But you sense it's time to step forward.

That's where I found myself. Waking up was only the beginning. So, I studied. I kept searching. Through science and psychology. Through books and ancient texts. The signs were there, hidden across lives, cultures, time.

Slowly, something began to take shape. Not a finished system. Not yet. More like tools forming. They surfaced during late nights, on black sand beaches, in alpine winds, in the stillness of the trail. Like pieces of a puzzle sliding into place, they offered a hint of a new structure. Not answers, but signs that a deeper order might exist beneath the surface. I didn't yet know what it all added up to. But I could feel it gathering. And soon, you'll feel it too. Subtle forces that shift how you move, decide, and align.

What emerged was the beginning of a new way of seeing. At first, it was faint, like a prism catching the light just right. But slowly, the architecture of life began to reveal itself. A living structure was forming beneath the chaos.

And though I couldn't see it yet, I felt it pulling me forward.

Toward a Quest that would change not just my path, but the way I saw the world.

Part 3
THE QUEST

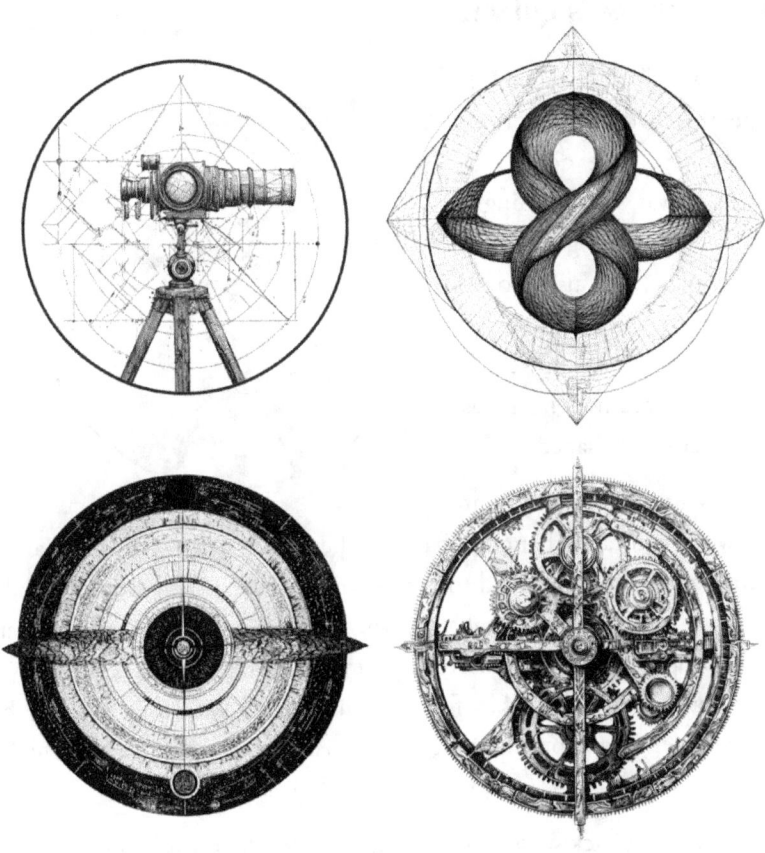

CHAPTER 8
The 7 Pillars

The Architect's Dilemma

The spell had broken. The blueprint had cracked open, but clarity alone doesn't lay bricks. I was still standing in the rubble, holding only fragments of what I used to believe. That's when a question emerged: How do you rebuild a life when you no longer trust the system that shaped it?

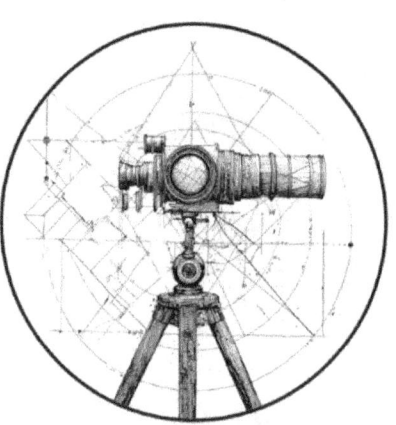

There's a point in every journey when you can either circle back to where you started—the familiar, the comfortable, the trap of old routines—or start anew. You are faced with a decision: keep drifting, or take the wheel and steer into uncharted terrain. Most people never make that turn. They see it, they know they could, but they don't. Even when they feel something is off with their life. So they work harder. Try to optimize their habits. And still, they end up where they started.

For me, going back wasn't an option. The old blueprint had failed, and I could no longer live inside it pretending. But awareness is a double-edged sword. Seeing the illusion didn't set me free. It made me feel more trapped than ever. Before, I played the game without questioning it. Now I saw the rules for what they were: a loop designed to keep me chasing, never arriving. And that made the walls feel even closer.

So what now? What do you do once you wake up and realize the script you've followed was never written for you? If the model was broken, what is the alternative? I didn't have answers, just a growing urgency: I needed a way out, a path I could actually walk, one step at a time. So I stopped looking for relief out there and let the pull turn my search inward.

Seeing the World Through a New Lens

I've always been a doer, wired to act, to fix, to move. But here's what I missed: real change doesn't begin with momentum. It starts by seeing, with the courage to question before rushing forward.

For months, I consumed it all: scientific literature, philosophies, and ancient wisdom, like I was trying to read my way out of a trap. My apartment was a mess of research, stacks of books, pages filled with notes and underlined passages, and my own scribbles in margins. I filled entire notebooks with techniques, models, and theories, each addressing some part of life. Some focused on mental models, others on high performance, others on well-being. Each one promised improvement. But nothing brought it together. No holistic framework. Just isolated concepts.

The clarity didn't come all at once. It arrived in small pieces, quiet realizations in late-night thoughts, in the moments when I felt like I was chasing something just out of reach. I tried out different ideas, some of them backed by rigorous research, some by personal anecdotes, some by self-proclaimed gurus. I changed my morning routine. My diet. My focus techniques. I experimented with deep work, with mindfulness, with the science of peak performance. I made changes, but in a random, disorganized way. One day, I optimized productivity. The next, I restructured my workouts. Then, I tested mental shifts. And still, I felt like something was missing.

One night, under the low light in my now-cluttered apartment, the weight of it all finally settled on me. I had read enough to fill a library.

Techniques, personal improvement tools, and models for well-being, but none of them spoke to each other. It felt like holding pieces from different puzzles, with no way to tell what they were supposed to form. I was drowning in insight but starving for clarity. Yet, I couldn't give up, as this had morphed into something more, an obsession with finding the answer. Because I knew deep down that if I didn't make sense of it, I'd drift further into a life that felt increasingly foreign to me.

That's when the thought hit me: What if I was looking at it all the wrong way? Maybe the disarray wasn't random but following a logic. I kept searching for one answer, one single truth, one ultimate tool that would explain it all. But what if it wasn't one thing? What if the answer had been in front of me all along, just dispersed, waiting to be assembled?

I pulled a blank page toward me and sat there, listening. Like waiting for a thought to finish forming before interrupting it. Then, my hand moved, as if on its own. Scribbles. Arrows. Words scattered like fragments waiting to connect. At first, it was messy. Lines crisscrossing each other. Concepts that felt related but didn't quite fit. I scratched things out, started again. I needed clarity, but the more I searched for it, the more elusive it felt. I wasn't drawing a plan. I was sensing for shape.

Then, I froze. My pen hovered mid-sentence. I looked down and, in that instant, I didn't just see a pattern, I felt it. A faint click inside. The shapes, the categories, the questions, they weren't random. Every problem, every frustration, every pain point I had ever encountered, and every solution that science pointed to, fit into core areas. And I could organize them. Group them. Still, I didn't immediately trust it. I tried to tear it apart. I threw moments from my own life at it, failures, arguments, decisions that still hurt. I looked for where it would give way. But it held.

And as I wrote them down, one by one, something started to emerge. What I saw wasn't just a list. It was a system. Each area of life wasn't isolated. They were all interconnected, influencing one another in ways I hadn't fully grasped before. I counted them.

Seven.

I exhaled, staring at the list. How to call them? I instinctively scribbled the word Pillars. Somehow, it just felt right. I hadn't invented them. They had simply emerged, like a truth that had been waiting, patiently, to be seen. The answers weren't hidden in a single theory or school of thought. They lived in the quiet connections, holding it all together.

And just like a telescope aimed at the sky, the more I adjusted my focus, the more the scattered became visible. Patterns emerged where there had once been only blur. This way of seeing that didn't just explain life. It illuminated it.

I sketched a circle with the outline of a human figure at the center, life unfolding within and around it. I placed each Pillar there, intuitively. At the center: the heart, our emotions. Above it: the mind, our thoughts. Below: the body, our physical form. At the bottom: our environment and the material world we move through. On one side, the people we love: our partner, family, friends. On the other: our work, interests and passions. And on the top, like the sky above, our spiritual connection: our search for something deeper.

I looked down at the drawing. It was just a circle, a figure, a few scattered words. Strangely simple. Yet somehow, it held everything. I had drowned in research, in models, in endless frameworks. But now, here it was, on a single page. The theories, the tools, the insights, they all found a home in this shape. They didn't clash. They clicked.

I sat back, my eyes following the lines, not just seeing them but feeling them. The weight of what I had uncovered pressed gently against my chest, like something sacred being revealed. And once I saw the connections, I could not go back to thinking life was just chaos. Because now, I had found the outline of something larger.

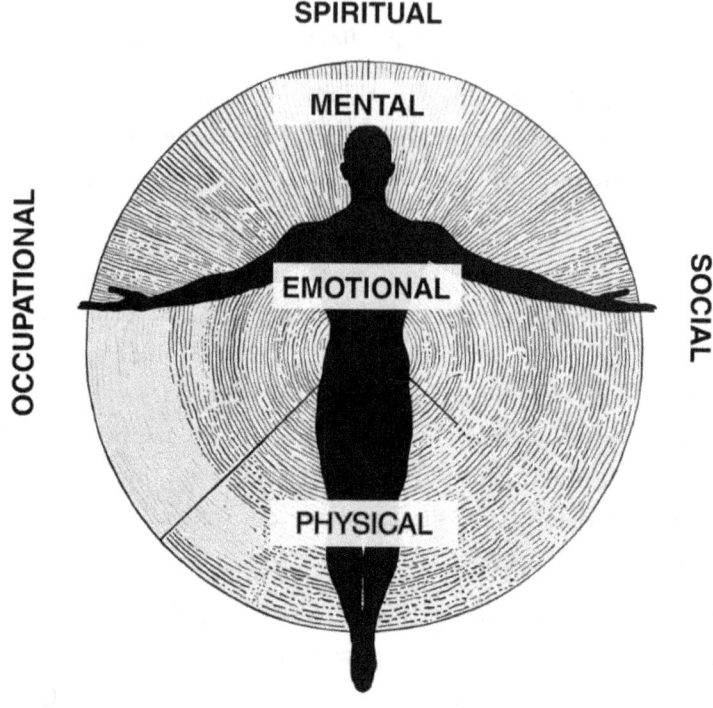

SPIRITUAL
MENTAL
OCCUPATIONAL
EMOTIONAL
SOCIAL
PHYSICAL
ENVIRONMENTAL / MATERIAL

The Lens

I leaned forward. That was it. The Lens, the hidden scaffolding behind the key choices I'd made. It made sense now. Not just intellectually, but viscerally. Flexible, yet rooted. It was like adjusting a camera lens and suddenly seeing the whole frame come into focus.

As I paused, looking at the drawing, something else landed. It explained my life with unsettling precision. I could trace the collapse, my need to escape, the parts that felt overwhelmed, back to one or more of these areas being ignored or left unattended. The pain I had felt hadn't been random. And for the first time, I could see it.

What the Pillars revealed was more than an answer. It reorganized how I perceived and understood my life.

I breathed in, contemplating it all. The Pillars weren't just theory; they showed the hidden architecture of life. Like a prism catching the light just right, refracting chaos into clarity. In that moment, what once felt scattered now had a deeper logic. Rhythm. Flow. Alignment. A way to see what had been influencing my decisions and reactions, and begin, finally, to rebuild with intention. Each success and setback traced back to one or more of these Pillars. I could see the weak points now. Even name them, not just feel them. I wasn't lost; I had been following the wrong map.

And yet, this was only the beginning. A new Lens doesn't create change. It reveals what's been hidden: the patterns out of sync, the places we break, and the ones we can begin to rebuild. What came next was the real work. I needed to understand what each Pillar truly meant, not just as a concept, but in the fabric of everyday life. This was the moment the story stopped being only mine. What I was looking at wasn't personal anymore. It went beyond me. To move forward, I had to lay the map out clearly.

From that day on, I kept returning to the Lens, testing it, seeing how it held up against science, against stories, against the lived messiness of real life.

The 7 Pillars: A New Map for Life

What follows is a simple introduction to the 7 Pillars. These aren't just ideas. They're structural, hidden forces that shape how you feel, how you move, how you live. You don't need to master every detail to begin. Even a basic understanding can spark real change. As you read further, you'll start to recognize where the gaps are, and how to begin bridging them.

The goal here is simple: to show you the system. A new way to trace the contours of your life with clearer eyes, so you can begin to see it differently.

Let's take a look at the 7 Pillars, one by one.

1. Emotional

I used to think emotions were like the weather, sudden, unpredictable, something to endure. But emotions aren't just moods. They're signals. They're shaped by what you do, how you think, and who you're around. You don't wait to feel better to act. You act your way into feeling better. This Pillar is about emotional agility: learning to shift how you feel through proven tools and techniques. Because once you understand and learn to regulate your emotions, you change how you experience everything else.

And here's what most people miss: emotional strength isn't about always feeling good, it's about feeling fully. Pain, when channeled, becomes clarity. Even grief and anger carry energy. If you learn to listen, not suppress, you'll find that the hardest feelings often hold the deepest truths.

2. Mental

Your mind is a filter. Every thought you have, every story you tell yourself, shapes how you see, what you believe, and how you act. In a world full of noise, one of the hardest things is to reclaim your attention. This Pillar is about mental clarity, choosing what you allow in, how you process it, and what you build from it.

This isn't about chasing positive thoughts. It's about thinking clearly. Your mind is an architect. It builds your reality from what you feed it and the meaning you assign. Change what you consume, and you change the materials you build your thoughts on. Change how you interpret events, and you change the very structure of your experience.

3. Physical

When you're burned out, numb, and stuck, it's easy to think the problem lives in your mind. That if you could just think differently, everything would change. But the fastest shifts don't begin with thoughts. They begin in the body. Movement, rest, nutrition, these aren't just wellness tips. They're chemistry. They're how your system resets.

This Pillar is your core. Without it, nothing sustains. But with it, your energy rises, your mood lifts, and your days become manageable again. The most reliable way to shift your emotional state isn't by thinking harder. It's by moving differently. A single workout. A walk at sunrise. A night of real sleep. Even one week of true rest and movement can reboot your entire system. Your body speaks in hormones, rhythms, and signals. When you learn to listen, you stop spiraling and start rising.

4. Social

Every joy and every heartbreak in your life has one thing in common: other people. Connection is the heartbeat of fulfillment. And yet today, many of us feel disconnected, lonely in crowds, scrolling for belonging. This Pillar is about real connection: friendships that fuel you, relationships that ground you, communities that hold you when everything else falls apart, because the quality of your relationships is the quality of your life.

The science is clear: connection isn't a luxury, it's a lifeline. Real, supportive relationships buffer stress, regulate emotions, and even extend life. Without them, we fray quietly. With them, we become more ourselves. Stronger. Seen. Known. Loved.

5. Occupational

You spend more waking hours working than doing almost anything else. If that time drains you, it impacts everything: your energy, your health, your joy. This Pillar is about redesigning that time to fuel you. Not through perfect jobs, but meaningful ones. Shifting from the endless hustle to work infused with autonomy, purpose, and flow. It's more than just escaping distraction; it's about engaging in what lights you up. Because when what you do aligns with who you are, life stops being a grind and starts becoming art.

What I didn't yet understand was how narrow my definition of "who I was" had become. I had reduced myself to a role, a function. But I was so much more than that. Your aliveness often hides in the spaces you're not paid to pursue, that don't fit your current title or the labels you've taken on.

6. Environmental/Material

The places you inhabit forge you. The light in your room, the city you wake up in, the clutter in your life, they're not background noise. They shape your thoughts, energy, and nervous system. Your environment isn't passive. It's alive. And it affects you, moment by moment. It isn't only about space; it's about rhythm. Nature isn't a luxury. It's a reset. Science shows that even a short walk in a forest can lower stress hormones, steady your breath, and clear your mind.

And then there's your material base, your finances, your possessions, your basic needs. Because survival stress doesn't just live in the mind. It lives in the body. If your environment drains you, if your material life feels unstable, or if you're trapped in the endless chase to accumulate more and never feel fulfilled, it ripples through your entire system. This Pillar invites you to create environments that support calm and clarity, and that feel secure. Because when your world feels steady, grounded, you finally have room to expand.

7. Spiritual

There's a part of you that's always reaching, beyond your aspirations and desires, for something deeper. It feels awe in the face of beauty, aches for connection not tied to the material. It's the voice inside that wonders why you're here. This Pillar is about anchoring yourself in something greater; whether that's faith, spiritual practice, or simply a sense of purpose beyond yourself. Without it, even success feels hollow. With it, even the storms have meaning. When you are rooted in something deeper, the noise falls away.

Seeing the Structure Clearly

This isn't just theory. It's structural. Because when a few Pillars are weak, the whole system is strained. You might be physically strong but emotionally unraveling. Financially successful but spiritually starving. That was where I stood. I learned it the hard way. When I looked back at my life, the gaps were glaring. The fractures weren't random; they traced perfectly to the Pillars I had ignored for too long. As poet and teacher Victor Webster reminds us: "Everything we do, even the slightest thing we do, can have a ripple effect and repercussions that emanate."[28]

And that was the turning point: finally facing the questions I had avoided. Because realizing the system exists? That's one thing. But confronting where you actually stand within it, that's something else entirely.

Versions of the Pillars have existed for centuries, in philosophy, psychology, self-development, and ancient spiritual teachings. Entire libraries explore each domain in one form or another. People have divided life into categories before, into similar or other subgroups. But the magic isn't in the labels. It is in the living of them: how each choice, habit, and action either strengthens the system or quietly destabilizes it. Naming the Pillars was only the surface. The real power emerged when I turned the lens inward. When I stopped treating them as abstract ideas and started using them as a mirror. That's when it got personal. Because the moment I aimed it at my own life, the gaps became impossible to ignore.

The Hard Truth: Where You Stand Now

I had to face the full picture, no more excuses. Just me, a blank page, and the truth I'd been avoiding. I pictured it like a sound engineer's mixing board, seven levers, each one tied to a Pillar. Some cranked high, others barely audible. The tone of my life, its balance, intensity, and richness, came from each channel.

Every decision is like adjusting the soundboard. Slide one lever up, and your energy improves. Slide another down, and your relationships distort. Without realizing it, weak channels blur the whole mix. But with intention, you can tune the frequencies of your life, aligning choices that strengthen you and bring harmony within. Over time, the pattern becomes clear. You're either composing something that uplifts or a loop that leaves you stuck.

So, I sat down with pen and paper, staring out at the skyline of Miami, the life I'd built, now half-lived, half-abandoned. And as I rated each Pillar, the story came into focus.

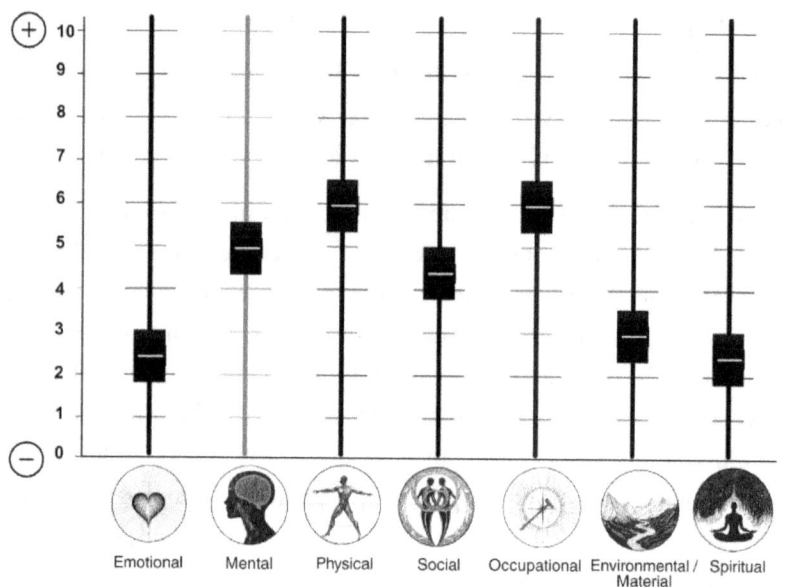

- **Emotional:** Fragile. The breakdowns came in waves, especially on weekends when the silence of missing my children was deafening.

- **Mental:** Scattered. My thoughts looped in negative circles. I couldn't focus. I was feeding my mind junk by doomscrolling, overthinking, and avoiding.

- **Physical:** Neutral. I squeezed in a workout here and there, tried to stay active with my kids, but my energy was low.

- **Social:** Disconnected from friends across the ocean. I had messages, group chats, but no one to call when the sleepless hours stretched on.

- **Occupational:** Unbalanced. My work inspired me, but the rest of what fed my soul was gone. Writing. Music. Wonder. At first faded, then buried.

- **Environmental/Material:** Chaotic. My apartment was a mirror of my mind, boxes half-unpacked, walls bare, closets full of things that no longer belonged to this version of me.

- **Spiritual:** Silent. I had once felt a connection to something larger, beyond myself. Now? Just static.

No wonder I felt hollow. The assessment took minutes, yet it explained the ache I'd been carrying and why the symptoms weren't random. Your life is the sum of your Pillars, and I'd been trying to fix the surface without seeing the full system.

That night, as I sat there looking at the chart and grasping what it all meant, I made a new commitment: I was going to rebuild. No more shortcuts or surface-level fixes. I would methodically strengthen each Pillar, one by one. Piece by piece. Choice by choice.

Your Reflection

Before we go further, take a moment. Strip away the noise, the routines, the roles you play. The need to be constantly in motion.

And ask yourself, honestly: Where do I stand in each Pillar? Don't overthink it. Let your body answer. It already knows what's out of alignment. Which Pillars feel solid, anchoring you? Which ones feel brittle, ignored, or empty?

Grab a notebook or your phone. Rate yourself from 0 to 10 on each Pillar. Zero means the weakest. Ten means thriving. The only requirement? Be brutally honest with yourself. No filters. No pretending. You can't build on fiction. Because before you can rise, you need to see where you stand. This is your starting ground.

When you stop to look, really look, something unlocks. You start to notice what's been missing, not just goals unmet or habits skipped, but something more subtle. A sense of alignment, of energy. You can feel it within you. The gaps. The weight. And now, you don't just feel, you see, and know what you must do.

Life Through the Pillars

Many people live in a fog, drifting forward. Choices feel random. Emotions swing without warning. Direction? A guess at best. And then they wonder why they feel lost. I know. That's where I was: I kept moving, but without any real intention.

Then I found the Lens. It cut through the blur and showed me the entire terrain of life. Without it, I was chasing progress without a sense of where I was headed. With it, I could see what to do next. Decisions sharpened. I wasn't just reacting anymore; I was choosing. Deliberately. Powerfully.

A simple question guided me: Which Pillars does this choice impact? And does it strengthen or weaken them? This changed the way I saw my decisions.

- A workout wasn't just for my body, it built energy (Physical), and boosted confidence (Emotional).

- Going on a bike ride along the boardwalk with my children wasn't just exercise (Physical), it deepened our connection (Social), and created memories that nourished the heart (Emotional).

- Blocking off an afternoon to write wasn't only about producing words. It pulled me into a flow state where time disappeared (Occupational), sharpened my thinking (Mental), and left me with a deep, settled sense that I was aligned with what mattered (Emotional).

- Picking up the kinds of books I once lived inside, those that invited me to see the world differently, did more than feed my mind (Mental). It reawakened a part of me I'd let go quiet for too long, pulling me back into a deeper reflection about life itself (Spiritual).

- Or simply going on a walk outside. It cleared my mind (Mental), lifted my spirit (Emotional), and reconnected me with the world around me (Environmental).

Every choice either lifts you or drains you. That was the missing piece: no secret, no mystery, only a system that was clear, grounded, and usable by anyone.

The Pulse Beneath

I began practicing the Pillars daily, not just thinking about them, but living them, testing them in real time. Each choice, each moment, each action, I ran through the Lens. It wasn't natural at first. I had to retrain my mind to organize my life not by to-dos or outcomes. I paused before a decision and felt which Pillars were impacted.

It didn't arrive all at once. Days blurred together. Some felt focused, others scattered. I kept returning to the Lens anyway, not searching for anything in particular, just staying with it long enough to see what surfaced. Slowly, as time passed, it became less of a concept, and more of a rhythm.

Then one afternoon, I was sitting alone by the window in Miami, watching the world move on outside: cars, voices, light shifting across buildings. I sat still, closing my eyes, just to sense it all from within. I wasn't trying to think. I was trying to feel. How each Pillar lived inside me. How each one rose and fell depending on how I moved, what I did, and how I connected. They weren't separate; they were woven together.

And then, almost without noticing, I sensed it.

Not a thought. A sensation. Like a current. A quiet hum running through me, linking everything I'd been working toward. It was subtle, almost imperceptible. But it was there. I had just never tuned in far enough to notice it. My breath slowed, my awareness deepened, and I turned my attention inward, letting myself simply observe. Everything quieted. Then, out of the depths, an image formed in my mind, blurry at first, but unmistakable.

I saw myself standing on a frozen lake at dawn.

The surface was smooth as glass, light bending gently across it. Perfect calm. But beneath that stillness, a pressure. The faint sense of movement, slow and unseen. An ancient force moving beneath the ice, so faint it could be missed. But it was there. It had always been there. Silent. Unseen. Waiting. And for the first time, I could sense it clearly.

And that current moved through me as well. Not just through my mind, but through my whole body. The Pillars had given me shape. A prism. But this... this was a movement inside the structure. As if the system I'd built wasn't just a framework, but something alive, resonating through it.

I opened my eyes. I didn't know what I had just experienced, only that it mattered. That I had touched something deeper than theory.

It felt like the beginning of something new.

I didn't have words for it yet.

Only that it was real.

And it was calling me deeper.

CHAPTER 9
The Equation

When the Land Whispered Back

The Pillars gave me clarity, a full map of life's terrain. Seven core domains. A holistic Lens. By then, I wasn't just learning to see through the Lens, I was trying to live it. I had made a choice: not to wait until the system was perfect but to step into it, with all its rough edges and unknowns. To begin applying it beyond theory, in everyday life, with all its mess 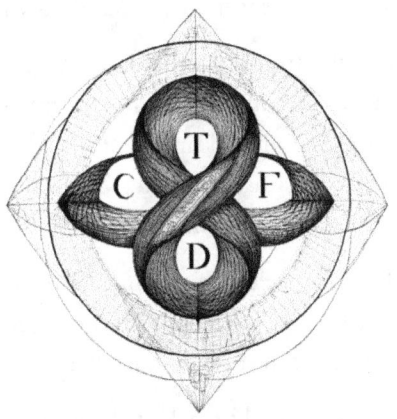 and beauty. Especially in the kinds of places that could nourish the parts of me I'd neglected, the ones rooted in nature, in movement, in wonder. I began noticing the small decisions: what lifted me, what drained me, what aligned with a Pillar, and where one was eroded.

Years earlier, my father had handed me a camera, an Olympus OM-10. That gift had sent me across continents, chasing light. Volcanoes in Indonesia. Waterfalls in Bali. Rainforests in Costa Rica. Monasteries perched on the cliffs of Greece. Always with my camera and a tripod strapped to my back. But somewhere along the way, I had lost that version of myself. Swallowed by deadlines and meetings, by a life of pressure and performance. But something in me remembered.

So, I picked up where I left off. I bought a new camera, a tripod, and filters that could darken light, slowing time just enough to turn the flow of water into silk. One by one, I laid the pieces out before me, like old tools, waiting to be used. I packed the gear with care, as if acknowledging a part of me I'd nearly forgotten.

And then, I left.

Iceland. An island of black sand, glaciers, and deep canyons that swallowed sound. I landed in Reykjavík and drove east, the road unwinding like a ribbon through moss and mist. That evening, I pulled into a gravel lot near a waterfall I'd only seen in photographs: Skógafoss. Nearly 200 feet high, its water thundered down, relentless, the spray filling the air.

I hiked up toward the base, breath rising, the light already beginning to shift. The sun hovered low, casting gold along the spray. As the whole fall came into view, I unfolded the tripod, and adjusted the frame. The wind pressed against my jacket. The shutter opened, and the water flowed into stillness. For a moment, time paused with it.

That faint electric thrill. Like recognition. As if that younger version of me, the one who once chased light across continents, had returned, just long enough to show me what I'd left behind.

Later that night, back at the guesthouse, the world outside had folded inward. The ink-dark sky stretched wide over the hills. I sat on the porch, my journal open, half habit, half instinct. I would jot down the moments that felt charged, a line from a poem, a strange coincidence, a lyric from a Leonard Cohen song, one of those meaningful lines that stayed with me, full of depth and resonance, waiting to be understood later.

Outside, the night settled in, pinpricks of light slowly blinking into view. And there they were, shapes I'd sketched with a kind of absent reverence. Cassiopeia's W. The Big Dipper. Constellations I'd learned to find as a child, simple lines, rich with meaning. I used to write down their stories, the old legends woven into each one, passed through generations.

As a boy, I didn't grasp that we were peering across time. The stars symbolized everything we didn't know, and everything that might still be possible. And yet, there they were, just dots in the night sky. Or maybe something more, I wasn't sure.

The days that followed took on an unhurried rhythm. No agenda, just motion and pause. I drove with the changing light, stopping whenever the land called to me. I slept in remote farmhouses, ate simple meals, and let the days unfold without force.

The road curved through green valleys shaped by wind and time. In the car, I let my thoughts drift. Revisiting what I'd learned. Noticing what still didn't make sense. Slowly, as time passed, the Pillars stopped feeling like a framework I had to remember, and became something I could feel, a pattern in how I made choices, moved, and rested.

I hadn't come here to solve anything. But Iceland gave me space. And in that space, something started to take shape. Not a neat answer, more of an intrinsic connection to the land, to myself, to something that existed within it.

Back home, I would walk friends through the model, Emotional, Mental, and Physical, all the way to Spiritual, and their eyes would light up. "This is so clear," they'd say. "It explains so much." But then, the comment would follow, "It's great, but now what?"

I found myself reciting these seven areas like a checklist, like categories in a filing cabinet. But I could feel it: something was missing. If the Pillars were the Lens, what was that element that connected them?

The Pattern That Moved

I was sitting outside a guesthouse near Diamond Beach, the black sand still clinging to my hiking boots, the air crisp and clean. The sky finally shed the morning fog and opened into an impossible blue. The ocean shimmered in the distance, calm, watchful, alive. I wrapped my hands around a cup of coffee, steam rising in the cold air. Everything around me was quiet, as if the world were listening.

My mind had been juggling contradictions. Clarity had come through the Pillars, but applying all seven at once felt like trying to tune every string of an instrument while playing a symphony. I was improving, yes, but it still felt scattered, disjointed. I kept asking: Where do I begin? What do I do next? In what sequence?

I kept grappling with competing truths. "All that we are is the result of what we have thought,"[29] said Buddha. But then came Will Durant's voice: "We are what we repeatedly do."[30] And the scientists pointed elsewhere entirely, to our surroundings, our habits, our relationships. Each view felt compelling. Each claimed to be the source. But none gave me a way to bring it together.

Through it all, one question kept returning: What actually changes how I feel? That was the heart of it, not perfection, just the ability to feel whole again, alive and connected. I needed a process. Something I could use, when nothing else worked, to shift how I felt. And as my mind tussled with that question, I paused. Maybe I was trying too hard to mentally force a solution. I sat for a while in silence, taking in the view.

Then I reached for my notebook. Something had quieted inside me, and in that stillness, fragments began to rise. My hand moved without hesitation. First, a figure eight, stretched wide and horizontal. Then another, crossing it vertically. Around them, a circle. I kept tracing, again and again, letting the lines coil like a current. There was no plan. Just motion. Flow.

I didn't know what the shape meant, only that it held an energy, like a system tuning itself as it moved, each part influencing the next.

I sat in silence, unsure. The symbol looked beautiful, but hollow. Was I just circling? Was this another dead end? My pen hovered. Then, without warning, my hand moved again. The order wasn't linear; it was alive. These four forces moved in a dynamic loop. Think fed Do. Do opened Connect. Connection transformed Feel. And Feel, in turn, shaped how I thought again. My pen flowed across the paper, and then I paused.

It wasn't a diagram. It was a circuit. And then, almost without thinking, I wrote…

+ Change what you THINK

+ Change what you DO

+ Change how you CONNECT

= Change how you FEEL

It landed with weight. Not a conclusion, but a key.

UNLOCK.

The First Key

A current, always there, just beneath the surface, running through the Pillars. Thought. Action. Connection. These weren't isolated elements, but parts of a living circuit, pulsing, adapting, feeding each other in real time. Not separate lanes, but a single living network. Like synapses firing in a brain, each Pillar lit up, thought feeding action, action opening connection, connection reshaping how I felt. Suddenly, it wasn't seven disconnected areas, it was one dynamic system. The current didn't just connect the Pillars, it activated them.

This was the First Key. The link I had been missing.

I grabbed my notebook and wrote down: The Equation.

Over the next week, driving past mossy lava fields, hiking by caves with dripping stone, and standing beside glacial rivers, I tested the Equation in my mind like a key in every lock. I twisted it, challenged it, pressure-tested it. And still, it worked. But something else began to happen too: I started to see it at play in everything around me. In the curve of the trail, in the rhythm of my breath, in the way water carved through rock. Each landscape became a metaphor. I wasn't simply taking photos. I was capturing proof. Of movement, of how everything connects.

I brought back to Miami more than photographs of wild places and scattered notes. I brought back the current itself, the twin infinities, the looping lines, and the circle enclosing it all. The Equation. Thought feeding action. Action shaping connection. Connection shifting feeling. A living rhythm.

Here's what I'd come to realize: everything we do, every habit, every goal, every sacrifice, is driven by a desire. We want to feel better. We chase money not for the currency itself, but for the sense of security or freedom it represents. We pursue success for the validation it brings. We seek relationships for how they make us feel: alive, seen, connected.

I stopped asking, what do I want to achieve? And started asking, how do I want to feel? Because when you change how you feel, consistently, your life begins to change too. It sounds obvious, almost too simple. But the more I lived it, the more undeniable it became. Every breakthrough I had ever experienced didn't come from chasing feelings, but from changing the inputs that shaped them.

And those inputs were now clear. Change your thoughts, your actions, your connections, and you'll change how you feel. That's the Equation. Elegant. Simple. But powerful.

Happiness is like a weather pattern. It moves in and out. What I needed was something steady, not fleeting highs, but rather a grounded sense of fulfillment. The kind you don't stumble into. I realized it wasn't about chasing joy; it was about creating the conditions where it could emerge. When I aligned how I thought, what I did, and how I connected, my emotional landscape began to recalibrate, without me needing to force it. This became the through line that connected it all. The Pillars weren't just categories; they were channels. And now, with the Equation, I had the current that made those channels flow.

What the Equation Reveals

At first, it felt almost too simple to be true. A part of me resisted it. How could something so basic hold the key to something as vast as fulfillment?

But then I remembered the research that had stopped me cold. Psychologists Brett Ford and Iris Mauss had discovered something that shattered conventional wisdom: the more people actively try to be happy, the less happy they actually feel.[31] It even backfires. The pursuit itself, what so many of us have been taught to chase, is often the very thing that pushes happiness further away. And study after study echoed the same strange paradox. When happiness becomes a goal, it becomes a ghost. It slips through our fingers the moment we try to grab it.

Eric Hoffer said it more bluntly: "The search for happiness is one of the chief sources of unhappiness."[32] It didn't just feel true. I had lived it. I had spent years chasing the feeling, through ambition, through achievement, through escape. And the more I chased, the more elusive it became.

That's what made the Equation so different. It didn't ask me to pursue a feeling. It gave me a way to build the conditions where the feeling could rise naturally, consistently. But it only worked if I understood what it was made of. I had to slow down and move through it, piece by piece. What did it really mean to change a thought, an action, a connection?

Decoding the Equation

1. Change What You Think (Mental Pillar)

Nobel Prize–winning psychologist Daniel Kahneman once observed, "Your emotional state has a lot to do with what you're thinking about and what you're paying attention to."[33] Your thoughts shape your emotions. Your brain is constantly interpreting the world around you, assigning meaning, predicting outcomes, filtering reality. And yet, most people never pause to question their own thought patterns. We assume that the way we think is just... how things are.

But if you've ever replayed an embarrassing memory from years ago and felt a pang of shame, even though nothing actually happened in the present moment, you know that thoughts don't just reflect reality.

They create it.

That's why changing what you think is so powerful. Cognitive Behavioral Therapy (CBT) has shown that simple shifts, like reframing how you interpret setbacks or controlling what you focus on, can profoundly alter your emotional state.

If you can control your input (what you expose your mind to) and your interpretation (how you assign meaning to events), you can fundamentally impact how you feel. That's why one of the first and most effective levers in this equation is your Mental Pillar, the thoughts you cultivate, the information you consume, and the way you train your brain to interpret life.

But thinking alone is not enough. If insight doesn't translate into action, transformation stalls. This is where the next phase begins, aligning your Physical and Occupational Pillars.

2. Change What You Do (Physical and Occupational Pillars)

Historian Will Durant distilled Aristotle's wisdom into a single line: "We are what we repeatedly do." Excellence isn't an act. It's a habit. And every habit is a lever that shapes how you feel. Most people think emotions come first. That we act based on how we feel. But what if it's the other way around? Studies have shown that something as simple as changing your posture, standing tall instead of slouching, can instantly affect confidence levels. Exercise is one of the most powerful natural antidepressants, not because it changes what you think, but because it changes your physiology, which in turn shifts how you feel.

Every action is a message, to your brain, to your body, to your sense of identity. Work drains or fuels. Hobbies awaken or numb. Movement isn't optional; it's emotional.

When I realized this, I saw that I had slowly removed all that once brought me joy. I used to play guitar. I stopped. I used to go mountain biking, and that faded too. I used to write for the simple joy of writing, until that went quiet. And with every abandoned pursuit, a part of me dimmed.

It wasn't until I started doing things differently, reintroducing the activities I loved, shifting my focus back to creative work, and rebuilding my Physical and Occupational Pillars, that my emotions started to change.

Action isn't just something we do after we feel better. It's often the thing that makes us feel better. You see, it was not only about the external forces, the world out there, the work I did, whether I picked stability, or went for adventure, or whether I followed the Analyst or the Seeker. It was also about the choices I made that strengthened or weakened my Pillars. And that was within my control.

3. Change How You Connect (Social, Environmental/Material, and Spiritual Pillars)

We are wired for connection. And yet, modern life has left many of us more disconnected than ever. Even the National Action Alliance for Suicide Prevention concluded that therapy, medication or hotlines on their own aren't enough. What's required is a multilayered reconnection of a person back to life itself: "the solution lies in social, economic, spiritual, and other connections."[34]

Decades of research echo this truth. Relationships, more than wealth or success, determine our well-being. The Harvard Study of Adult Development, a 75-year-long study, found that the single greatest predictor of happiness and longevity isn't money, fame, or success. It's the quality of our relationships.

When I looked at my own life, I saw that I had neglected this. I was connected to my children, but beyond that? I had distanced myself from deep friendships, as I lived thousands of miles away from them. And I had not taken the simple steps to nurture them. I had filled my free time with entertainment instead of meaningful relationships.

And it showed.

The places we inhabit don't just reflect our inner world. They help create it: a cramped apartment, an uninspiring office, a life detached from nature. These aren't just inconveniences. They quietly chip away at our energy and clarity.

And finally, beyond the material and social, spiritual emptiness creates a low-level background dissatisfaction that no amount of external success can fill. Without it, we drift.

When I started intentionally strengthening my Social, Environmental/Material, and Spiritual Pillars, my entire emotional state began to shift. Because we don't exist in a vacuum. Everything around us is shaping us, whether we realize it or not.

4. Change How You Feel (Emotional Pillar)

This is the heart of it all. Every thought, every action, every connection feeds into one thing: how you feel. And if you change the inputs, the output, your emotions, will follow. Psychologist Daniel Goleman put it simply: "Biological impulses drive our emotions. We cannot do away with them, but we can do much to manage them."[35] It reinforces one of the Equation's core truths: we can't erase the storms, but we can learn to steer through them. This isn't about suppressing emotions or pretending that life is always positive. It's about understanding the levers you can pull, so that when you feel stuck, you know how to move forward. That's what makes the Equation so powerful. It's simple enough to remember. But profound enough to drive deep and lasting change.

When Clarity Isn't Enough

The world doesn't change. But our way of moving through it can. The Pillars provide a clear Lens. The Equation reveals how the pieces of life connect, and why we feel the way we do. It shows the hidden drivers of emotion.

Suddenly, it makes sense: why people chase things yet never feel fulfilled. Why every achievement seems to fade. Why even success can ring hollow. Because no matter how much we gain, if the inputs stay the same, our thoughts, our actions, our connections, our emotional patterns will keep repeating. The chase continues, but the desired feeling never arrives.

I understood all this. But knowing still wasn't enough.

I had to live it. To make real choices, every single day. To apply the system in real time, when doubt crept in, when the way forward blurred. It sounded simple: change what you think, what you do, how you connect. But knowing the path is not the same as walking it. And walking it, not just once, but over and over, requires something steadier. Something I hadn't yet found.

So I gave it time. I practiced. I tested the Equation quietly in the background of my life. Some days it worked. Other days I stumbled, unsure what to do first, what order to follow, what sequence mattered most. But I kept returning to it, adjusting, refining, and listening.

And then, months later, far from home, high in the Alps, I looked up, catching a movement I almost missed. The same rhythm I had sketched in my notebook months earlier. Only now it felt different. An arc cutting through the sky.

I froze.

I wasn't just seeing the pattern. The spiral wasn't static—it rose. I sensed something I hadn't seen before. Not the full answer, not yet. But a clear direction. A pull upward, where before there had only been questions.

CHAPTER 10
The Ascend Wheel

Finding the Updraft

The valley stretched out beneath me in breathtaking vastness, green slopes giving way to jagged cliffs, a stream slicing the land like a blade of light. Far above the Swiss alpine village of Grindelwald, the sky was a perfect blue, vast and still. Then, movement. Paragliders dancing overhead, suspended on invisible lines.

But despite their acrobatics and maneuvering feats, they too were caught in gravity's pull, in a slow spiraling descent toward the valley below. But then, something invisible took hold. A slight change. They found an updraft. And suddenly, the dynamics shifted. Instead of plummeting, they began to rise, higher and higher, spiraling upward, defying that physical force that was pulling them down.

I watched transfixed. And in that instant, I saw it clearly: this was the difference between those caught in a descending spiral and those who rise. Because I had felt the pull downward, the negative loops, the endless overthinking, the feeling of sinking despite my best efforts. A downward spiral isn't a choice. It's automatic. The brain is wired to focus on avoiding pain, so it replays our fears and amplifies doubts. It's just a survival mechanism, but it's also why we get stuck.

But rising? There is no such automatic upward force in our lives. That requires intention. It takes effort to shift your trajectory, to move upward instead of getting pulled under. I saw that it wasn't about struggling against the pull. It was about finding the forces that lift you. And that's when I realized: I needed to create my own updraft. A structured way to break free of negative loops. A decision-making process that didn't leave me trapped in "analysis paralysis" or emotional spirals.

Even with the Pillars and the Equation, I was, at times, still stalling. Not lost, but oscillating. Gaining ground one moment, then slipping the next. That's when it clicked. The spiral wasn't just a pattern; it was a process. A way to turn awareness into movement. I sketched it in my journal: five points of motion, five words. Strangely, each one began with the same letter. It wasn't just a diagram. It was a rhythm, a wheel designed to rise.

As I returned from that alpine escape in Grindelwald to my life in Miami, something stayed with me. The image of that spiral in the sky. Built for lift.

The Decision Dilemma: Why We Get Stuck

The Pillars gave me a Lens to see my life clearly. The Equation showed me how all that I did, my thoughts, actions, and connections, shaped how I felt. But perspective alone didn't break the loop. Every day, I faced decisions, some small, some large. I needed a tool to help me move when the doubts crept in. A reliable way to break hesitation before it pulled me back into old patterns.

The problem was clear: life throws choices at you, messy, complex, and layered with emotions and uncertainty. And if you don't have a system for making decisions, you either freeze or default to the familiar. So, I built one.

The 5 Steps to Break Free and Rise

I began with three simple questions:

Where do I want to go?

Where am I now?

What do I need to do to get there?

That became my baseline. It wasn't elegant, but it gave me a cycle I could run whenever I felt off track. I tested it in the places that mattered most. At the time, I was deep into rebuilding my life. My days were full, and many areas had been neglected. So I took little steps. I set Saturdays aside for adventures with my kids, and I picked up the phone and called old friends. Not a grand reinvention. Just small actions. And they worked— at first.

But something was still off. The changes didn't always stick. Even when I had a clear goal and some momentum, things would stall. I started looking closer. What was I missing?

That's when it hit me: I'd skipped something critical. Acceptance. I hadn't fully faced where I was. I was pretending I'd moved on, but part of me was still clinging to a version of life that no longer existed. And the second insight came just as fast: I was moving too quickly. Not choosing, but reacting, jumping into action without pausing to really assess the options.

That was when I finally saw it. When I made lasting progress, it wasn't random; I had been moving through the same five steps. That's how the Ascend Wheel was born.

1. **AIM** — The Power of Knowing What You Want

2. **AWARENESS** — Seeing Clearly Before You Move

3. **ACCEPTANCE** — Release the Weight Holding You Back

4. **ASSESSMENT** (+/−) — Choosing the Right Path Forward

5. **ACTION** — The Step That Brings It to Life

It was time to move from discovery to use. From what I had uncovered to how it could be lived, step by step. Bringing insight and method together, to understand how to rise.

1. AIM — The Power of Knowing What You Want

If you don't know where you're going, you drift. And when you drift, external forces decide for you. Every decision should start with an Aim. A direction. A desired outcome. Michelangelo warned of this centuries ago: "The greater danger for most of us lies not in setting our aim too high and falling short, but in setting our aim too low, and achieving our mark."[36]

Your Aim doesn't need to be grand or lifelong; it just needs to be clear. What are you really trying to achieve? What matters most right now?

Some people call this the power of manifesting. But what is it, really? It's the clarity of Aim, so strong and so focused, that your entire life begins to organize around it. Things begin to show up. Not because you're forcing them, but because your direction becomes magnetic. And over time, you'll notice: this can't just be a coincidence. Jordan Peterson shares the power of Aim: "What happens is that the world shifts itself around your aim (...) You're an aiming creature, it's built right into you. (...) It organizes what you see, and what you don't see. It organizes your emotions and your motivations. So, you organize yourself around that aim, and then what happens is the day manifests itself as a set of challenges and problems, and if you solve them properly, then you stay on the pathway towards that aim."[37]

It's not about having all the answers; it's about knowing where you're headed. Many people struggle with this because their aims aren't really theirs: they're borrowed from family, culture, or old versions of themselves. Your Aim should come from within, from what genuinely pulls you forward. It can be specific, linked to one of your Pillars, or something larger. A deeper thread. A kind of North Star. One that, as you'll see later, has the power to shape the direction of your entire life.

To define your Aim, start with two simple questions: *What am I aiming for? And why do I want this?*

2. AWARENESS — Seeing Clearly Before You Move

Once you define your Aim, you need to understand your starting point. Awareness means looking at the full picture, your current reality, and the broader patterns in your life. This is where many stumble. They jump into action without fully grasping their own obstacles. And it's no surprise that we'd rather avoid discomfort than face it. But as Socrates warned, "The unexamined life is not worth living."[38] Without that honesty, we repeat the same loops, blind to the patterns shaping us.

At the time, I thought Awareness meant mostly looking inward. Taking inventory. But even as I tried to rebuild my life deliberately, there were things I still couldn't account for, gaps that didn't make sense. Sometimes, the clearest view doesn't come from introspection at all. It comes later, sideways, through someone else's life.

A year after I moved to Miami, I was blindsided and struck by a loss that arrived without warning. My father was gone. The days that followed felt out of sync as I tried to make sense of the hole that had opened in my life. Soon after, I found myself driving through the canyons of Southern Utah with my uncle. My heart was heavy, my mind unmoored, trying to process the loss of someone who had shaped so much of my story, yet remained partly a mystery to me. We were headed to a small, sleepy town called Blanding, where my dad had recently settled, just one more move in a lifetime of constant searching. He had spent his life reading, writing, and teaching, pouring himself into ideas. But there was always a restlessness to where he lived, the houses he chose, the way he never quite stayed.

The same raw, wild landscape I'd explored with him as a child now felt different. Sharper. Nature hadn't changed, but something in me had. As we drove, I kept replaying the same scenes. He'd buy "fixer-uppers." Old houses full of problems, but he saw only the potential. Each time, he'd dive in with energy: new tiles, fresh plans, stacks of new windows waiting to be installed. He'd fill the garage with materials, talk about the vision, the future. But the work never got finished. The projects dragged on, then faded. Eventually, he'd give up, sell the house at a loss, and move again, starting the cycle all over. To everyone else, the pattern was obvious. But to him, it seemed invisible.

Seeing his pattern so clearly forced me to look for the ones I hadn't been willing to see in myself. That's the strange thing about awareness. What we refuse to face inside often becomes visible only when life mirrors it back.

Developing awareness means noticing thought loops, questioning assumptions, and becoming an observer of your own life. A key question to ask: *What's really happening right now?* Most of us avoid this step because we don't want to face what it reveals. But if you don't see clearly, you'll never navigate effectively. I did this by assessing all 7 Pillars, analyzing where I was strong, where I was weak, and what needed to change. This level of honesty was necessary because you can't change what you don't acknowledge.

Ask yourself:

- Which areas of my life feel strong?

- Which areas feel neglected or empty?

- What's really happening beneath the surface?

3. ACCEPTANCE — Release the Weight Holding You Back

At first, I focused mostly on Aim, setting my goal, Awareness, seeing where I was, and then taking action to move forward with intention. That should have been enough. But every so often, I would get hit with something that sent me spiraling, a derailment that knocked me off course.

The reality was, for quite some time after moving to Miami, I hadn't fully accepted what was happening. I was making plans, setting goals, even reacting, but underneath it all, I was resisting. Clinging to the life I thought I was still going to have.

Then, one day, a friend who had been through a brutal divorce sat across from me, looked me straight in the eye, and said: "You have to accept the new reality. Let go of everything else. None of it matters, the house, the things, what you thought you'd have. It's all gone. The only thing that matters is that you and your children are healthy, that you love each other. Focus on that. Let go of the rest."

His words hit me with blunt force. I had been carrying this invisible weight, a tight grip on what once was, an unwillingness to fully face what had already changed. And that weight was holding me back. I would never heal if I couldn't truly accept my new reality. That was the missing piece. Acceptance. Psychologist and meditation teacher Tara Brach, who has guided thousands through the practice of Radical Acceptance, puts it this way: "When we put down ideas of what life should be like, we are free to wholeheartedly say yes to our life as it is."[39]

Letting go of what should be is where real power begins. I wasn't just resisting the pain; I was draining myself by being stuck in the past. Acceptance wasn't defeat. It was the release that allowed forward motion. Ralph Waldo Emerson wrote, "Finish each day and be done with it. You have done what you could."[40] Studies confirm it: people who accept their reality rather than resist it report lower stress, reduced anxiety, and more adaptability. Acceptance doesn't just ease pain; it frees up energy to build again. Only when I stopped clinging to the version of life I thought I'd have, and fully faced the one I was actually living, could I begin to move forward.

Most people misunderstand acceptance. They think it means giving up. It doesn't.

- **Acceptance is not passive.** It's not about sitting back and resigning yourself to a situation. It's about fully seeing reality as it is, without excuses and without blame, and then making the best possible decisions from that place.

- **Acceptance is not weakness.** It's the opposite. It takes immense courage to face what you've been avoiding, to stop telling yourself the comforting lie that things will "go back to normal." They won't. And that's okay.

- **Acceptance is about regaining control.** When we refuse to accept reality, we stay stuck. We wait. We hope circumstances will magically shift. But when we accept, we free up the energy to assess and adapt.

If you don't accept where you are, you can't move forward.

4. ASSESSMENT (+/–) — Choosing the Right Path Forward

Many decisions feel small at the time, almost insignificant, a split-second choice you barely register. After long days at work, they feel harmless, relaxing, even deserved, though deep down, we know better. And that's when it became clear. Every choice came down to this:

Was I choosing what strengthened me... or what weakened me?

Most people never ask that. Not because they don't care, but because they don't realize the real consequence of their decisions. A single choice might not seem like much, but choices aren't isolated. They stack. They accumulate, and over time, they shape the entire trajectory of your life. You don't wake up lost. You drift there, one unexamined decision at a time.

So I began assessing every choice by its true impact. Not just in the short term, but across time. Because every decision either fills or depletes, lifts you or pulls you down. But there's a critical piece many people miss: some choices benefit you while harming others. What seems positive in the moment can come at a cost to those around you. I needed a simple, visual way to see the ripple effects—not just the immediate gain, but the broader consequences. And I found it.

Every decision had two effects. One on me. And one on the people around me. When I laid it out visually, it formed a simple grid.

The +/– Grid

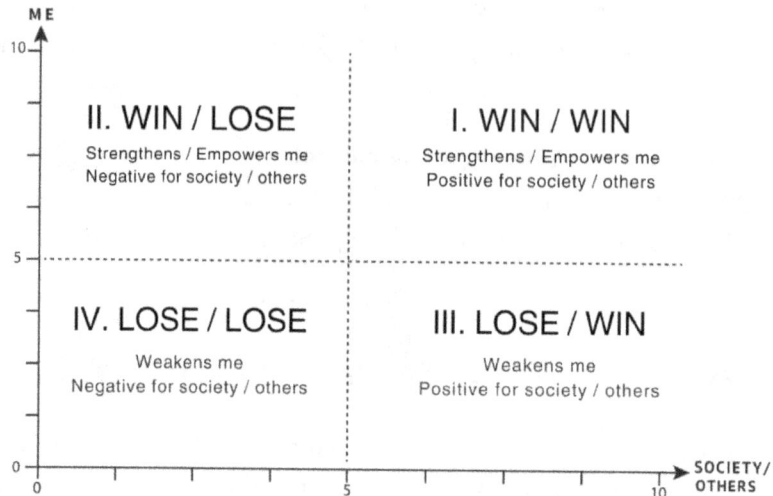

And just like that, the model came into focus. Some decisions lift both you and others. Those are your true north: WIN / WIN. Some reward you but hurt someone else. Those are the ones that feel smart now but leave regret later. Others deplete you, even if they help the world. That's noble once, but unsustainable as a way of life. And some… harm everyone involved.

The grid made it clear: this wasn't about making the perfect choice every time. It gave me a clear way to see the true impact of my decisions. Not chasing temporary comfort but choosing what strengthened me over time. Not all good decisions are easy, and not all hard ones are bad. What matters is direction. So instead of guessing, I updated my approach and ran every decision through two checks:

- Is this strengthening or weakening me?

- Is this strengthening or weakening others?

Many people don't struggle because they lack options. They struggle because they don't assess. They drift forward, never pausing to consider where their choices lead. As Thomas Jefferson warned: "Whenever you are to do a thing, though it can never be known but to yourself, ask yourself how you would act were all the world looking at you, and act accordingly."[41]

The most successful, fulfilled people don't just act. They evaluate. It doesn't have to be perfect; it just has to move you in the right direction. Assessment is like scanning a map with a compass. You're not just looking at what's ahead, you're gauging whether this path takes you toward your Aim.

So, before you make your next decision, ask yourself: Is this strengthening me or weakening me? Strengthening others or weakening them? And once the answer is clear, choose wisely.

5. ACTION — The Step That Brings It to Life

Goethe captured it centuries ago: "Knowing is not enough; we must apply. Willing is not enough; we must do."[42] There's a point when the plan is ready. The options are clear. You know what you need to do. But then, you hesitate. Doubt creeps in, disguised as logic. Maybe you should wait. Perhaps now isn't the right time. The mind spins stories of why it's safer to stay still. And just like that, you remain stuck, not because you don't know what to do, but because action is often the hardest step.

I've been there.

After the breakdown, the realization, and a new system taking shape, I still found myself hesitating when it came time to act. I had the Pillars, the Equation, and now the Ascend Wheel. But none of it mattered if I didn't move. I was standing at the edge of a new terrain, clear on where I needed to go, but still frozen. Because here's the truth: you can't think your way into a new life. You have to move your way into it.

Why We Stay Stuck

Science backs this up. Psychologists call it *the intention-action gap*, the space between knowing and doing. Studies show that even when people are fully aware of the right choice, they often default to inertia. Because action requires energy. And even positive change triggers resistance.

Neuroscientists have found that the brain perceives *uncertainty* as a potential threat, activating the same survival circuits that warn us of physical danger. This is why we hesitate, and why we find excuses to put things off until "the right time." But waiting for the right time is the surest way to stay exactly where you are.

As Don Miguel Ruiz wrote: "Action is about living fully. Inaction is the way that we deny life. Inaction is sitting in front of the television every day for years because you are afraid to be alive and to take the risk of expressing what you are."[43] The way to break the cycle is to move, even if it's small, even if it's imperfect. Once you start, momentum builds. And those small changes can shape the course of your life.

Fear, doubt, worry, like gravity, pull you down. The slide happens without effort. But there is no automatic upward force, no effortless rise. You have to create it. And that's what the Ascend Wheel is for.

When I was stuck, I learned something that changed how I approached action forever: I didn't need massive leaps. I just needed to break inertia. So instead of overhauling everything, I focused on the next smallest step. Then another. Until action became automatic. Psychologist BJ Fogg calls this the *Tiny Habits* principle: when an action is too big, the brain resists. But when it's small, ridiculously small, it bypasses resistance and creates a natural starting point.

That's how I pulled myself out. I stopped thinking about exercise and simply put on my shoes. I reached out instead of debating whether I should. I started, without waiting for the perfect strategy. Because forward is still forward, and even a stumble carries more power than standing still.

At some point, a deeper change happens: you stop *trying* to change and *become* the kind of person who moves. Behavioral scientist James Clear puts it simply: "Every action is a vote for the type of person you want to become."[44]

That's what The Ascend Wheel became for me: a way to generate momentum on demand. Understanding and planning weren't enough. I needed to actually move forward. And once I felt it, I saw I had not been stuck in the way I thought. I just hadn't known how to create lift. Now I did.

The Second Key

The sound was not a lock clicking shut. It was turning open, and something larger, waiting all along, came to life.

UNLOCK.

A new chamber was giving way. The Second Key had turned. A deliberate movement, guided by aim, like a wheel finding its rhythm on a steep incline. It was earned, not granted. One rotation at a time, it carved upward through gravity's grip.

I paused, letting it all settle. I looked back, not just at what I had uncovered, but what I had built. Every major breakthrough in my life had followed the same cycle: small, sustained, intentional efforts. The wheel spun. I hit bumps in the road, but I knew now how to keep it moving, and over time, I rose.

And in rising, I saw it more clearly:

The Pillars: the Lens. The structure to see life in a new way.

Key One, the Equation, reveals how everything connects and how to change what you feel.

Key Two, the Ascend Wheel, provides a clear path to rise.

Each one had emerged through a mix of insight and experience, tested in silence and forged in pain. Together, they revealed a living architecture, an organized rhythm inside the chaos of life. I stood there, feeling the exhilaration of something broader taking shape.

But then, a faint shift caught my attention. Nothing dramatic or obvious, just a strange echo, a pattern I couldn't yet identify. A few small actions, barely worth noting at the time, triggered disproportionate results. The wheel was turning, but other forces were driving the acceleration. At times, the system hummed louder than expected, like an engine running hot. I had filled the tank, but this felt supercharged.

The engine had caught something hidden. A configuration of subtle dials turning together.

And that… is what I was about to uncover.

CHAPTER 11
The GearShift

Where the Map Ends

There are places that resonate
deep within you. You hear about
them in the quiet hours of travel,
when the day's activities finally
still, the conversations soften, and
people speak in the kind of voices
reserved for stories they keep
close, never meant for the crowd.
More than names on a map.
Places that mark you. That follow
you home.

The Palawan Islands, where the water glows in a hundred hues of turquoise. The high deserts of Bolivia, so vast they erase the idea of bounda-
ries. Bunaken, a small island north of Sulawesi, where the reef drops off
into an underwater cliff so sudden, it feels like falling through liquid sky.
The list grew slowly over the years, each name a promise I made to myself
that I would one day see with my own eyes.

One destination kept surfacing in my mind: Patagonia. The edge of the
map. A land where glaciers move like time, and the earth feels ancient
beneath your feet. I had felt drawn to that region carved by ice and stone
since I started exploring the outdoors, though I couldn't say why. Maybe

it was the name itself, passed around campfires and stitched into the backs of jackets. I didn't know what I'd find there. I only knew I needed to go.

The pull was steady, and I stopped resisting. I chose the W Trek, a five-day journey through raw terrain. No phone signal, no digital distractions, just the trail. I had spent too many years surrounded by noise and chasing luxury. Now, I was seeking something more authentic. A way to connect to nature, to my body, to the part of me I had neglected. And it would bring me back to what I loved: hiking, wild landscapes, majestic vistas, the patience of long exposures.

But even as I mapped the route, my mind remained elsewhere, still working through the Pillars and the patterns I was seeing. Whatever I uncovered, I wanted to test it in the dirt, in the ache of my legs, in real terrain. At the time, I was devouring everything I could find about performance, human potential, decision loops, and habit systems. The deeper I read, the more one specific question haunted me: why do some people achieve extraordinary results, with the same resources, while others struggle to move the needle?

As I buried myself in research, the trek and the tools began to knit themselves together. Every great outcome is like a trek. To be successful, it requires the right gear, the right preparation, the right fuel, and the right conditions. Details you don't always think about, but ones that decide whether the journey flows or grinds to a halt. When you're packing for a multiday trip through shifting weather, every ounce counts. Toothpaste. Socks. Waterproof gear. Do I really need this? Will this help or hold me back?

What I didn't know then was that the Ascend Wheel wasn't the whole engine. It was the surface, the rotating rhythm you could see and follow. But beneath it lay a hidden layer. The mechanics where gears and teeth meshed together, creating acceleration. And that deeper force, the trail would help me uncover it.

Before I even knew it, I was on my way, packed up and airborne, heading from Miami to the far reaches of the southern continent, where the map thins out.

Clarity Through the Climb

The trail hugged the turquoise lakes, crossed stone-carved valleys, and climbed beside glaciers that ground their way through the land. Some days blazed under clear skies, others drenched us to the bone. And through it all, our trekking group moved in step. Wind at our backs, then in our faces. Pack straps digging into our shoulders. There were long stretches of silence where no one spoke, because there was simply nothing that needed to be said.

And somewhere in that rhythm, something began to settle. The trek wasn't just about endurance. It was about alignment. The right pace. The right use of energy. Having the right moments to refuel and recharge. What struck me was how the terrain mirrored everything I had been trying to understand. Each step a principle. Each choice a reflection.

That night, after our longest stretch, we reached a camp cradled between two towering cliffs framing the sky like figures standing watch. My legs ached, but my mind kept moving. I sat by the fire, the cold etched into my skin, my fingers barely moving. The wind fell silent, like the whole land had drawn a long breath. I opened my notebook to record what was surfacing before it slipped into the night. My mind kept returning to specific forces that showed up everywhere. Five of them, I'd later realize. But that night, I could only feel them pulling, like a compass trying to find north.

When I returned home, I unpacked more than just gear. I unpacked the choices we'd made. What we brought. How we rationed time. How we adjusted when the terrain shifted. Beneath it all, I saw the logic. These weren't just decisions. They were levers, forces shaping how we used what mattered.

I wasn't the first to notice this pattern. Across disciplines, habit formation, neuroscience, and behavioral economics, researchers found that when you make small, sustained improvements across multiple areas of life, the effects compound. This idea, known as the aggregation of marginal gains, was the philosophy behind one of the most dramatic turnarounds in modern sports.[45]

Sir Dave Brailsford didn't try to overhaul British cycling with a single breakthrough. His team focused on making tiny, 1% improvements across everything: bike aerodynamics, sleep quality, nutrition, and recovery. The result? They went from decades of mediocrity to winning multiple Tour de France titles and rewriting Olympic history.

I saw the same pattern in the Pillars. A 5% shift across multiple Pillars outperforms a 25% shift in just one. Strengthen one, and you feel it stabilizing the whole. Like adding an anchor point on a climb, the load redistributes. When small changes happen across multiple Pillars, they don't just add up. They compound, and the system begins to work with you. For you.

That was the secret I had missed: it wasn't about trying harder, but about activating the right forces at the same time. The trail had revealed the terrain. But now I needed to understand the mechanics. How to move through it faster, smoother, with less strain. It was time to uncover the system behind the stride. Five fundamental forces emerged. When aligned, they could multiply effort into results.

The Levers

You know this feeling. That moment when you're doing everything right, working hard and staying committed, and yet... progress is slow. Results are scattered. Something's missing. The levers are the forces that either weigh you down or propel you forward. The idea isn't new. Archimedes once said, "Give me a lever long enough and a fulcrum on which to place it, and I shall move the world."[46] He was naming a universal truth: with the right leverage, the impossible shifts.

1. Time: The Finite Factor

Time doesn't ask for permission. It moves, silently and irreversibly. Every wasted hour is gone forever. But when we move with it, intentionally, fully present, it becomes an amplifier. That's why every minute matters. Time is the one resource you can't buy, borrow, or extend.

Even Steve Jobs, who took Apple from near bankruptcy to one of the most valuable companies in the world, reminded us that the greatest resource isn't money. "My favorite things in life don't cost any money. It's really clear that the most precious resource we all have is time."[47] Jobs knew what we too often forget: when you spend time well, everything else compounds.

So, ask yourself: Are you spending shallow time, half-distracted, or deep time, fully engaged? Are you consistent or sporadic? Are you focused on what moves the needle?

2. Resources: The Amplifiers

Resources can either hold you back or help you rise. They may look like cold nouns: money, tools, human capital, networks. But in truth, they're force amplifiers. You can struggle alone or learn from someone who's already walked the path. Build a company slowly, brick by brick, or leap ahead with technology. Resources don't guarantee success, but they change its speed and scale.

One of the most overlooked resources? Relationships. We've all heard it: "It's not what you know, it's who you know." The right introduction opens doors you didn't know existed. The right community lifts you higher than you could ever go alone.

Some people make the mistake of thinking success is purely an individual effort. It's not. Nearly every great achievement in history has been built on the foundation of relationships, collaboration, and access to resources.

Money: The Most Misunderstood Resource

Among all resources, money is the one most people fixate on and often misunderstand. You'll notice it isn't one of the Pillars. That's intentional. Most personal development books treat money as an objective, something to be pursued in itself. But money isn't an end goal; it's a means to an end. It's a resource, just like time or knowledge, that you can use to accelerate and expand what truly matters, and reach what you wish to achieve.

Ask someone why they want more money, and you'll always get an answer beyond money itself: the security, the ability to provide for loved ones, the freedom to choose where they live, work that excites them, or experiencing more of the world.

This is why money belongs here, not as a goal, but as a tool. If your goal is to master a skill, it allows you to learn from the best. If your goal is to get fit, it enables you to hire a world-class trainer. If your goal is to live wherever you want, it can help deliver that. Money alone does nothing. It's what you trade it for that matters.

And history proves that wealth alone does not create fulfillment. Viktor Frankl, a psychiatrist who survived the Nazi concentration camps, found meaning even when stripped of every worldly possession. The key question isn't, "How can I make the most money?" but rather, "How much do I need to achieve the life I truly want?"

Chasing money for its own sake can become a trap, one that can steal your time and even health. But when used wisely, it's an accelerator. It can fast-track your progress, open doors, create opportunities.

As Tony Robbins puts it: "It's not the lack of resources, it's your lack of resourcefulness that stops you."[48] A reminder that resources themselves aren't the difference-maker: it's how creatively and courageously you use them.

3. Energy: The Force That Drives Execution

Energy is your internal flame. It doesn't show up on to-do lists, but it determines whether you crawl or fly. When energy is steady and focused, every move becomes a multiplier. You don't need more hours. You need more voltage in the ones you already have.

Two people can work the same amount of time, yet one gets exponential results. Why? Energy. A fatigued mind takes three hours for what a sharp, rested one can do in thirty minutes. Even the best strategies collapse when energy is low. But when you're charged, everything shifts.

The pattern became clear. Energy had three dimensions that mattered most: depth, sustainability, and replenishment. Was I truly immersed, or just going through motions? Could I maintain this pace, or was I headed for burnout? And was I refueling my mind, body, emotions, or just running the tank dry?

Cal Newport calls this state Deep Work, the ability to focus without distraction on cognitively demanding tasks. His research shows that even brief periods of deep work lead to significantly higher output than scattered effort.[49] The point is simple: deep focus multiplies output.

Even Aristotle, more than 2,000 years ago, recognized this truth: "The energy of the mind is the essence of life."[50] Today, neuroscience echoes the same reality: energy shapes everything.

4. Knowledge: The Intelligence Multiplier

Knowledge is your navigation tool, but it only matters if you walk. You can study maps for a lifetime, but they mean nothing if you never move your feet. Those who thrive don't just collect insight, they test it, stress it, reshape it. The ones who move the farthest? They don't hoard information. They turn understanding into action.

Knowledge alone does nothing. Application is everything. It's what shifts results. Someone performing CPR might have watched videos or read about it, but in a real emergency, theory alone won't save a life.

I reflected back on the hike, and not just effort or mindset, but knowledge had shaped so much of what we were able to achieve. That's why we had a guide. Someone who could read the terrain. Who knew when the clouds would just pass by, and when they signaled a storm. When to pause. When to push.

5. Number of Variables: The Compound Effect

What mattered most wasn't any single lever. It was the number of variables working together, and how well they aligned. When gear, weather, team energy, and terrain came into sync, everything began to move as one. The climb became almost fluid. But when even one variable dropped out of harmony, the system faltered.

Most people make changes in isolation. They focus intensely on one area of their life, believing that a single major improvement will change everything. It doesn't. True transformation comes from small, coordinated shifts across multiple areas. That's when the real magic happens.

As Robert Collier, one of America's great early self-help writers, observed: "Success is the sum of small efforts, repeated day in and day out."[51] It isn't one heroic push—it's the compounding rhythm of consistent steps.

Back to the Trail

My mind drifted to Patagonia. What stayed with me wasn't the distance I covered. It was the moments when things flowed, when motion felt unforced. Out there, effort alone wasn't enough. It had to be amplified. And now I saw it: five levers. They move through you when the pressure is high and the way forward is unclear. When all five align, you don't just make progress. You accelerate.

So, I wrote down what I had learned, without thinking: Time. Resources. Energy. Knowledge. Variables.

I stared at the words in my notebook. This hadn't started in a lab. It had formed out there, on the trail, under pressure. Etched into the cadence of the natural world. Not new, simply uncovered.

I circled the first letter of each word, and the shape began to reveal itself, a way to name what I'd already lived.

TREK-V = Time × Resources × Energy × Knowledge × Variables

My breath caught. I'd found it, the very pattern I had walked, now made visible.

The Third Key

The Ascend Wheel had moved me. But this key made that movement efficient. Smarter steps and better leverage. This was the GearShift.

UNLOCK.

It clicked: clean, precise. This was the mechanism I had missed. The hidden system inside the Wheel, the part that turned rhythm into acceleration. Less friction, more thrust. Teeth interlocking, tension syncing, each lever amplifying the next. On the trail, under pressure, I'd felt it. Five forces working as one, creating momentum.

It was the Third Key. The multiplier that unlocked the entire system.

I let the realization settle. From all of it, the windswept valleys, the glaciers and black beaches, something finally emerged. All the fragments aligned like bolts sliding into place. The pieces were keys. A sequence that had always been there, waiting to be unlocked.

All three keys, finally together.

And when they turned, a door opened.

CHAPTER 12
The Framework Comes Alive

The Vaulted Chamber

I had crossed the threshold. The moment I'd been chasing for years, through journals, late nights, and the ache of unanswered questions, was no longer out there. It was here. Complete.

I closed my eyes and let go of the instinct to steer or analyze. Instead of reaching for ideas, I allowed space for whatever had been waiting to appear. Noise fell away. Thought softened. Time blurred. The images formed on their own, unforced. Shapes emerged in that inner darkness, blurry at first, then becoming sharp. A vision, yes, but more than imagined. Remembered. As if I had spent a lifetime circling it, only now seeing the door.

And then, I found myself inside a vaulted chamber, high and circular. The space felt different. Structured, yet breathing. It wasn't rigid; it felt rooted, like a living architecture that was timeless.

Despite the darkness, the light carried a kind of presence. I stood still, barely breathing. This was a room I had always carried within me, but only now could I step into it.

Around me, a sequence of tall, radiant panels of stone and shadow, each one inscribed with a symbolic shape. Forms I had uncovered now stood before me, whole and clear. Each wall revealing its truth.

On the first wall, a fluid geometry, drawn like a double infinity, its lines glowing faintly. It was the Equation. Where thought, action, and connection impacted emotion. The hidden pulse beneath the Pillars. It made the invisible connections visible.

I turned and saw the giant carved Wheel. Not decorative, but dynamic. Five "A"s etched in sequence, forming a rhythm: Aim, Awareness, Acceptance, Assessment, Action. I could feel it turn, breathing, as if the chamber itself exhaled through its rhythm. This was the process that moved me forward when clarity wasn't enough.

The last wall was gleaming like stone polished by centuries. It rose before me, marked with a pattern of interlocking rings: nested gears like the inner workings of a clock. Each of varying sizes, engraved with a single letter, symbolizing the forces I had once felt but only later named: Time. Resources. Energy. Knowledge. Variables. But here, they weren't words. They were instruments that multiplied, a hidden engine. This was the GearShift: the mechanism beneath momentum.

I stood there, breath still, heart pounding, as the chamber shimmered. The panels curved upward into a domed ceiling, where everything converged. Traced above me were the 7 Pillars. It was the arch that held everything together, the Lens that made sense of the journey in this world.

For a moment, I hesitated. What if I had imagined it? What if it disappeared the instant I tried to name it? But then I opened my eyes. And it was still there. Not a fading vision, a memory made clear. I reached for my journal, and without overthinking, I captured everything I had seen so clearly. I looked down at my notes, my rudimentary drawings, and let the details find their shape.

I saw clearly the two separate but tightly interconnected layers.

The 7 Pillars: the Lens that shapes how you see and make sense of life.

The Three Keys: the tools that operate inside that Lens to create movement and change.

Together, they formed the Framework. No longer loose fragments, but a coherent structure for living.

Inside the Architecture

In that silence, with every piece now in place, the Quest ended. It was time to start building. The old map, the one that no longer matched reality, couldn't guide me anymore. I had stepped into the inner scaffolding itself, rising above the surface, with its ceiling and walls surrounding me. The Framework fully formed: a Lens to see clearly, and the tools to move deliberately.

This was the 2nd Shift.

I now had a way to interpret what was unfolding, through the Pillars, and a set of tools to respond, through the Equation, the Wheel, and the Gear-Shift. Not ideas to consider, but a system to act from.

And once inside it, how you move changes. You no longer push blindly or chase the next answer. You act from within the system itself. Decisions have context, effort has direction, progress becomes intentional. From here on, the work is no longer about finding the path. It's about walking it. Each day becomes part of the climb.

I won't pretend it was simple. I had years to let these pieces settle, to strengthen and integrate each part. At first, it felt like too much at once—like learning to drive for the first time, too many parts moving, nothing fluid yet. That's why I revisited certain concepts deliberately to refine them. Repetition was how the framework became second nature.

The Pillars became my reference point, a way of seeing my life through that Lens. I'd pause during decisions and ask: Which Pillar does this touch? Does this choice strengthen it or weaken it? A late-night scroll might numb me for a moment, but I could see how it weakened my

Physical Pillar the next morning and quietly eroded Mental Clarity. A 10-minute walk at lunch, or calling someone I cared about, lifted several Pillars at once. Slowly, I started choosing more of what strengthened multiple parts of my life.

At the same time, I kept working on the tools together, in real situations. The Equation showed me the interconnections. The Wheel guided my next steps. When that rhythm felt natural, I brought in the GearShift to increase momentum. Over time, these stopped feeling like tools I reached for and became the way I moved.

Eventually, something subtle but powerful took hold. The Framework no longer needed constant attention. I didn't have to think through every detail. It shaped how I noticed opportunities and made decisions. I now stood inside a system I could return to, again and again, as life unfolded.

However, the Framework doesn't resolve everything. It doesn't remove uncertainty or friction. But it replaces the broken advice and guesswork with a clear process.

The Mirror and What Lies Beneath

But sometimes, just when you think you've arrived, when you've walked the trail, you realize you've only rebuilt what's visible, what sits above the surface. There's still a layer you haven't touched. Not another step forward, but a step downward.

I thought I had seen the whole landscape, but I had only charted what was already lit. That was the mirror: beautiful, crisp, and clear. The Framework worked. The pieces had locked into place, holding it up. But mirrors only show what is visible.

They do not reveal what lies beneath the surface. Sometimes the most dangerous ruptures don't strike from above. They rise from below. What happens there doesn't stay contained. It leaks into decisions, relationships, and the quiet moments when you're left alone with yourself.

I hadn't yet named or understood the dynamics of what lay beneath, though they were already at work. I would painfully realize that what rises above is always shaped by what lies unseen.

And that is when the camera flipped.

Part 4
THE DEPTHS

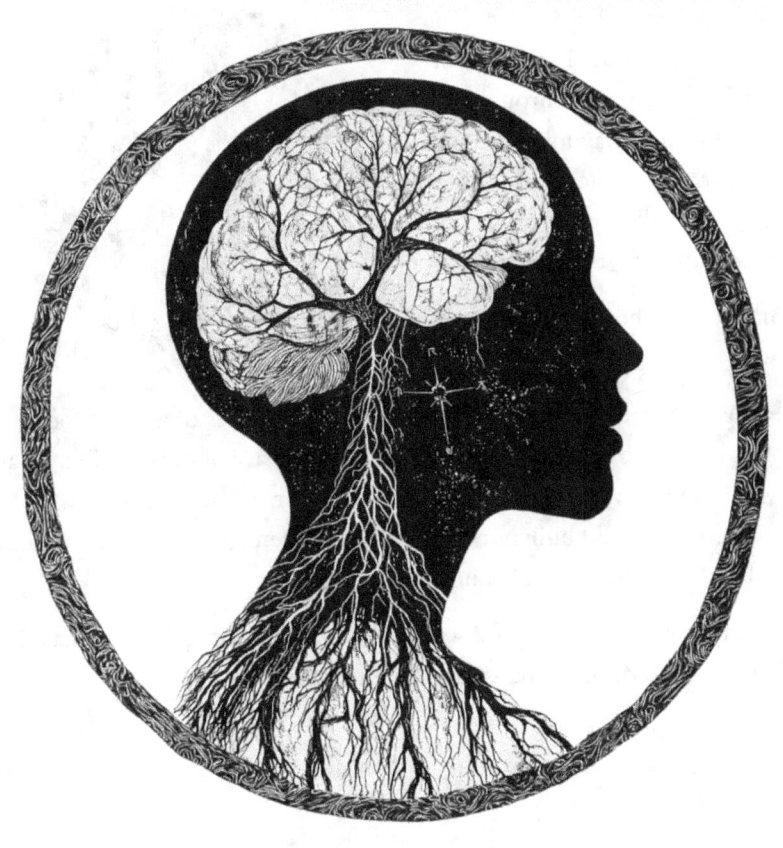

CHAPTER 13
The Systems Running Your Mind

The Camera Flips

In Iceland, the Lens opened wide. Landscapes stretched beyond the eye, water crashing like time, volcanic peaks cutting through the night sky. In Patagonia, the trek became rhythm, each step a question, each valley a lesson. I had turned outward, seeking clarity.

But then... the wide shot narrowed.

The light shifted, from vast blue skies to the confines of a small room. I wasn't hiking now. I had dropped below the surface of my own life. That is where I went next. Not in the mountains, or in the gear on my back, but in the rooms I'd built as a child. Walls plastered with unspoken rules, lined with images that still controlled me.

I felt the pull inward. The landscape narrowed, becoming less predictable. There were no detailed maps for where I was going.

The Moment That Opened My Eyes

It was Sunday evening. The light was low, the house heavy with silence. I had just zipped up my bag when I felt a tug, small hands clutching my shirt, as if trying to keep me anchored in place.

"No, Daddy. No."

My daughter's words tore through me. She stood in the doorway, shaking her head, her cheeks streaked with fresh tears. I crouched down, tried to smile. "I'll see you soon, my love. You're going to have so much fun this week." But what I said felt thin, like a bandage over an open wound.

"I don't want you to leave," she said.

Her face twisted with grief too big for her size. I bent down, kissed her forehead, and brushed a strand of hair from her face. And then I did the hardest thing. I let go and turned away. A thousand doubts screamed inside me. Was I doing the right thing? Or just learning how to live with the distance between us? I walked through the door, out of the house. Slipped into the car and closed the door behind me.

As I pulled away, the pain rose hard and sharp. My throat tightened, an emptiness spreading through my chest. My hands gripped the wheel. My eyes stung. And then I did what I always did in these moments. I played that song. The one I always turned to when grief came knocking. A slow aching melody about saying goodbye.

Later that night, I called her on FaceTime. To my surprise, she was all smiles. Bubbly. Chatting away about something funny that had happened. Meanwhile, I was still carrying the heaviness of walking away.

And that's when it hit me with a clarity I couldn't ignore. She was okay. I wasn't. She had a loving home, stability, parents who adored her. She had probably cried for a few minutes, then run off to play. The brokenness wasn't in her. It was in me. Why did my system react like this? Why couldn't I shift my emotional state as naturally as she did?

In that instant, I realized the ache wasn't just about saying goodbye. It was about something deeper: an old system pulling my strings. Automatic processes shaping how I experienced reality. No matter how much I learned about the Pillars, the Equation, the Ascend Wheel, and the GearShift, there was something deeper. I had questioned and challenged so much, but there was still one question I hadn't answered: What was truly operating within me when I wasn't looking?

The Hidden Forces Controlling Your Mind

Most people believe they're navigating with logic, making conscious, rational decisions. I did too. But forces wired long ago were still pulling me back, directing me beneath my awareness. I was running on outdated software shaped by beliefs and fears I had unknowingly absorbed. I believed my decisions were my own. I was wrong. My conscious mind wasn't in control.

I had two options: either confront the world beneath or keep repeating the painful loops on the surface. What I hadn't seen until then was that these reflexes and stories weren't scattered. They were organized, layered into the base on which everything else rested. And unless I addressed it, what I had built, the Pillars, the Equation, the Ascend Wheel, and the GearShift could falter under pressure.

This is what I call the Foundation.

It's the code beneath your choices, the hidden architecture of brain processes and stored data. No matter how strong your tools, your climb will falter if the bedrock beneath is fractured. And until you understand it, you can't influence it.

The Two Systems

Even when we think we're steering, something older and faster is already in motion. Psychologists Daniel Kahneman and Amos Tversky showed that over 95% of our daily behaviors aren't conscious at all. They're automatic. They arise from two competing systems inside the brain: one fast and instinctive, the other slow and logical.[52]

They're different from the Seeker and the Analyst, which are inner motivational drives linked to your identity. These two systems, by contrast, are processing modes. They explain how your mind handles information. It's the way you're wired to process what's happening in your life, moment to moment, and how that wiring hijacks your decisions before you even realize it.

And understanding these two systems explains why you keep falling into the same patterns, and why change, real, lasting change, feels so hard. It's because two very different forces are at work inside your mind. They're called System 1 and System 2.

Here's how they work.

System 1: The Instinctive Mind

It's ancient and fast. It doesn't think: it reacts.

System 1 is the primal, automatic part of your brain that senses danger before you consciously register it, that flinches when a ball is thrown at your head. It's both emotional and deeply intuitive.

It's also the part that accesses your deepest fears, your childhood conditioning, and the scars of past wounds. It's why a certain tone of voice can trigger a disproportionate reaction. Why you find yourself repeating destructive patterns even when you know better. And it's the reason rejection can feel unbearable.

System 1 is survival-based. It's wired to protect you. But in doing so, it often locks you in patterns that no longer serve you. It's also predictive. It doesn't wait for proof of danger; it anticipates it. That's why a shadow in the dark makes your heart race before you even confirm what it is. Neuroscientist Lisa Feldman Barrett discovered something radical: your emotions aren't just reactions, they're simulations.[53] Your brain runs a constant prediction loop, guessing what will happen based on the past. If

System 1 accesses an old association of something it tagged as dangerous, it will keep reacting to that ghost, even when the danger is long gone.

So, if you learned early that closeness wasn't steady, System 1 might cause you to pull away in relationships, creating distance before you even register why you're doing it. If you grew up in scarcity, it may drive you to hoard money, even when you're financially safe. Or if you were told you weren't good enough, it can lead you to sabotage opportunities so you don't have to risk the pain of failure.

System 1 doesn't reason. It's trying to protect you, even when that protection harms you.

System 2: The Rational Mind

It's slow and effortful. It plans, reasons, and evaluates, but only in small doses.

System 2 is the conscious part of your mind, the part that reflects before acting, and helps you weigh pros and cons. It's what we associate with reason and self-control. But here's the catch: System 2 handles only a small slice of what your mind is dealing with. The rest has already been handled by the faster system underneath.

And System 2 tires easily. The more pressure you're under, the less it shows up. You can know exactly what needs to change and yet struggle to act on it. This is why you still avoid the conversation even when you know what's right. Still text instead of speaking. Or you say yes when you mean no.

The Rider and the Elephant: Why Willpower Alone Fails

Psychologist Jonathan Haidt, in *The Happiness Hypothesis*, describes the two systems like a rider and an elephant:[54]

System 2 (the rider) is logical and rational, trying to steer you toward good decisions.

System 1 (the elephant) is instinctive, emotional, and immensely powerful.

The rider can plan ahead. Set goals. Analyze options. But it's a bit like sitting in the passenger seat, giving directions to a stubborn driver who often ignores you. You can advise, you can point out the turns, but when emotion surges or fear kicks in, the elephant takes over. And the truth is, the rider isn't really in control. The elephant is.

That's why we so often feel torn between what we want to do and what we actually do. Why we promise to stop procrastinating, leave toxic relationships, and yet, when the moment comes, we slip back into the same familiar patterns.

I used to believe willpower was enough. That if I just tried harder, forced myself to act differently, I could change. But that's not how the mind works. Because lasting change doesn't come from trying to wrestle the elephant into submission. It comes from retraining it. And to retrain it, I first had to understand what it runs on: the invisible code beneath every decision, every hesitation, every repeated mistake.

What Your Systems Are Running On

To change the script, you have to understand the deeper architecture within. Without that, no amount of tools or willpower will hold. You'll keep repeating the same loops, no matter how much you learn. Because your mind isn't reacting randomly. It's pulling from an internal database you never consciously chose. This is what System 1 and System 2 are actually running on—the data beneath the processing. Some of it is ancient, written into your DNA, and some of it is absorbed through childhood, trauma, and the environments that shaped you.

I realized I had to go one layer deeper. Without knowing it at the time, I was about to pull back the curtain and get a glimpse of what lay hidden on the other side. And what I found fundamentally changed how I understood myself.

CHAPTER 14
The Hidden Code

The Story You Didn't Choose

I was 12, visiting my father during the winter holidays. The wind cut through the air, sharp enough to sting. I remember tugging at my scarf, pulling it tighter around my face, as he walked a few steps ahead. My father didn't seem to notice the cold. I stared at his sweater and asked, "Dad… where's your jacket?"

He smiled, as if it were nothing. "I gave it away," he said, like he'd just handed someone a napkin. "There was a man outside the church. He needed it more than I did." He chuckled, his blue eyes warm yet piercing. But I didn't understand, not really. I tensed, as if I had just witnessed a moment both beautiful… and unbearably sad. That was my father. Brilliant. Lost in bigger questions, often missing the practical ones. Generous in ways that left him exposed. At times, his open heart made a difference. Other times, unfortunately, he was taken advantage of.

That summer, my sister and I visited him in the United States. He had sublet his little studio while on an assignment abroad. When we arrived and opened the door, we froze. There was nothing. No furniture, no dishes. Just a bare mattress on the floor, the only thing left. The students who had rented his place had sold nearly everything. "Why didn't you do something?" we cried out. He shrugged. "They needed it more than me. Those poor kids have nothing. It's fine, it's just things." He wasn't upset, not even a little. He carried a quiet peace, as if the ordinary burdens of the world passed straight through him. As long as he had his books and his students, he was fine. But I wasn't. I was furious. Not just at what had been taken, but that he let it happen. How could they strip him of so much? How could he offer no resistance, and let them take advantage of his beautiful heart? What hurt most wasn't the emptiness of the room; it was how easily he accepted it.

At the grocery store, he turned his meager financial situation into a game: the hunt for the ultimate deal. "Three cans of tuna for a dollar," he'd beam, holding the prize aloft like a trophy. "Or five packs of ramen, you can't beat that." And I would nod, smile, play along. But something deeper than logic was forming inside me. A vow. Quiet but absolute: I will never live like this. I didn't want to give away my coat in the snow. I didn't want to be taken advantage of and sleep on a bare mattress. And I refused to teach my children to survive on the cheapest meals imaginable.

And so, in my life money became a trigger. Despite what I learned in Guatemala, that I needed very little to feel alive, everything began to change when I started a family. My perspective shifted. Suddenly, safety and predictability became the priority, not just preferences. That need for control was etched deep in my nervous system. A belief that stability was essential. That being a good father meant shielding your children from uncertainty, that risk was selfish, and that following your passions without protection, like my father so often had, could be dangerous.

Epictetus wrote, "It is not events that disturb the minds of men, but the view they take of them."[55] I didn't know it then, but that was exactly what had happened to me. The events themselves, those early moments with my father, weren't what bound me. It was the meaning I attached to them. I didn't consciously choose that story. Yet it was recorded within me.

And like all the stories we carry without knowing, it became more than a memory. It became a program. In every reaction, in every hesitation, you're not just responding to the present moment. You're running code from childhood. Your mind pulls from that old file, even when you don't know it's there.

That's why I couldn't move on when my daughter did. Her sadness passed. Mine didn't, because I wasn't just feeling her grief, I was carrying my own. A pain I'd locked away, until she touched it.

Your Mind Is Running on Pre-Loaded Data

I didn't know it then, but that moment with her wasn't just about her. It was a reflection of a hidden part of me, a truth that revealed itself in the most unexpected way.

For years, I tried a variety of books and strategies. None reached the root. That's when I realized: the beliefs driving me were deeper. They were emotional, subconscious. I needed insight I couldn't reach through intellect alone.

So, I went to Sedona, Arizona. I was looking for answers, but not the kind you find in everyday advice. I booked a session with a spiritual counselor named Elizabeth. Sedona is known for its energy vortexes, for transformative internal work. I went there with no big expectations. Just a faint hope that maybe, somehow, she could help me see what I couldn't.

What I uncovered in that dimly lit room splintered a part of me I didn't even know existed, something that had long been sealed shut.

The Two Types of Data

What that moment revealed wasn't unique to me. In everyday life, we reference a database of old experiences and buried rules. A file system we don't even know exists. One that is pulling the strings before we have a chance to think.

Before you even process a situation, your brain has already retrieved from its internal storage and determined how you should react. Your mind is like a processor, running not only on two systems, but accessing from two types of data. One is hardwired into us, etched into our DNA before birth. The other is written over time, shaped by life, experience, and memory.

Finally, I saw it. The operating system I had felt beneath the Pillars, that quiet force pulsing through everything. This was what had defined much of my life without my permission. And now that I could name it, I could finally change it.

This stored information comes in two forms; I call them hard and soft data:

- Hard data: The instincts and survival mechanisms wired into your DNA.
- Soft data: The beliefs, values, and experiences you've absorbed over a lifetime.

The first is fixed, forged over millions of years of evolution. The other is fluid, influenced by your personal experiences. And whether you realize it or not, this is what's running your life.

Hard Data: The Ancient Code

Hard data is the ancient memory stored within your mind. It's not chosen; it's inherited. This core programming prioritizes survival. Neuroscientists call it "adaptive memory"[56]: the reason certain fears and biases feel automatic. Your brain is doing more than reacting; it's retrieving scripts designed to keep you alive.

Fear of falling. Fight-or-flight. The need to belong. These aren't quirks, they're survival code. Even your brain's tendency to make snap judgments? That's energy conservation. All of it worked… once.

But in the modern world? They often hold us back. Fear of rejection once kept us safe from being cast out of the tribe. Now, it makes us afraid to speak up or take risks. The instinct to store food helped our ancestors survive famine. Now, it can turn into hoarding or binge-eating behaviors. And the impulse to conform keeps us following societal norms that don't actually serve us.

You can't delete your hard data. But you can learn to spot when it's steering. The goal isn't to overcome your instincts. It's to work with them, without letting them run the show.

Soft Data: The Mental Code You Can Rewrite

Not all your programming was hardwired at birth. Some of it was written over time, by the people who raised you and the moments that broke or uplifted you.

This is your soft data: your acquired programming.

It's the baseline code imprinted in childhood, often in the half-light of bedrooms, car rides, or raised voices overheard behind closed doors. It's when you learned what love looked like, or didn't. It's the story etched into your nervous system after being laughed at in class, rejected by someone you trusted. You didn't choose this programming. You absorbed it.

And over time, it became invisible: the belief that you're not enough, the idea that risk equals pain. These aren't conscious decisions. They are conclusions drawn by a younger version of you trying to survive.

But here's the truth: just because it was written, it doesn't mean it's permanent. Your brain is changeable. Beliefs can be rewritten. Pathways reshaped. Just like a forest trail fades if you stop walking it, those old scripts lose power when you stop repeating them. And with every conscious thought, with every new choice, you carve a new path forward. Your mind can rewrite its internal files in the same way a software patch corrects errors in a program, if you know how to access them.

Soft data determines how you see yourself and the world. Among its most powerful elements are three that shape nearly everything:

- Beliefs – The deeply held assumptions you have about yourself and the world.
- Values – The principles that guide your decisions and sense of purpose.

- Memories – The emotionally charged moments and stories you carry from the past that mold how you react in the present and what you expect from the future.

Soft data is personal; no two people have the same set of experiences, beliefs, and values. And here's the kicker: soft data is often absorbed unconsciously. You didn't decide your earliest beliefs about what love meant or how success looked. They were modeled for you. You didn't choose your first fears. They were formed by experience. Your values? They came from culture, family, and environment.

And yet, while you may not have chosen your original soft data, you do have the power to rewrite it. That's not just a hopeful idea. Cognitive neuroscientists have found that beliefs are simply thoughts repeated so often that they become embedded as reality. But the same process that created them can also undo them. When you consciously introduce new thoughts, over time, you weaken old patterns and form new ones. And in doing so, you're not just rewiring your mind, you may be reshaping how your genes express themselves in response to the world around you.[57]

I think of my father sometimes. How he spent hours at the table, sketching house plans he never built. Pages of outlines, paragraphs, ideas. Notes for a whole series of books he never finished. As a child, I didn't understand it. As a teenager, it frustrated me. I'd visit him in the summers, hoping for more time together, but many days, he was lost in the manuscripts. For years, I saw it as dysfunction, a kind of self-sabotage.

But when I began examining my own internal programming, I realized something I had never named. Those summers had quietly influenced me. Watching him start so much and complete so little wrote a belief into me long before I could articulate it: that stability depended on finishing everything, that I had to hold things together. Drifting meant danger. That was the soft data being formed.

And then a thought surfaced that unsettled me: What if, for him, the meaning came not from the finishing… but in the act of creation itself? That possibility lingered, refusing to settle.

Beliefs: The Powerful Mental Code

A belief is a thought that's been repeated so many times, your brain treats it as truth. Not a preference. A law. Neuroscientist Joseph LeDoux showed that emotionally charged memories can physically reshape neural pathways.[58] Beliefs formed under stress or strong emotions become hardwired into your fast-reacting, automatic System 1.

That's why even when you "know better," it can feel impossible to act differently. If you were told over and over, "You have to work hard for money," or "You're not good at this," your brain both stores the statement as fact and filters every experience through it. Your mind shows you the world through what you already expect to see, not as it actually is. This is why two people can experience the same event and interpret it completely differently.

Values: The Compass Guiding Your Life

Beliefs shape how you interpret the world. Values guide how you navigate it. Your values determine what you prioritize, how you make decisions, and what you're willing to fight for or let go of. But here's the catch: Most people never consciously choose their values. Instead, they inherit their sense of what matters from parents, culture, and the voices they were taught to trust.

If you grew up in a family that valued stability, you might resist change, even when growth requires it. If success was defined as status and wealth, you might chase achievements that don't actually fulfill you. And when independence was prized above all else? You might struggle to form deep relationships, even when you crave connection.

Until you consciously choose your values, you're living by someone else's. What was handed to you can start to feel like truth. Values, if left unexamined, can keep you stuck in place. Are your values truly yours, or were they handed to you? And if they were handed to you, are they still serving you?

Memories and Experiences: The Echoes of Your Past

Memories aren't neutral. They determine how you predict the future. Neuroscientists call it predictive coding.[59] Your brain is constantly anticipating what comes next, using the past to fill in the blanks. That's why trauma lingers. When something is highly emotional, your brain encodes it as a survival rule. The more intense the experience, the deeper the imprint, and the harder it becomes to overwrite.

Childhood painful experiences, heartbreak, public humiliation: these moments don't just fade… they dictate how we expect life to unfold. If you were abandoned once, your brain prepares for it again. And if you were told you weren't enough, and failed? It braces for the next fall, scanning for proof.

These shortcuts are meant to protect you. But left unchecked, they become traps. You're not reacting to life. You're responding to ghosts, old scripts you never chose.

In my own life, I could now see both systems at work clearly. The automatic, instinctive, emotional System 1 and the rational, logical System 2, and the data they ran on: hard data (wired within you) and soft data (formed by beliefs, values, memories, and experiences). But among the soft data, one layer had tremendous power: the wounds I carried.

These weren't episodes that just passed through me, they reshaped me. And sometimes, the trigger looked like my daughter's goodbye, but the pain actually belonged to the child I once was, still holding more than I could carry.

The Risk to Be Alive

I didn't fully understand it, not until that moment in Sedona unlocked what lay beneath the choices I made. The room was dim, soft light spilling across the floor, the corners fading into shadow. Elizabeth wasn't what I expected, no mystical airs, no cryptic pronouncements. Just a calm, unwavering presence, with eyes that carried a depth beyond words. It was there, in the thin, dry air of that red rock town, that I finally recognized what I'd been unknowingly carrying.

We sat in silence, the sandstone glowing just beyond the window. I had talked about my life, my dreams, the spark that had now dimmed, and the suffocating reality of obligation. I told her I had so many ideas, projects, visions of who I could become. But I couldn't move. I was frozen by the weight of responsibility.

"If I take the risk," I said, "I could lose everything." Elizabeth didn't flinch. She just looked at me with steady eyes and asked: "What's the worst that could happen?"

I paused. "I could fail," I said. "Leave a stable job, try something bold, and fall flat."

"And then?" she asked gently. "Then what?" "I'd probably have to start over," I said. "Earn less. Lose some comfort." "And do you believe," she asked, "with your background, your experience… that you wouldn't land on your feet?"

"No," I said. "I'd find a way." "And your family?" she asked. "They'd adjust," I admitted. "We'd live with less, but we'd be okay." She nodded. "Then what are you really afraid of?" I fell silent. My pulse accelerated. I knew.

I wasn't afraid of failure. I was afraid of reliving what I had never let go of. Of becoming the man with no coat in winter. The man who gave until there was nothing left and asked for nothing in return, who turned a grocery store trip into a bargain treasure hunt and smiled with pride at what he found. Who shrugged off poverty with a smile and a story.

I built my life in rebellion to that image, but in doing so, I gave fear the steering wheel. I convinced myself I was being responsible; that sacrifice was virtue, that putting my dreams on hold was what good fathers do. But underneath it all was a vow I'd made years before.

Breaking the silence, Elizabeth leaned in.

"You've built your life on a distorted story," she said softly. "One where the only choices are sacrifice or selfishness. Protection or freedom. But that isn't reality. That's conditioning."

Then she said something I'll never forget: "You're carrying the fear of a child. But you're no longer that child. You're the father now. With responsibilities, yes, but also with the right to dream, to create, to want more than just getting by."

I felt my throat tighten. She continued. "Now imagine everything you worry about. The financial fears. The pressure. The risks. Take it all to the extreme. What's the absolute worst that could happen?" I swallowed hard, then finally answered. "Death."

She nodded. "And are any of these choices about life or death?" "No," I said, barely audible. "Then why are you letting them steal your life?" Just like that, a wall I'd built started to fracture. For years, I had blamed my family, quietly and unfairly, telling myself they were the reason I'd set aside my passions. But they hadn't taken those passions from me. I had. Out of fear. Out of programming.

Elizabeth was right. I lived like disaster was just around the corner and any wrong move would bring collapse. As if dreams were luxuries I couldn't afford. None of it was true. The real threat wasn't failure. It was this slow erosion of the soul. The gentle fading of who I could become, strangled by the illusion of safety.

All those old fears, of not providing enough, of not being enough, weren't based on facts. They were ghosts from a story I never chose but kept living.

Don Miguel Ruiz wrote: "Death is not the biggest fear we have. Our biggest fear is taking the risk to be alive, the risk to express what we really are. Just being ourselves is the greatest fear of all."[60]

Those lines hit me with force. The danger wasn't dying.

The danger was never really living.

CHAPTER 15
Rewire Your Mind

The Invisible Wounds

A few years after the cliff and the end of my marriage, as I rebuilt my life, I tried to piece together my love life, too. I wanted a steady relationship, one that could last. And yet, something kept happening. Things would go well until suddenly, I would end it. Or sabotage it. For no real reason. I told myself: maybe I just wasn't built for deep connection anymore, that it wasn't the right fit, that I needed space. But in my gut, I knew there was more to it.

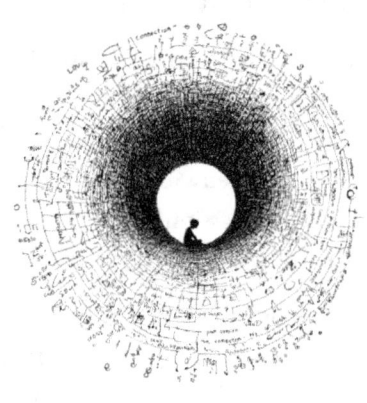

Finally, I managed to stay in one relationship for two years. She found me when I was broken, and stood by me through the hardest chapters of my life. Her laughter lit up the apartment. Her warmth steadied me. But I couldn't meet her where she was. I kept my distance, without realizing it. When she asked about the future, I'd deflect. "Let's not plan too far ahead," I'd say. "Let's enjoy the present." I wanted love, yet something in me still held back.

And so, it ended. She walked away. And I was alone again.

Sitting there with Elizabeth, I realized that the sense of an unseen force shaping my choices was what had brought me to Sedona in the first place. After our first conversation, Elizabeth motioned for me to follow her. We descended a narrow staircase. The light grew fainter, the air cooler, and with each step, it felt as if the world above us was slowly receding. She led me into a low-ceilinged room, the walls lined with shelves of worn books and softly glowing stones. The scent of incense clung to the air, earthy and steeped in ritual. She motioned to the padded table and asked me to lie down.

She studied me for a while, letting the silence settle, then asked gently,

"What do you want to understand about yourself?"

The question hung between us. What did I want to understand? I had spent years untangling my thought patterns, mapping out the Pillars, the Equation, the Ascend Wheel, the GearShift. But despite all of it, despite the clarity, the systems, and the knowledge, there were still places in my life where I felt stuck.

So, I told her the truth.

"I feel like there's something I can't see that's holding me back. I don't know what it is, but it keeps derailing me. Especially in relationships. It's like... there's a blockage I need to unlock, but I can't access it."

She nodded, as if she had already seen it. "Close your eyes," she said softly. "And just listen to my voice. I'm going to take you somewhere." My mind resisted. Thoughts fluttered. But her voice pulled me inward. Down. As if I were descending into an interior landscape with no markers, no sense of how far it went.

And then, just like that, I was gone.

No longer in the dimly lit room in Sedona. I was in a dark bedroom that smelled like fear. There, on the edge of a bed too big for him, sat a boy, folded into himself, knees drawn tight, face streaked with tears. I didn't recognize the room, but the feeling rose through me with painful clarity.

I knelt in front of him and met his eyes. In an instant, the distance between us dissolved. I wasn't just witnessing him. I was inside his small, breaking world. I could feel everything he felt, until the line between us faded.

And then, I wasn't just seeing him. I was him. All I felt was pain. The sting of a heart that learned too early how love can turn to absence, the shock of someone leaving while you were still holding on. Pain from the hurt of loving so deeply that the loss made everything feel unsteady.

My body was frozen, my heart pounding, my stomach twisted in knots. The emotion was so consuming it swallowed the room, my breath, and any sense of time. There was no sound, only the unbearable sense of being left. Of not being enough. Of waiting for someone who would never come back.

And in that moment, I knew. This was the wound. At one point, love had fused with pain, and opening up fully felt like stepping toward hurt. It was a script I lived for years without ever realizing it. I had built walls around myself, not because I didn't crave love, but because, somewhere in my core, I learned that love could vanish. That it could shatter without warning. That one day I'd laugh over dinner, and the next, I'd stare at a door no one would ever walk through again.

So, I protected myself. I played the part, yes: I gave affection and shared laughter, but I always kept one foot out the door. Because a part of me came to believe love wouldn't last. It never could. It would hurt. And if it was destined to disappear, it was better to stay slightly distant, to leave first before being left.

Jon Krakauer once wrote about this same hollow self-deceit in *Into the Wild*: "I had convinced myself for many months that I didn't really mind the absence of intimacy in my life, the lack of real human connection, but the pleasure I'd felt in this woman's company... exposed my self-deceit and left me hollow and aching."[61] I knew that ache. I lived it. And I carried it into every relationship, even when I pretended otherwise.

How Pain Becomes Identity

Some wounds heal. Others become part of us. Psychologist Carolyn Myss calls this woundology, the invisible process of shaping our identity around our deepest wounds.[62] We don't just remember pain. We relive it. And then we mistake it for fate, when in reality, it's just remnants of an old hurt pulling the strings.

In those years, I believed deep, loving connection just wasn't for me. I had mistaken self-protection for independence, slowly building armor that kept me safe, but also alone.

This is how a wound becomes part of the default setting running your life. A painful experience, such as abandonment, rejection, or failure, becomes more than just a memory. It turns into "proof" of how the world works. Your mind then writes a survival rule. "Love is dangerous." "I'm not enough." "I can't trust people." Your brain filters reality through that rule. You stop noticing proof that contradicts it, and unconsciously act in ways that reinforce the cycle. You push people away. You self-sabotage. You stay small. And the only way to change those rules is to go back and re-write the code.

Recoding: The Four Steps

The way you see yourself, your strengths, flaws, and limits, wasn't born in you. It was programmed through words, experiences, and the beliefs you absorbed. But just as it was written, it isn't permanent. Soft data isn't static. It's code you can edit once you know where to look.

Over time, I built a powerful practice for doing exactly that: a process I still return to whenever a belief no longer serves me. It comes down to four steps:

1. Identify the Wound

Many limiting beliefs start with a wound. That moment in Sedona had revealed the wound that shaped how I moved through the world. What other wounds had I unconsciously absorbed that were holding me back?

2. Expose the Lie

Is this belief actually true? Is love really dangerous? Was I really incapable of deep connection? Or was it a false equation I had carried for years? Love = Pain. Connection = Loss. Had I proved these beliefs right, or had I just looked for confirmation?

3. Challenge the Evidence

What proof had I gathered to support this narrative? How much evidence had I filtered out without even realizing it? What about the people who stayed? The ones who loved me fully? Had I built a life around protecting myself from something that wasn't even real anymore?

4. Provide New Data

Once the lie was exposed, it had to be overwritten. This meant consciously collecting proof of the opposite. People who stayed. Love that lasted. Safety that didn't require walls. Every new experience became a patch in the old system, proof that the old story no longer defined me.

The Science of Change: Why Knowing Isn't Enough

You might know exactly what you need to do, you may even picture the solution, even rehearse the conversation. But you still get stuck. Because logic doesn't override programming.

I had read countless books on personal transformation, psychology, and neuroscience. I had studied the concepts, even named the beliefs that held me back. And still, I regularly slipped into old reactions.

Psychologists call this the Knowing-Doing Gap.[63] It explains why people struggle to apply what they learn. It's not that we lack knowledge. It's that knowledge alone doesn't create change. Our behaviors aren't just intellectual choices. They're neural loops. The Foundation is so powerful because it works at the level of circuitry. And the more a loop is repeated, the stronger it becomes.

Change happens through what you practice, through repeated responses and experiences. Habits are like rivers carving through terrain. Every time you repeat an action, you deepen that riverbed. A misleading belief, if repeated enough, becomes a conviction. A small bad habit over time can lead to a major addiction.

So, until you interrupt the old pattern, until you break the flow of that river, your brain will default to what it knows. And that's why, even in a world overflowing with advice and information, many people still don't get better.

Disrupting the Cycle

The real breakthroughs don't come from adding more analysis; they come from collisions, moments that shake you out of the old rhythm long enough to choose a different response. In my case, it took an interruption to force my brain to update its map. Because when logic and experience contradict each other, experience carries more weight.

That's what ultimately changes your internal wiring. Not thinking. Not willpower. But breaking the old pattern, again and again, until the new one takes hold.

Many people don't realize that they're living inside an old script filled with scars, built on stories they tell themselves about who they are. "Everyone is necessarily the hero of his own life story,"[64] said novelist John Barth, who spent much of his career exploring how stories shape the lives we live. Too often, though, it isn't a story we ever consciously chose.

But even then, breaking free wasn't instant. It wasn't a switch I could flip overnight. Yet over time, something started to shift. The more I looked for new evidence, the more I saw through the veil that covered my eyes. The more I stepped into experiences that felt foreign, allowing love and embracing risk, the more my mind updated its filter. And the strange thing is, this new approach lit a spark in my life. I moved from feeling lost to feeling alive. Suddenly, I wanted to open up my heart fully and take a risk.

Then, it happened. After Sedona, I felt a strange lightness inside me, like someone finally opened a window in a house that had been sealed shut for years. I didn't just feel different; somehow, I knew I was different.

It was Easter Sunday. The space was alive with shrieks of children, mine among them, scrambling for pastel-colored eggs, lost in the whirl of movement and laughter. The sky above was that brilliant Miami blue, bold and cloudless.

And then I saw her. She stood at a distance, sunlight catching in her long brown hair, her deep blue eyes finding mine for an instant. It was as if the world slipped into slow motion. Everything else fell away. I wasn't analyzing. I wasn't calculating. I just looked at her. Each fine detail: how she moved her hands, how her hair shifted in the breeze.

Finally, I just walked toward her. No mask. No strategy. No protection. For the first time since I could remember, I felt ready to give all of me, from the start. To be all in, no games, no holding back.

Normally, I would've hesitated. I would've analyzed, maybe even waited too long until the moment passed and was gone. But not this time. I went straight to her, with my heart wide open. That was the day I met Claudia. The woman who became my wife, and who taught me how to love fully and fiercely.

Rewiring the Foundation

Slowly, decision by decision, I started seeing and experiencing the world and myself differently. The old patterns were disrupted. Because in the end, we are not trapped by our past. We are trapped by the stories we refuse to question.

Sedona opened a door within me. So many years trying to change my life without realizing I was building on the same damaged foundation. That night with my daughter at the door, I thought I was breaking her heart. It was never her pain. It was mine.

But now? Now I had proof that it could be rewritten. I was living on new terms. I wasn't trapped in my old story anymore. I had begun to rewrite it. And so can you.

This was the 3rd Shift. And it wasn't a mountaintop. It was an excavation.

I didn't rise. I descended into the unseen. Through a fracture. A narrow split in the bedrock of my story. And down there, in the dark, I found buried instructions. Old agreements I never consciously made.

I used to think transformation was about rising. About learning more. Becoming more. But this part was about uncovering what had been there all along. The old code, misguided fears and inherited stories still steering the ship.

The Lens, the Framework, the Equation, the Ascend Wheel, and the GearShift were the breakthroughs. But they would all collapse if I kept building on a cracked floor. That's the part most people skip. They try to climb without first going down. But if you want lasting change, this is the shift you can't avoid. Not the peak. The base.

I sat in silence. Pen in hand. And I wrote down every rule I inherited but never agreed to. One by one, I named them. And as the list grew, they loosened. Their grip weakened. They had been exposed.

The world inside me had shifted. Nothing dramatic. Just subtle rearrangements at the tectonic level. Nothing outside had changed. But my wiring had. The light felt different now. As if a fissure had opened in the ceiling, just enough to send a shaft of light into the darker corners within me. The camera didn't pan away. It leaned in, closer than ever, peering into the depths. This time, I didn't flinch.

But there was something I didn't see coming. Even the strongest foundation can begin to give way when something powerful, just out of sight, falls out of alignment. I didn't know it yet, but there was an unseen frequency permeating it all. A signal that everything else quietly followed. And when that signal began to fade… the whole system started to tremble.

I went downward on purpose. To heal, to understand, to rewire. And it worked. At least for now. I emerged with new eyes and firmer footing.

But not all descents are chosen.

And soon, I learned the difference.

Part 5
THE ABYSS

CHAPTER 16
Calm Before the Storm

The Summit

I had ventured deep into the roots of my life. But before I could unearth what was brewing beyond the map I'd drawn, life gave me a moment to pause. A breath. From the outside, everything looked intact. The systems were holding.

But inside the calm, something began to shift. Not urgently. It was like a compass nudging off course by just a few degrees, barely noticeable, yet enough to alter the entire direction if left unchecked. A thread was beginning to loosen. But I refused to see it. Not yet. I had finally arrived, and the peace was too hard-won to disturb.

I stood on the balcony of the chalet in Grindelwald, a small plate in hand, aged Gruyère, cornichons, a few slices of bread still warm from the toaster. The late afternoon sun spilled across the valley, illuminating the snowcaps with a subtle glow. I breathed in the cold, pine-scented air.

And there, in all its towering silence, stood the North Face of the Eiger: monolithic, eternal. A cathedral carved in stone. I gazed at it, not as a peak to conquer but as a witness. It had seen empires rise and fall, beliefs rewritten, blueprints abandoned. And yet, it stood, unmoved. A reminder of the power of simply enduring.

I breathed it in, color, light, and sound. No striving. No next step. Just a lingering stillness, one that comes only after the climb. That moment on the balcony, I sensed it for the first time: the summit. Not the top of the mountain, but a return to myself, a dawning recognition that I had made it through. And not just survived but changed.

The voices of my children drifted from within the chalet as they darted through the rooms. But out here, the silence wrapped around me. I took another slow breath. Finally, in what seemed like years... I felt at peace. Not a fleeting pause, but a deep, profound exhale. I looked out at that mountain, at the play of shadows across its face, and thought: this is what all the pain was for.

I paused, taking in the journey behind me. I had come a long way in every part of my life, each Pillar strengthened in its own way. What once seemed scattered now looked unified, as if seven parts of my life were finally rising into alignment.

Emotionally, I was lighter, more hopeful, as if a weight I'd carried for years had loosened at last.

Mentally, the old negative loops no longer ran the show; my mind was clearer, steadier.

Physically, I had rebuilt myself with better food, consistent workouts, and real rest.

Socially, I had grown closer to the people who mattered most. I had opened my heart, allowed love back in, and remarried.

Occupationally, I had returned to the work and projects that energized me; my career was thriving again.

Environmentally and materially, my life was grounded: regular time in nature, a stable home, finances no longer under strain.

Spiritually, I felt reconnected to something larger than myself.

Standing there, watching the last light shift across the Eiger's face, my life felt just as solid. After years of dismantling, I had finally rebuilt something real. The Pillars held. The Equation delivered. The Wheel guided my choices. The GearShift gave me acceleration. Combined, they didn't just work, they remade me.

I had finally made it.

And for a while, I let myself believe the climb was over, that I'd finally become whole.

The First Tremor

But here's what no one tells you about reaching the summit: the peace is temporary. The quest that once consumed you, suddenly over. And in its place? A motionless plateau. You expect to feel victorious. Instead... you feel the absence of movement. The silence after the storm. Not peace, but a pause. A space wide enough for the questions you'd been too busy to hear.

At first, I barely noticed it. A slight unease I kept brushing aside. A sense that something no longer fit the way it used to. I tried to ignore it, to stay focused on what was working.

And so, I did what had become my default response when discomfort appeared. I dove into the next project, the rush to solve the next riddle. I asked myself: How do you master the mind? Can you regulate your emotions? I thought to myself: if the 7 Pillars are the scaffolding of my life, I need to understand their essence, their components. They aren't abstract ideas. They are the working parts of change itself.

I went deeper. I immersed myself again in research, books, and models. Positive psychology, long-term life satisfaction studies, performance and emotion regulation, neuroscience, systems thinking,[65] and evidence-based therapies like CBT and ACT filled my days.

Every insight lit me up. I chased each one like it held the next key. And I didn't stop. I couldn't. Because somewhere along the way, the search became a place to hide. As long as I was digging, I didn't have to face the real question I was circling. The notes piled up. The documents grew.

But the feeling didn't disappear. It stayed with me, quiet but persistent, as if something essential still waited just beyond reach. And then, one night, lying in bed, I heard it. That voice. I ignored it, pushed it away. But it returned, again, and again. Undeniable. A weightless gravity tugging at the edges of what I'd built.

The next morning, I opened the Word document, the one that was supposed to be this book. The cursor blinked at the bottom of the screen: 1024 pages. I stared at it. And felt... empty. Not pride. Not excitement. Just numbness. All those years, all that furious gathering and compiling. And yet... the book was nowhere and everywhere at once. Somewhere along the way, it had become a maze.

That's when I almost quit. In one final move, I sent it to a friend. Someone who worked with authors and whom I trusted to tell me the truth. I expected feedback: how I should structure the flow, some parts to edit out, which parts worked. What came back hit like a punch in the gut:

"Nathan, this isn't a book. It's an academic dissertation. It's too much. Your story is powerful. But the deep dive into each of the Pillars? The piles of research. It doesn't fit together. You either have to cut it out entirely, or completely rewrite it."

I read her note twice. Then a third time. My chest tightened. Cut it down? Rewrite? After all this? The years of work, the obsession, the nights I couldn't sleep? Was it all... useless? I didn't respond. I didn't argue. I just sat there, paralyzed.

And so... I walked away. I saved the file in a folder, closed my laptop. I told myself it was enough. My life was steady now, I wasn't the man on the edge anymore. The insights lived in me. That had to be enough. For a while, I even started to feel free.

Until the doubts returned, questions I thought I'd buried by setting aside the file. They lingered, soft and insistent, at the edges of my awareness, refusing to disappear.

For years, the climb was the only rhythm I knew. I pushed forward, overcoming, researching, becoming. Then the urgency faded, and I didn't know what to do with the space it left behind. The drive that once kept me moving, the hunger, had thinned out. I couldn't tell where it had gone or why.

Momentum Without a Destination

I had fought my way back from rock bottom and rebuilt my life. The system worked. The proof was undeniable. Yet, this lingering, gnawing feeling remained.

So, I pivoted, shifting from research to real-world momentum. I filled my days with movement. New challenges. New environments. I chased adventures, convincing myself this would reignite the fire. Looking back, I can see it now: there was a silver thread running through it all. Thin. Vital. Almost invisible. It was holding something essential together, and it was starting to fray.

At first, I blamed exhaustion. Maybe I just needed rest. But as the weeks passed, the weight grew heavier. The habits that once felt effortless, the workouts, the deep work, even the momentum, now felt forced. Why did I suddenly struggle? Why did I wake up without the urgency that had once been automatic? Nothing I had built was broken. But something inside me had come undone. I pushed harder. The resistance only grew stronger.

The Hollowing Begins

I lay in bed, eyes open. The air felt wrong, stale. The questions came back. Flickers of doubt came and went. But then, they started multiplying, seeping into my thoughts like water through a crack in the ceiling. At first, just a few drops. Then a steady leak. And then... the flood.

How much time do I really have left?

Losing my mother, and later my father, had already shown me how quickly life can change, but only now did I feel time moving in my own body: in the lines on my face, in the way exhaustion lingered longer than it used to. I had lived as if there would always be more time. More time to write. More time to build. More time to chase the dreams I had set aside.

Suddenly, the illusion of endless time shattered. It happened as I was attending a conference, listening to Professor Dan Cable speak.[66] As I sat in the hall, he looked around the room and suddenly asked, pulling everyone into the moment:

"Raise your hand if you know your grandparents' names."

Most hands went up.

"Now, raise your hand if you know the names of their parents."

Almost all hands dropped.

"And their parents?"

Not a single hand remained in the air.

The room went silent. Three generations. That's all it takes before most of us are forgotten. I sat there, stunned. That realization, so simple, yet so profound, tore through me.

The work we pour our lives into, the dreams we fight for, and the words we write, do they even last? My father spent years working on books. Ideas he wrestled with, notes scattered across pages, many of them never becoming a final manuscript. He had stories to tell. Wisdom to share. But the day he died, much remained unfinished. Undone.

And then, in that conference room, I muttered to myself: "Would I be the same?" The weight of that question settled into my chest. Because now, time wasn't an abstraction. It was real. And running out. I thought of my book. Still sitting in that folder, massive yet incomplete. Just there, countless years of work. Would I let it fade away, too?

The Price of Protection

My work contract in Miami was ending. I now had to find a way to ensure my family was provided for, and that responsibility pressed on me like a cold, unrelenting hand on my shoulder. But no good options were available. The pressure was mounting. And so, I made the hardest decision of my life. I accepted a new position overseas with the company.

Paris. The city of light. But it didn't feel like a dream, more like a gamble. My mind was a storm, rationalizing. I told myself this was the best option. A better future for the children. Security. They would have a good education, and stay in the schools they loved. But was it?

I made precise arrangements. I'd be with my children as much as before, just longer stretches during the holidays. More uninterrupted time. I convinced myself this was the right call. But the truth? It felt like leaving everything that mattered behind. And when I boarded that plane, my heart ached. I felt a tear in the very fabric of my life.

One of those early nights in Paris, I sat on the edge of the bed. The room still felt unfamiliar, its air carrying the sharp scent of the recent cleaning. From the living room, I could hear Claudia and her son Alex unpacking boxes, their voices a low murmur through the half-open door. Outside, the hum of traffic drifted in, voices in French echoing off cobblestone. And suddenly, it hit me, not the logic of everything stable that I provided, but the ache of a family split across an ocean.

I couldn't shake the thought that I had traded presence for the family's security. That I was giving my children a provider... but losing the man they needed most. A father who was close by. That question haunted me: Had I escaped the fear that Elizabeth had helped me expose in Sedona, or just rebranded it as sacrifice for those I loved?

The silence in that room was suffocating. I tried to sleep but lay still, my thoughts spiraling. I pulled out my phone, stared at a photo of the kids smiling, arms flung around each other. The ache in my chest wasn't abstract. It was physical. Like something essential had been torn from me.

What if, in chasing security, I had broken the very thing I wanted to protect?

And then, before I could answer, before I could rebuild, before I could find my footing in this new life, everything came to a halt.

The World Stops

Just like that. The streets emptied. Borders closed. Flights were grounded. A silent wave swept across the globe, relentless and invisible. And I was caught in its wake. This city that was supposed to be filled with life, bustling with experiences, slowed to a trickle. I stared out the apartment window. The streets were cold and damp, the sky a muted gray. The light felt colorless, like the world had drained itself of contrast. Everything paused. The pandemic hit. And whatever chapter I thought I was entering... disappeared.

For years, my life was forward motion. Rebuilding. Creating. Every day, I knew my next step. Until suddenly, there wasn't one. The momentum vanished. And in that stillness, when the world froze, the thread that connected me to what mattered kept slipping. Quietly. Invisibly.

I woke up to the same four walls, the same routine, the same dull flicker of back-to-back Zoom calls. Days stretched, indistinguishable. The vividness of life lost its color. At first, I told myself it was temporary, a pause before the world picked up again. But as news spread of hospitals overflowing, people losing loved ones, this time, something was different.

When the noise stopped, the questions began. And not just for me, I saw it everywhere. People who had spent years grinding, chasing, pushing, now forced into stillness. Conversations that had once been about what to do tomorrow, where to escape to, turned into honest doubts about the lives we were building. I sensed it wasn't just me. It showed up everywhere, in friends, in coworkers, behind grainy webcams, speaking from cluttered desks and half-lit rooms. A simple, unavoidable question taking shape: What is all of this for?

But I didn't have the answer. Not yet. I tried to convince myself it was just a phase.

It wasn't. It was the beginning of the fall.

CHAPTER 17
The Undoing

Falling into Darkness

It unfolded in the small, ordinary motions of the morning. Breakfast, emails, headlines, the stacking of dishes in the sink. Daily life was familiar. But a slight distortion crept in. It felt like watching life unfold through frosted glass, muted, distant. The days began to blur. I kept doing all the things, answering calls, setting goals, and checking boxes.

But somewhere underneath, I felt it, that subtle fraying. The calm of the summit hadn't lasted. I filled the void like I always had, with action, projects, and the next goal. But the warmth that had lit those pursuits was fading. Light still filled the rooms, but it carried no warmth.

I couldn't see it yet, but I was no longer building. I was patching over. Reacting. Spinning. And the air around me felt heavier. There were mornings I couldn't pull myself out of bed. I lay there, numb, trapped in my own mind. I kept setting goals... but the fire was gone, and I didn't know why.

At first, I blamed the world. The pandemic. The pressure. The endlessness of modern life. The move. I kept adding to the list.

The Cracks Turn to Fractures

Maybe it was fatigue. Or perhaps the stillness around me made everything inside louder. The light in the apartment sat flat across the walls. Claudia and Alex were settling into their new routines, while inside me the unease grew a little more each day. A week passed. Then two. Then six. I wasn't tired, I was coming undone.

And that was when I started questioning what I had built. The Lens and tools I trusted like a compass now resembled a map whose lines had faded, the path no longer legible.

And the worst part? On the outside, I still looked "fine." No one knew. I answered emails. Led meetings. Smiled in Zoom calls. But I felt it, my own sense of self fading. Like color draining from a photograph left in the light too long.

And then came the final blow: full lockdown. Confined within the apartment walls. Everything I had built my life around, freedom, travel, adventure, and seeing my kids, was gone. And this gray city suddenly felt like a prison.

The World Fades Away

I had spent years building a system I believed would withstand any storm. Clarity, control, habits I thought were unshakable. But now, everything started to slip. It didn't happen overnight; it crept in with the slow ticking of the clock, the days tightening around me. A kind of soft, unrelenting dissolve.

Waking up felt less like beginning a day and more like resurfacing into something static. Coffee lost its taste. Music lost its rhythm. The world wasn't silent; it was muffled. Like someone had padded the walls of my life. I scrolled through the news. Image after image, nurses wrapped in gowns and shields, eyes ringed with fatigue. It wasn't the shock that got to me. It was the dull sameness of it all. Even a crisis, when played on a loop, starts to lose its edges. And within that blur, I stopped feeling.

I was once a man who burned brightly. And now... I barely flickered. My own world was eroding. Every day, it got worse. I woke up exhausted, no matter how much I slept. I was still doing everything right, but something had stopped responding.

The force that once fueled me, the relentless drive that pulled me forward, was gone.

And without it, the entire system collapsed. One night, Claudia asked if I was okay. I told her I was tired. That I just needed a reset. She nodded, but I saw it in her eyes. She knew. She could feel it. The descent into the abyss had begun.

The Questioning

For weeks, I tried to believe this was temporary. But deep down, I knew it wasn't. Because when I looked in the mirror, I didn't recognize the person staring back. I wasn't lost. I was empty.

For all the work I had done, I had overlooked something fundamental: we are not designed to operate in a constant state of self-improvement. We're not machines built for endless output. And when nothing is pulling us forward, the weight of the lull can pull us under.

The hardest part wasn't the questions. It was realizing that despite all that I had uncovered, I did not have the answer. No matter how much work I had done, how many Pillars I strengthened, how many lessons I learned, when the momentum stopped, what I'd built went silent.

I had overcome so much, or at least, I thought I had. The bad habits, the self-destructive tendencies, the search for external validation. But here's the thing about old patterns: they don't need much to return. All it takes is a pause. A crack in momentum. Suddenly, they're back, automatic and easy to justify. Not because you're weak. But because they're still wired within you. Practiced over time. Comfortable.

And sure enough, they returned. Not with a warning. Just the attraction of the familiar. That restless edge. The hollow ache. The old wiring firing up again. I could feel it happening before I even made the decision. The pause before the pour.

And then, I let go.

Not in surrender. In weakness.

The first lie before a relapse is always the same: "Just this once."

CHAPTER 18
The Glass and the Stone

The Relapse

Over the years, I had built a life designed for control. Like glass, it was
clear, precise, and meant to impress.
I trained myself to move through
chaos without letting anything
show. I kept things tight. My
rhythm steady. It looked flawless
from the outside. But pressure
doesn't care how perfect things appear.

When the first slip happened, I barely noticed. I told myself I was just
unwinding. But that's the danger of having made it through before; it
makes you think you're immune. The final fall rarely starts loudly. It
shows up as permission. A small decision you don't bother arguing with.
"Just this once."

And once it began, it was fast. The first drink. Then the second. The sharp
burn down my throat, the warmth spreading through my chest, the rush
of something loosening inside me. Relief. I exhaled, long and slow, like I
had been holding my breath for months. It didn't matter that I knew better. It didn't matter that I'd promised myself I was past this. At that point,
I didn't care. I wasn't drinking to celebrate. Or to enjoy the taste. I was
drinking to silence the questions. To feel something other than this emptiness.

And that was the part I didn't want to admit. Because I had built my life around control. Structure. Mastery. I had proven, over and over, that I could take anything, pain, loss, and failure, and turn it into fuel. But now? I didn't want to master it. I didn't want to reframe it. I didn't want to find a solution. I just wanted it gone.

And for a few hours, it was.

It wasn't the drink itself that undid me. People drink for a thousand reasons: celebration, connection, and release. Many can do so without any negative consequences. At times, I could, too, still drink socially, without a second thought. But this was different. This wasn't about the taste, or the company, or even the moment. It was the hidden intention behind it. I wasn't sipping. I was escaping. And that's what unsettled me. Not the drink, but what I was using it to avoid, and the cycle it began to feed.

In that moment, it softened the pressure. The doubt. The questions that wouldn't let go. But the thing about escaping: eventually, it always catches up with you. And when it did, the weight was still there. Heavier than before. Because now it wasn't just the questions. Not even the emptiness. Now, it was shame. And shame is a weight that drags you under faster than anything else.

The same voice that once inspired me, the one that said, "You can rebuild," was now silent. In its place came another, darker one, that said, "You're a fraud. You talk about transformation… but look at you. You haven't really changed. None of what you built matters."

I just stood there. Stunned. My life's work reduced to nothing.

I didn't argue with it. I withdrew. I reached for whatever could keep my mind occupied, anything that dulled the edge of that thought. I could see my life narrowing. I could feel things slipping. And yet, I couldn't stop it.

The Quiet Collapse

I woke up with a dull, pounding headache, my body heavy, my mind in a deep fog. The regret was there. That sickening, quiet realization: I did it again.

I lay still, the ceiling blurring above me, exhaustion weighing me down. I knew this feeling. I had been here before. Years ago, when my life was unraveling, when I was trapped in a cycle I swore I'd never return to. But I had.

And that was the worst part. Because this wasn't rock bottom. It wasn't a dramatic collapse. I had a great life. I was not like so many unfortunate people around the world. I was the lucky one, not struggling financially. I had a healthy family. A beautiful wife. A great job. So, there was no real excuse. Yet, there I was.

The undoing happens in ordinary, unnoticed moments. A tiny compromise. A small justification. And then, one day, you wake up and realize you've slid further than you ever thought possible. At first, it is just skipping a workout. Then hitting snooze. Sometimes, it's just reaching for one more glass. Pushing off the deep work, telling yourself, "Tomorrow. Tomorrow I'll reset." And that's how it happens. A slow, steady descent.

I was still functioning. Still working. On the surface, nothing looked different. But inside, something was coming undone. I could have intervened. But I didn't stop it. I let it happen.

The Breaking Point

It was late one Friday night. Outside, a dark mist blurred the edges of Paris. Streetlights cast faint halos, their glow swallowed by the damp air. Gazing out the window, I poured another drink. Not thinking. Just… coping. The glass was cold against my palm. I didn't taste it. I didn't even want it. I was just trying to mute the noise. Or maybe escape the silence, I couldn't tell anymore. Then I caught my reflection in the window. The half-empty bottle on the counter behind me. The hollow look in my eyes.

And in that reflection, I saw it, not a dramatic warning, just confirmation. I wasn't lost. I was retreating. Slipping into something darker I never fully left behind.

I couldn't sleep that night. The ceiling dissolved into darkness, the room closing in until all I could feel was the weight of my own mind. Eyes wide open, thoughts churning. The question circled above me, silent, patient, waiting to strike: What changed? Why, despite everything I knew... was I sinking?

I must have drifted off at some point. And in that half-sleep, I slipped into a dream, so vivid it felt like a memory. I found myself standing alone in a field. A vast, dry, windswept expanse. The sky had this strange color, part ash, part gold, like the day had a sepia filter over it.

In the distance stood two houses. One was all glass and steel, sleek, perfect, geometric. The kind you see in architecture magazines. Every line clean. The other was made of stone, worn by years, crooked in places, yet still standing.

I felt pulled toward the glass one. Somehow, it carried the promise of possibility. As I approached, the doors slid open. Inside, it was silent. Controlled. Every surface immaculate. Not a single object out of place. I walked through endless corridors of accolades and framed successes, all that I had achieved. But as I walked deeper, the stillness started to press in. The air grew stale, almost suffocating. And then I saw it: a hallway of mirrors. Each one reflected a version of me. Older. Polished. Accomplished. But none of them looked back at me. Their eyes were blank. Something was missing. They were all me, but emptied out. And that's when I realized: this wasn't a home. It was a showroom. A life made to be admired, not lived.

Suddenly, the mirrors splintered.

Then, I was outside again, now facing the second house. It was much smaller. Crooked. Cracks between the stones. Some paint peeling from the walls. Tools were scattered in the yard. As I stepped inside, the floor creaked beneath me. The room smelled of wood and something else, a distant memory. Nothing was finished. Exposed beams. Unhung shelves. A sink still sitting in its box. But something in it felt familiar.

And that's when I saw him. My father, sitting on a worn couch, his hands wrapped around an old mug. He looked up at me, not surprised to see me there, and smiled. Not a sad smile. Not even nostalgic. Just… content.

Everything slowed. We didn't speak. But something passed between us. I saw it in his eyes. A knowing. Something I had never understood. He wasn't failing to finish the houses because he was broken. He loved being inside the becoming. Seeing the potential. Dreaming of the building. He didn't need it to be done. He needed to feel its shape in his hands. It's what pulled him forward. Gave meaning to his life.

And then he chuckled, looking at his hand-drawn plans on the coffee table, with all the changes, the modifications.

That was him. Always sketching. Always rewriting. Not just architectural plans, but books, ideas, and whole systems of thought. He had journals stacked high with notes, chapters, reflections. He never published most of them. But maybe he didn't need to. Because the ideas lived elsewhere, in the classroom, in the lives of his students, in the way he listened and made people feel understood. The manuscripts may have stayed in drawers, but the message didn't. That was his real work. Unfinished, yes. But alive.

And then, I saw it in the room around me, echoes of him, everywhere. This house had many flaws, yet it felt simple, warm, true. An old worn-out rug. A corduroy jacket draped over the chair. Pieces of a life I once knew, quiet reminders of where I came from. Then, softly, as if rising from the room itself, I heard him say: "You can't live in both houses." I turned to face him, but he was gone.

And that's when I woke up, gasping, heart racing. The silence, unmoved. But something about that dream stayed. Not the houses. The choice. I had always thought the choice was between striving and achieving, or standing still. Glass or stone. But maybe it was never about that. Maybe it was about the kind of life I was willing to claim as my own. Not one built to impress, but one I could actually live inside.

That was the pattern I was trying to outrun, the belief that meaning only arrived at the finish line. That fulfillment came after the work was done. But maybe the truth was simpler. I didn't need perfection. I needed something that I could feel and shape, something that carried meaning. My father didn't fail to finish the house. He just chose to keep building. What lit him up wasn't the product; it was the presence he felt inside the process. The silent joy of shaping what held meaning for him. That was his way. It was never about the endpoint.

And maybe it was time for me to return to what's real. To step out from behind the polished glass. To build something imperfect but true. Not to prove anything. Not to get anywhere. But to feel it again, that pulse that once moved through me. The sense of aliveness I felt as I rebuilt after the cliff. The forward pull. The meaning that came not from the outcome, but from the making.

I got up from bed and walked to the window. The morning sky was a heavy gray, the kind that presses down on the world. Rain tapped against the glass, soft and rhythmic. The streets below were still, no movement, no people. Just wet pavement. The world paused.

And that's when I felt it.

I closed my eyes and let it come. Not as words. Just the weight of knowing. I had lost something. I didn't even feel it coming. My chest tightened, pulled inward by the memory of his quiet smile, the worn couch, the smell of coffee. It wasn't sadness. It was a deeper ache. A longing for what I had lost, and for the path I had somehow stepped away from.

In that instant, it hit me. A quiet click, the last piece of a puzzle I didn't know I was holding slipping into place. It wasn't motivation I had lost. Or knowledge. Or the right framework.

No.

What vanished was the very thing that steadied me and pulled me forward. The quiet force I had rebuilt my life around, the one I followed after the cliff.

The thread that held everything together.

It hadn't snapped. It simply faded and frayed, buried beneath the noise, the striving, the emptiness. And over time, it slipped out of sight. I hadn't lost my edge. Or my tools. Or even my belief.

I had lost my purpose.

Seeing it, finally naming it, shifted something. Not a solution, just the faintest moment of clarity, like noticing again the silver thread stretching across the abyss. Too thin to grasp, yet unmistakably there. But it was just enough to make me turn toward the path instead of the escape.

I wasn't whole or healed, but for the first time in a long time, I stopped drifting.

At last, I was ready to face the biggest question I had been circling all along.

Part 6
THE SILVER THREAD

CHAPTER 19
The Void

The Missing Piece

I kept doing what I was supposed to
do. But somewhere between one
task and the next, the days lost their
shape. I couldn't tell anymore where
I was going, why I was doing what I
was doing, only that I was still moving. The emptiness was there, like a
low, gray static that fills the background of your days.

The structure still stood, walls up-
right, tools intact. But the light had gone out. A life without the pull.
From the outside, nothing was broken. But inside, a part of me had faded.
I was moving, but not going anywhere. I was working, but not truly building. Alive, and yet not fully living. I had lost something essential. Not
money. Not relationships. Not even health. What slipped away ran
deeper.

I had lost the why.

Not in the motivational sense, or the career-coaching, brand-strategy
"What's your why?" way. The real thing, that internal force that connects
every other part of you. The invisible thread that gives structure to pain,
meaning to effort, and coherence to your days.

And I wasn't alone. People who had spent years working, striving, and grinding, suddenly found themselves staring into the void. The world had stopped moving. For the first time, they asked why they got up every morning. Why they kept pushing at all.

I had spent my life building systems. But a system without a purpose is like a vehicle without a destination. It doesn't matter how fast you go if you don't know where you're headed. And for me, the force pulling me forward had simply... vanished.

Finding Purpose

As I stood there that Saturday morning in the Paris apartment, I was contemplating my options. Another weekend trapped inside. No flights. No restaurants. No gyms. The world still on pause, I had nowhere to be. I poured a cup of coffee, the rich scent filling the room. The city outside remained frozen, silent storefronts, a world suspended in limbo.

I walked over to my desk, pulled open a drawer, and ran my fingers over the stack of black leather-bound Moleskine notebooks. Years of thoughts, half-formed ideas, and equations etched on the paper. I grabbed one at random, sat down on the couch with my coffee in hand, and flipped it open. The pages felt familiar. A past version of me, captured in ink, staring back through the handwritten lines. And then I saw it. A name scrawled at the top of a page: Paolo Morrison. A man who had walked straight into the emptiness instead of running from it. I had almost forgotten him. But as my eyes moved across the ink, suddenly I was brought back there, five years earlier. The blinding sun, the haze of the heat rising off the ground, the still rhythm of a desert town. Todos Santos. A small haven along Mexico's wild Pacific coast, where artists, wanderers, and poets drifted through the streets, each answering a calling of their own.

The Man Who Went into the Desert

The dry, dusty heat pressed against my skin, the air shimmering in waves under the relentless sun. A deep, endless blue sky stretched overhead, vast and cloudless. The streets were quiet, life moving with a slow, steady hum.

A small café stood tucked between an art shop and a bookstore. The walls were covered in paintings, some loud with color, others simple sketches. The café smelled of baked bread and hints of coffee roast. I walked in, looking for nothing in particular. But then, I saw him.

A man, probably in his seventies, wiry and sun-worn, his straw hat resting beside a tattered backpack. His face was carved with lines that spoke of years spent under an open sky. He sat at a small wooden table, an old typewriter in front of him, tapping the keys with unhurried precision. He looked settled, like a man with no more battles to fight.

"Still works?" I nodded toward the typewriter. He looked up, a slow grin spreading across his face. "A dying machine," he said, patting it fondly, "but still breathing."

We exchanged a few words, just the usual pleasantries. But there was something about him. An ease. A presence. The kind of steady confidence that comes from a man who has seen enough of life to stop pretending. Some people don't require effort. There's no posturing, no small talk, just an unspoken understanding.

Quickly, the conversation shifted. We talked about the world changing too fast. About how people spent their days running, and yet never arriving anywhere. About the constant hum of distraction, always connected, but never really present.

He told me about the first time he came here. There were no newspapers, no cell phones, no rush. Life wasn't about the filled schedules, but the rhythm of the day. "People simply lived," he said, his voice calm, like he was stating something obvious.

And then he told me a story. He leaned in, his intense eyes peering through me. Twenty years ago, Paolo drove with his camper van into the desert with no money, no food, and no plan. He had reached his breaking point. If life were only about money, about chasing, about surviving, then what was the point? Why continue? He sat there for days, alone under the vast sky. On the fifth day, a part of him opened. He felt a strange pull: an urge to paint.

He had never painted before. Never considered himself an artist. But in that moment, he felt a calling. Maybe it was desperation, maybe it rose from a deeper place, a pull he couldn't explain, yet he chose to follow.

So, he got in his truck, drove back into town, and with the last few pesos in his pocket, bought a set of brushes, some paint, and a thick pad of drawing paper. It made no sense. But then again, neither did anything else.

"I painted because, for the first time in my life, I listened," he said, his blue eyes locking onto mine. And then, he sold his first painting. Then another. For over 10 years, he lived off his art. But he never painted for money. He painted because it was the only thing that made him feel alive.

Paolo turned and pointed toward the back of the café, where a small painting hung on the wall. "That one's mine," he said, smiling. Then he leaned in further and shared something that didn't land right away. A truth that had faded into the background of my mind, waiting to be rediscovered in the pages of my notebook.

"People try to fill the emptiness inside with anything they can get their hands on," he said. "Drugs, money, things, relationships. They think if they find the right thing, the right person, they'll feel whole. But the emptiness doesn't go away. Because it's not about what's out there, it's about what they build from within."[67]

The Thread Within

I sat there on the couch in my apartment, Paolo's words staring back like a message I wasn't ready to hear then. But now? Now, they hit differently. Once the world stopped and distractions were gone, what had been background noise became unavoidable. Millions of people were left alone with themselves. No commuting back and forth to the office. No social events. No gathering with friends and family. Just silence. And without anywhere left to run, the questions changed. Why am I doing any of this? What meaning does it hold?

Paolo hadn't gone into the desert to find art. He had gone there to die. But something else met him instead: a thread. Fragile, unexpected, impossible to ignore. It pointed inward. Build from within.

I hadn't understood it then. But now, with the world forced into stillness for the first time in centuries, I could feel it.

The pause wasn't empty. It was a rupture in the fabric of our lives.

Something long ignored had begun to move.

Not just in me. In all of us.

And soon, millions would awaken.

CHAPTER 20
The Search

When the World Asked Why

The shutdown disturbed all of our routines. And in the process, it suddenly exposed the story we'd been living inside. Work hard. Keep climbing. Don't fall behind.

When the motion stopped, people began to question what they'd always assumed: that more was better. That effort alone would get you there.

And it happened all at once, on a massive scale. In the pandemic's wake, nearly 50 million Americans quit their jobs, the highest number ever recorded in a single year.[68] People walked away from careers they had spent decades building. Some packed up, moved to the mountains, bought vans, and lived on the road. Others just… stopped.

They called it The Great Resignation. I call it The Great Awakening. The world wasn't chasing more any longer. It was chasing meaning.

But what happens when you see for the first time that the life you've built is not the one you want, that the promises of the path you followed were illusions? Now, you see it. The gap with the life you ache for. But there's no clear way out. No map forward. That's when the spiral into the abyss begins. When meaninglessness isn't just a feeling, it's a downward force.

It pulls at everything you thought you knew. And you can't escape it. You feel it in the quiet of your home, in the way mornings blur into evenings without distinction. A dull ache beneath the routines.

The signs were everywhere. Alcohol sales skyrocketed. Depression spiked. People who had spent years running on autopilot were suddenly aware of the void they had been ignoring. They tried to fill it with Netflix binge watching, online shopping, endless scrolling, and yet the emptiness only deepened. Because for the first time in modern history, an entire planet asked itself the most important question of all: Why?

And that's when I saw what I had missed in Paolo's words. The thing I had been running from. Purpose isn't something you find. It's something you build. Not out there. Not in validation. Not in the glass house built to impress, but in the raw, unpolished work of creating from within. It emerges as the layers dissolve, the noise, the borrowed scripts, until only the core remains. That's what Paolo understood, sitting alone in the desert, staring at an empty canvas. He didn't *find* his purpose; he followed the signal that remained after everything else fell away, and he built it.

Purpose is created, piece by piece, choice by choice, instant by instant. Which meant, no matter how lost I felt, no matter how much I had drifted, I could build it again. But that raised the next big question: How do you build it? Paolo found his way. But what about the rest of us? What about me? I wasn't sitting in a desert, waiting for inspiration to strike. I was trapped in an apartment, in a world that was just slowly coming back to life. The silence wasn't offering me answers; it was pressing in, demanding them.

So, I reverted to the approach I followed every time I had hit a wall: I went looking for answers. I stared at the blinking cursor in the search bar like it owed me something. As if it could somehow explain why my world had come apart. I typed: "How to build purpose in life." Enter.

Tens of thousands of results. Blog posts. Self-help manifestos. Pages of promised breakthroughs, most vague, many contradicting each other. I was distraught. It can't be. There seemed to be no consensus. No shared map. Not even among the experts. And for a terrifying moment I wondered, what if there is no answer? What if purpose isn't something you can ever grasp... because it was never real to begin with? What if all the articles, all the TED Talks, all the books, they aren't doorways, but distractions? A question no one truly knows how to answer. Maybe purpose is just a concept we invented to quiet the questions.

And if that's true... then what's left? What happens when you finally stop running, and there's nothing waiting for you? If there's no deeper why, no structure beneath the striving, what's the point of waking up at all?

I didn't want to believe that. I couldn't. If there was even an ounce of true answers in everything out there, I had to find it. I needed more than hope. I needed proof. So, I turned where I always did when the world went sideways: data. If purpose was real, it had to leave a trail.

The Science of Purpose

If it could be built, then there had to be a formula. Something deeper than pop psychology quotes on social media. Something backed by research, by evidence. So, I decided to go first to the science. I pulled every major study, psychological model, and research paper I could find. I traced purpose through philosophy, neuroscience, and case studies of people who lived with unshakable clarity, and those who didn't. What made the difference? Why did some people wake up every day with a fire inside them, while others drifted aimlessly, feeling lost, untethered?

The nights blurred into each other, each question leading to another. But my mind stayed sharp, focused on the notes in front of me, on what I was uncovering. I didn't have answers, but somehow the work kept me moving when everything else had stalled.

Purpose, I would later learn, isn't just a feeling. It's a biological advantage. Psychologists and neuroscientists have found something remarkable: a strong sense of purpose doesn't just make life better, it makes life longer. One study followed nearly 7,000 adults for 14 years. The result? Those with the strongest feeling of purpose were 43% less likely to die from any cause.[69]

And it's not just about living longer, it's about how you live. People with purpose bounce back faster and take better care of themselves. In the Blue Zones, the places on Earth where people live the longest, there's one thing they all share: a strong reason to wake up each morning.[70] A purpose. And in other places? That reason adds up to seven extra years of life. In Japan, they call it *Ikigai*, "reason for being." In Costa Rica, it's *Plan de Vida*, "life plan."[71] Across cultures, across centuries, this pattern repeats. Purpose isn't a luxury. It's the basis for a life that feels whole. The science was undeniable.

Purpose Can Be Measured

If it can be measured, it has structure, and structure can be built. So, I kept digging. And what I found surprised me: the science was already there. Studies. Scales. Decades of research. Buried in academic journals almost no one reads. One of the most widely used psychological tools to measure purpose is the Purpose in Life Test (PIL), developed by psychologists James Crumbaugh and Leonard Maholick.[72] But it's not the only one. Over the years, dozens had emerged: the Meaning in Life Questionnaire (MLQ), the Life Engagement Test (LET), and the Ryff Scales, to mention just a few.[73]

At first glance, they seemed disconnected. Each with its own model, its own language, its own way of mapping purpose. But as I stayed with it, something unexpected came into focus. They weren't different. Not really. Underneath the surface, beneath the acronyms and academic jargon, there was a pattern. A set of core ideas, recurring forces.

If purpose is an ecosystem, then somewhere in that ecosystem... there's a formula. But the studies were sprawling, the language was dense, and the signal drowned in complexity. And yet, I couldn't look away. Because deep down, I wasn't just analyzing research anymore. I was chasing clarity, the answers to the most fundamental questions. If I could decode what held it all together... Maybe, just maybe, I could rebuild what I had lost.

Without realizing it, I was standing at the edge of a much larger truth. And what I uncovered next didn't just explain why we drift. It revealed how we return. Not just for me. But for anyone who's stared into the stillness and felt it stare back. For anyone who's ever asked "What now?" and heard nothing in return.

What surfaced was imperfect, unfinished, but impossible to ignore. It pointed somewhere. And it was enough to begin.

At its center were three hidden strands. Not answers. Not conclusions. But something strong enough to start rebuilding.

CHAPTER 21
The Formula

The Threads That Weave Purpose

I spent that whole Saturday afternoon at my desk, a steady urgency pressing in. I sifted through it all, page by page, study by study. Notes scattered across the desk. Research papers and highlighted sentences. Each alluding to an insight, but none of them enough. Not alone. Something was missing.

I was concerned. Because after all the confusion, the contradictions, and the failed answers, I didn't want another theory dressed up as truth. I needed more than theory. I needed tools I could test in real life. That would hold when the next crisis hit.

But I kept at it, trying to piece it together. The most widely accepted tools, like the Ryff and Keyes scales,[74] don't just ask if you feel purposeful. They break it down into components. Researchers don't look for bursts of passion or momentary motivation[75] when assessing purpose. They look for specific, measurable indicators repeated across cultures. I started tracing the lines between the various models, connecting the dots. I noticed that certain elements were present across multiple research frameworks. And slowly, a pattern began to take shape. A simple structure, a code interwoven through it all. Not abstract. Not vague. A clear, buildable formula. I grabbed my pen and wrote in my notebook:

Meaning from Past & Present

+

Life Direction

+

Supporting Beliefs

=

PURPOSE

At first glance, it felt... sterile. Clinical. Like something built in a lab, disconnected from the messy, aching thing I'd been trying to understand. Three variables. It read more like a class exercise than a doorway into something profound. I almost dismissed it. Just another set of boxes to tick. But I decided to lean into it and test it. Against the research. Against my own spirals. Against the stories of people who felt alive, and those who didn't.

Each time I looked, strangely enough, the structure held. When people felt lit from within, driven, and deeply engaged, these three elements were always present. And every time they fell apart, at least one of them was missing. This wasn't just another insight; it was something hardwired into human psychology. Like neural architecture.[76] These three interconnected elements didn't stand alone. They reinforced one another. They were the backbone of purpose.

The formula showed me that purpose isn't binary. It's not something you either have or don't. It's a dynamic force, alive, responsive, and fluid. It rises and recedes based on these elements. And when it fades, you don't have to search the world to find it. You can rebuild it. From within. When I let it touch the places I hadn't dared to look, something opened. Not just insight. But old memories. Forgotten pieces of myself began resurfacing, like photographs slowly appearing in the red glow of a darkroom.

What this formula unlocked wasn't just understanding. It triggered a deeper reordering. It didn't happen all at once. As I stepped into each of the three elements, Meaning, Direction, and Belief, I began to see not just one thread, but three. Intertwined so tightly, they seemed like one. Pulling through everything, my past, my present, my future. Suddenly, it all began to make sense, not as a straight line, but as something woven. A design I hadn't seen until now.

That was the moment I realized: this wasn't a conclusion. Because uncovering the formula wasn't the breakthrough. When I moved through the components, each one revealed something I hadn't seen before. Like an invisible magnet had been switched on, and the scattered pieces of my life began turning, one by one, toward the same direction.

Only then did I see what I'd missed all along. Without realizing it, I was already moving toward the next Shift.

But it didn't start with direction. Or belief.

It started with something far more elusive.

The first thread that runs through it all.

CHAPTER 22
Meaning

Deriving Meaning from the Past and Present

I used to think the past was fixed, poured like concrete, hardened by time. But it's not the past that shapes us most. It's how we've recorded it. "How you arrange the plot points of your life into a narrative can shape who you are—and is a fundamental part of being human," wrote Julie Beck, a writer at *The Atlantic*.[77] And that story? That's clay. Malleable.

Two people can live through the same episode and walk away with completely different memories. One sees the failure as proof that they weren't good enough. The other sees it as the moment that forged their strength and shaped who they became. Same event. Different lives. What happened matters far less than the meaning you give it. That ability to reinterpret your story is known in psychology as cognitive reappraisal.[78] The act of reframing doesn't just change how you think about the past, it changes how you feel right now.

How Meaning Shapes Purpose

If you believe your past is meaningless, your present will feel hollow. But if you see your past as something that shaped who you are, and the present as preparation, they become fuel. That's what Viktor Frankl discovered in Auschwitz, after being stripped of everything.[79] The people who endured the longest weren't necessarily the strongest; they were the ones who found meaning in their suffering.

Meaning doesn't come from a single source. It emerges across the main domains of life. The 7 Pillars are like the roots of your life, each one reaching into a different layer of experience, drawing meaning from what you've loved, built, given, and endured. The Social Pillar connects you to the people who matter, shaping how you show up in their lives. The Occupational Pillar carries meaning through what you create and contribute each day, how your work becomes part of something larger. The Physical Pillar keeps the tree healthy, grounded, and steady, so it can rise. The same is true across the rest of the Pillars.

Think of it this way: the tree is your life, the Pillars are its roots, and meaning is the nourishment that moves through those roots, giving the trunk its strength. And when life shakes you, and it will, it's these roots that determine whether you stand. You can't control the wind. But you

can shape how deeply your roots go. And the deeper they reach, the more resilient the tree is.

But roots don't deepen on their own. They require tending. You must come back, again and again, to the practices, people, and places that help you feel alive, connected, and grounded.

One of the most overlooked sources of meaning is contribution. Offering your experience, your strength, and what you learned through hardship in service of others creates a sense of purpose that accomplishments rarely match. We look for significance in what we achieve, yet it often emerges through what we give.

The Moment It Flipped

At my lowest, I asked myself a question that initially felt almost absurd: What if the setbacks, the detours, the pain weren't random? What if it was all preparation, shaping me for something I couldn't yet see? When I allowed that possibility to land, a switch turned inside me. I could reframe it, just not all at once. It was slow, messy. But gradually, I began to see how every struggle had left me with something real I could build on.

But insight wasn't enough. Knowing the theory didn't change how those old memories felt, the ones filled with regret, shame, or grief. I needed a way to take those tangled, painful stories and let them take on new meaning. And that's when I began a practice. A method I refined over time, when the weight of the past pressed in and the old stories were no longer just memories. They were chains. It didn't fix everything. But it gave me a place to start, and it can do the same for you. It came down to two steps.

Step 1: Name the Wound

Write down a painful experience you haven't fully resolved. Something unfinished that still lingers. Look inward, and search for the tension, the knot, that unresolved memory that still impacts you. Look at what happened, name the wound and the story you captured.

Step 2: Rewrite the Frame

Take that story and rewrite it as if it had to happen. As if it weren't a detour, but a doorway. A turning point that shaped who you're becoming. That despite the pain it might have caused, somehow, through it all you grew.

Ask yourself: What did this experience teach me? What did it prepare me for? What strength, insight, or truth did I gain because of it? And then, keep reading it back to yourself as if it were already true.

Why is this exercise so powerful? Because this isn't just mindset, it's biology. Neuroscience shows that when we assign new meaning to a memory, we don't just revise the story; we physically alter the way our brain stores it. [80] Over time, that rewiring changes not just how we see the past... but how we experience the present. The past doesn't have to haunt us, it can heal us. If we let it.

This Moment

The past holds meaning. But the present is the only moment you ever truly live in. It's the heartbeat of purpose. Many people are haunted by what's behind them or obsessed with what's ahead. But purpose is forged in how you show up, right here. In the big moments, yes, but more often in the tiny, unseen ones. A laugh with someone you love. A slow sip of a morning coffee. I call them Meaningful Micro-Moments, tiny pulses of presence that don't make headlines, but leave imprints. Not because they're big, but because they're real.

We assume the past defines the present. In *What Is Zen?*, Alan Watts wrote, "We tend to think that what happened in the past determines what is going to happen next, and we do not see that it is exactly the other way around!... The past trails behind the present like the wake of a ship and eventually disappears."[81] The present is where your story becomes alive, where the past becomes wisdom, and the future becomes direction.

So yes, honor where you've been. And yes, dream of where you're going. But never forget: purpose is forged in the daily. In the way you choose to show up, again and again.

Meaning isn't out there. It's here. Not someday. Now.

Suspended

By the time summer returned, the world had finally reopened. Travel resumed. Borders unlocked. Masks were no longer a constant necessity, but they still clung to us, lingering reminders of the storm we'd all just passed through.

Paris woke up, cautiously. Cafés spilled back onto sidewalks. The riverbanks of the Seine buzzed with laughter, the smell of freshly baked bread drifting from the boulangeries into the air. Life was stirring.

And then, my children arrived.

I had planned it carefully, our time together, long stretches meant to make up for the distance, for the empty months. Days spent wandering through Paris, summer trips to the mountains, late-night movies, their voices drifting softly through the apartment. Finally, they were here with me.

And yet, there were moments when something in me felt... off. It was supposed to be a return to normal. But I knew better. I had spent months locked in that silent war with myself, chasing answers, mapping out the pieces of purpose. I had written it all down, the formula, the elements. Meaning. Direction. Belief. But it was all so new, still fragile, starting to come together, but not yet fully assembled.

One night, the children were asleep. Their slow, steady breathing was a reminder of life beyond the walls of my own mind. I sat in my room hunched on the edge of the bed, thoughts churning. I felt like I was holding the architectural plans for a house I didn't know how to rebuild. It still felt like patchwork.

I had done the exploration. I read the books. I built the systems. I had the Purpose Formula. But that night, doubts took over. What if it didn't work? What if, in the end, it was all just smoke, an elegant formula that never became real? What if this is who I really am? A man always chasing light, but never truly exiting the shadows.

Then, an image. A memory from my childhood.

I must have been around 11, running wild through the woods with my friends, soft light slipping through the leaves. We had one mission: leap the widest gap. A place where the stream bit into the hillside, carving a narrow gorge. The bank on one side was higher, a perfect launchpad. The stream twisted below, a reflective ribbon cutting through the ground.

We sprinted, feet pounding the soft forest floor, hearts racing. Then we launched. For a heartbeat, we were weightless, suspended between earth and sky. A rush of wind, the blur of green. And then, impact. Our feet hit the dirt on the other side. Tumbling. Laughing. Crashing onto the ground. It wasn't just a game. It was a test. A dare to defy gravity, to stretch past the limits of what felt possible.

In that moment, I saw it clearly, something I had buried beneath years of doubt. When I was a child, I didn't wait to know I would land safely. I didn't wait for certainty. I went anyway. I used to believe I could create something the world hadn't seen yet. I moved before I was certain. But somewhere along the way, I stopped.

The strangest thing? Nothing really happened in that instant. And yet somehow, everything did. The boy who jumped was still there.

The past had been rewritten. I just wasn't moving yet.

The page was blank again. Waiting.

Meaning was there. What I lacked was direction.

Without it, nothing carries you forward.

You just stay suspended.

Still in midair.

CHAPTER 23
Life Direction

When the Path Disappears

If meaning connects and draws strength from all that you've lived, feeding the trunk of your life, direction is what gives your life lift. Without it, you drift. You wake up, go through the motions. You're "busy," but deep down, something's missing. The goals are still there, but they've lost their pulse. Days start to lose their shape. The 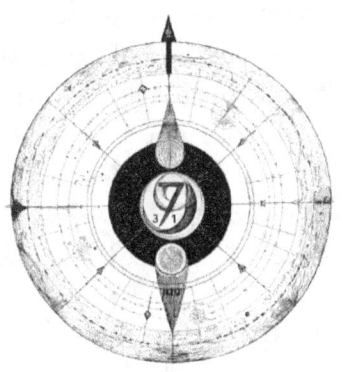 drive fades. Not because you're broken, but because the future stopped pulling you forward.

That's what happened to me during the pandemic. I still had meaning. I had a good life, a wife I loved, and a family I treasured. I was proud of my past, of the challenges I overcame, and of what I had built. But something was gone. Not discipline. Direction.

And when that vanished, purpose thinned.

Direction isn't a perfect map—it's a pull. Not rigid. Not a one-year plan carved in stone, but something real enough to walk toward. You won't always know where the path leads. It's not about certainty. It's feeling the forward pull, knowing your "why" isn't just an idea, but a force strong enough to move you, even when all else stands still.

Why We Need Direction

Psychologist Philip Zimbardo's research on time perspective found that the most fulfilled people don't just live in the moment, they view their past, present, and future in a balanced way.[82] But here's where direction gets distorted. We often start with how things feel right now, what's immediately fulfilling, and get hooked by short-term pleasure, by the quick dopamine spike. Or we focus too heavily on the past, where we've been, the events that shaped us, and begin to believe they define what we can achieve. In either case, the future quietly disappears from view.

When you truly have something to look forward to, something that matters, your days feel fuller. But what happens when what lies ahead goes dark? You can hold all the meaning in the world, every value still intact. Yet if you wake up and see nothing ahead, no peak to climb, no reason to move, that's when purpose dissolves. Days stretch without form. One morning becomes two. A week becomes a month. And before you know it, you're waking up... but not really living.

When the Future Vanishes

Among my circle of friends, Brian was the one we looked up to. Wild energy, always in motion. A smile that could lift any room. He lived in a renovated barn tucked in the Swiss Alps, a simple, beautiful space surrounded by nature. A life most would dream of. One day, he'd be heli-skiing with clients, the next, sailing the coast on a boat he renovated with his own hands. His life wasn't just adventurous; it had plenty of freedom. But the best part? He wasn't doing it alone. He had found love, the kind you build a life around. Their future was already written: the mountains, the travels, the dream they were shaping together.

And then, in a single moment, she was gone. No warning. No time to prepare. Just like that, the future vanished.

The Freefall

Brian was the strongest guy we knew. Physically? Unshakable, spending every day in the mountains. Professionally? Thriving, he had walked away from the corporate grind years ago, choosing passion over a high salary. Mentally? Steady, always upbeat, always finding the ray of light in things.

But when she left, his Social Pillar collapsed overnight. And with it, his Emotional one crumbled. His home became a museum of grief. Every shelf. Every mug. Every corner carried her name. The mountains he once climbed with joy now loomed like monuments to all he had lost. What was once breathtaking... now broke him. The future he dreamed of was gone. Not just altered. Erased. His life had been theirs: their plans, their vision. And now, there was no road left to walk, no reason to take the next step.

But the deepest collapse was his Direction. The parts of life that once tethered him to tomorrow, the shared dreams, the imagined milestones, the sense of where it was all heading, now cut deepest. It wasn't just his future. It was theirs. And when that shared future disappeared, so did his will to move forward.

The doctors who saw him said his depression was serious, even life-threatening. They urged him to check into intensive care, to begin immediate treatment with stabilizing medication. But Brian refused. Not out of pride. Out of fear of what that choice represented, a sterile room, a medicated fog, a version of himself he wouldn't recognize. He couldn't bear the thought of being parked in some clinical ward, his grief reduced to symptoms, his soul dimmed by sedation. So he walked out at his own peril. And the spiral downward continued, pulling him ever further into darkness.

One night, he climbed into his car and drove. The stars hung above the alpine valley, cold and indifferent. Wind rushed down the valley like a grim warning. He followed the winding road deeper into the night, the mountains' dark silhouettes pressing in on either side.

His destination: the Mauvoisin Dam.

A brutal slab of concrete carved into the edge of the earth rising like a scar against the alpine silence. By day, it's majestic. At night, it's a void. The wall plunges over 600 feet into the gorge below, where the river churns unseen in the blackness. A thin three-foot railing traced the edge, feeble and ornamental, the only barrier between breath and oblivion. No voices. No light. Just the sound of distant water crashing like time itself.

He sat there, just him and the silence at the cliff's edge. The end had come. There was nothing left to say, no reason to continue. The emptiness had hollowed him out. He had lost the map and with it, the will to navigate.

And then... a thought. His son.

The graduation he would miss. The look in his boy's eyes when he crossed the stage, scanning the crowd. That tiny thread, thin as air, almost invisible, pulled him back. Not with force. With a future.

He turned the key. The car's engine sparked. He drove back down the mountain, slowly, like waking from a dream he hadn't meant to enter.

The Fragile Thread

He spoke quietly to me. "I've never told anyone this," he said. "Not really." His eyes drifted, as if still watching the night unfold. "That night at the dam... that was the closest I ever came to stepping out of the story for good." Then, softer, almost to himself: "I never thought I could get that close... that life could push me that far."

In that moment, I understood the power of losing Life Direction. Brian's story showed me something I hadn't fully grasped in my own life: how one missing thread can cause the whole to come undone. He still had meaning. His past, his values, his experiences: they were intact. But without a future to move toward, the rest began to crumble.

In some way, that's what had happened to me too. Different story. Same pattern. Purpose isn't just about where you've been, it's about where you're going. And when that direction disappears, you don't drift forward. Everything stalls. Brian's story is a warning, a reminder that purpose is fragile. The whole system can easily begin to fray.

Defining Direction

The summer was fading, but the light still lingered, warm and diffuse, spilling through the narrow streets of Paris. The cafés were now fully alive; I could hear the hum of conversations rising from the terraces and mixing with the sound of the streets. There was optimism in the air.

And I sensed that I was getting closer. To what, I did not know. But I could feel it was important. I sat down at the living room table. It was time to get to work. To define my Direction. To name what mattered most.

But direction wasn't a grand revelation. It was slow. Fragmented. Scribbled on pages, scattered notes. In ideas that felt true, until they led nowhere. I kept circling the same question: What's that direction for me? Not as a vague concept, but in reality. Beyond the science or methods. What do I truly want?

I picked up my pen. And almost by reflex, I started building lists. Charts. Diagrams. Mapping out goals.

But this time, no matter how hard I tried, none of it landed, none of it moved me. So, I went deeper. I had to. I asked the hardest question I could imagine: If this were the end, if I were on my deathbed, what would I regret not doing? What is the life that could have been, but never materialized?

This was about options, possibilities, the full shape of what I could be. I thought this powerful question would unlock something, that this was the key. But no. It felt too far away, too philosophical. I couldn't feel it. So much could change between now and then. I zoomed in.

Ten years? Still blurry.

Five? Too close.

Seven?

Seven Years Out

Seven years felt right. Far enough for real transformation, close enough to stir movement today. So, I sat with the question: Seven years from now, what does my ideal life actually look like? I started to write; the words came fast, like they'd been waiting. But something still felt off. Not wrong, just distant. I paused and asked the uncomfortable question: Whose dreams are these? Are they truly mine... or just residue of what I've been told to want?

I scanned the list. Bigger house. More money. Recognition. It was all familiar. But was it true? I let the silence stretch. And then, word by word, I interrogated each one. Did I want a bigger house... or the ability to wake up anywhere on earth? Did I really want more money... or more freedom to do what I wanted? Did I want recognition... or to feel deeply, unmistakably alive?

What I had written wasn't wrong. But it wasn't me, not fully. It was too curated. Too expected. Half of it came from expectations I had inherited but never questioned. I picked up the pen again. This time, I listened to what rose from deep within me and let it pour out.

I turned to each of the 7 Pillars, Emotional, Mental, Physical, Social, Occupational, Environmental/Material, and Spiritual, and asked a new kind of question: Not what do I want to achieve, but who do I want to become? Not in the abstract. In seven years, across every Pillar, what would it mean to feel fully alive? And when I asked that, different answers came. Some had always been with me. Others surprised me. A few scared me. And they demanded a new level of honesty with myself.

I filled the pages without rushing, just letting it pour out. But eventually, the list grew too long, so I sharpened my approach: Why not select just three per Pillar? To focus on the essence.

The Realization: I Can Be So Much More

The list was still long, 21 items in total. Overly ambitious? Absolutely. It felt like a contradiction: How could I possibly live all of this? The voice came quick, stern, and all too familiar: "You can't. Be realistic. Pick one. Simplify." I had heard that practical voice before, echoing every leadership book and mentor who ever told me: "Clarity is saying no." But something in me pushed back. What if the problem wasn't that I didn't have enough time, but that I didn't understand what was truly possible? That question hung in the air, insisting on an answer.

As I looked ever deeper, I uncovered a thought pattern running in the background: I can only be a very limited number of things, linked to certain widely accepted labels: a father, a husband, a professional, with certain hobbies. But was that true?

And then, a thought emerged, tentative at first, then sharper. Maybe the issue wasn't the goals, but the beliefs beneath them? The quiet script that insisted I had to pick one lane. One title. One version of myself. But what if that was the lie? What if I didn't have to choose? What if the struggle wasn't about working too hard, but about working from the wrong story?

As that idea settled, something realigned. It was like finding a hidden hinge in the story I thought was already written, one that, with the slightest pressure, could swing my life in a new direction.

Becoming Multidimensional

Suddenly, I didn't feel split. I didn't have to choose. I could be both a father and a builder, an executive by day, an entrepreneur and writer by night. Whole. Integrated. I didn't need to shrink to fit someone else's mold. I could expand into the full, unapologetic truth of who I could become.

When I embraced that belief, something came alive again. Purpose. But not the old, frayed kind. A new one. Built from the inside out. The real transformation wasn't about narrowing my options. It was about unfolding, stepping into the person I was choosing to be, across every dimension. This wasn't a fantasy. It was already written in the lives of those who came before: Da Vinci, Franklin, Baldwin, those luminous figures who refused to be one thing. And once I researched it, I saw there were so many. Proof that a life could be vast, multidimensional, and fully alive.

In that moment, I thought of Elsa. Sitting across from me all those years ago by the shores of Lake Atitlán, her voice low, uncertain, as a breeze ruffled the surface of the water: "What should I do with my life?" The question had pulled at me for years, but it wasn't the question itself. It was the hidden assumption behind it. Back then, it felt like a cliff-edge decision. Like there was one right answer, and a thousand wrong ones. But now, I see it differently. The real question isn't which job or which country to choose. It's how many parts of yourself are you willing to bring alive?

Because life isn't a straight road. It's a mosaic. And purpose isn't a map. It's the invisible force that pulls at your core, guiding you forward. Elsa didn't need a perfect answer. She needed permission. Permission to expand. To become more. I realized then: these moments, the hesitation in Geneva, the uncertainty by Lake Atitlán, weren't isolated. They were chapters in the same deeper story. A rejection of the narrow choices offered by society. Everything was pointing to the same underlying truth: these aren't the only options.

And the real turning point wasn't just about what I did. It was about remembering who lay dormant within, not fully expressed, and daring to become all of it. Beneath the expectations and beyond the masks. I had felt it before, standing by Lake Geneva, stiff in a crisp suit, the script of adulthood clutched tightly in my hands. I thought I was stepping into my future, but deep down, something already knew: this wasn't it. I didn't have the words then, only a feeling, a quiet refusal to disappear into a version of life that didn't fit.

My head was spinning. I had been sitting there for hours. The sun had long ago sunk behind the outline of La Défense, the sharp silhouettes of the Parisian towers fading into shadow. The city dimmed into evening, streetlights flickering awake. Somewhere in the distance, a siren wailed, then faded.

I hadn't noticed when the stars first appeared, nor the coolness of the night settling into the room. I was immersed in the ideas, the stories, the possibilities that opened up within me.

Time didn't keep moving. It collapsed inward. Past and present blurred. I wasn't thinking anymore, or analyzing. I was inside it. The clarity was physical, alive in my chest. I was on the brink. The truth I'd been circling for years was right there, just beyond my grasp.

But the rush faded, and something else surfaced. A subtle recognition that the pieces were here, the insights and the possibilities, but they were scattered. Like stars strewn across a dark sky, bright, beautiful, yet disconnected. A constellation without form. Too many paths. Too many roles. Too many ways I could become. The sense of possibility felt electric, but also paralyzing. I needed a way to cut through the options and point me toward what mattered. Something simple and undeniable.

The Forgotten Riddle

I couldn't shake it. The puzzle of how to navigate a life with so many conflicting options haunted me. I had no sense of time. The night thickened around me, the city outside gone silent. A sliver of moonlight painted lines across the cluttered table, a quiet reminder of how long I had been sitting there.

I pulled open a drawer filled with old journals. Years of scribbles, fragments of thoughts, sketched symbols. To anyone else, they were nonsense. But to me, they meant something. Beneath the diagrams was a strange belief I couldn't explain: the world is littered with clues. Patterns and hidden laws repeating over centuries and across continents, woven into life's fabric. Fingerprints of something vast and old. I could feel them pulling at me.

I flipped through pages, the leather cover creaking beneath my hands. Then, suddenly, my fingers stopped.

A triangle.

The ink was darker here, with words I had scrawled onto the paper:

What pulls at you, lifts you up, makes you feel alive?

What moves you forward, even when it's hard?

What will you go back to protect, shelter?

I stared at it. That familiar feeling swelled again. This wasn't new. It was here, in ink. A question I had never answered.

The Creation Triad

Three forces. Three directions. A puzzle I had been circling for years. And suddenly, it wasn't a riddle; it revealed a path. I held my breath as the room seemed to press in, even as something in me expanded. I flipped to a fresh page and drew a new triangle, with a circle inside.

At the top, I wrote Love. The upward force, the source of inspiration, the flame that ignites passion.

On the right, I wrote Build. The force that moves us forward. Creation, craft, the work to make something real.

On the left, I wrote Care. This is the sustaining force, because it matters long after the shine fades.

It wasn't just a model; it was a way to navigate. To see which paths carried the weight. A guide for finding direction. When you're lost, overwhelmed, or paralyzed by options, these three forces help you cut through the noise. Love shows you what you truly want. Build reveals where you can create something that makes an impact. Care asks if it will still matter when the excitement fades. It's both a map and a filter. Not a list. A triad to reclaim direction.

Navigating the Choices

The rush of clarity was like a flash of lightning, brilliant, undeniable. But lightning fades. Life isn't a page from a journal; it's a maze of possibilities, each one pulling at you, each one promising something different.

I leaned in. It was time to apply the Triad in real life, to cut through the noise. It goes beyond eliminating choices, asking instead for clarity about which ones to pursue.

I drew three columns across the page, with each word at the top, and sketched out a symbol that represented it.

LOVE   BUILD   CARE

The Flame   *The Craft*   *The Embrace*

In the first column, I wrote what made me feel most alive: writing, nature, learning, building tools, decrypting the world, inspiring others, beautiful places, and time with my family. That was Love: the Flame.

In the second, I listed the things I was willing to struggle for. To create. To keep at it even when the work was hard. Projects, ideas, tools. Something real to put into the world. That was Build: the Craft.

In the third, I asked myself a harder question: If I built it, would it matter? Would it still hold meaning for me in the future? It wasn't enough to create. I needed to care enough to stand by it, to protect it, to keep shaping it even when the shine wore off. That was Care: the Embrace.

I went back to the list. The seven-year vision, laid out across each of the Pillars, spread out on the table. Line by line, I tested each aspiration against the Creation Triad, asking a single question: Which of them is strong in all three?

And that's when it became clear. Some options lit up Love but faded fast in Care, exciting, but shallow. Others were strong in Build, but lifeless; they didn't light me up. Only a few carried weight in all three—Love, Build, and Care—and that's where the signal was strongest.

This wasn't just about listing who I wanted to become. It was about measuring which possibilities had staying power. Sorting through them was no longer guesswork; it became a method. A way to see which options were just distractions, and which truly mattered enough to become part of my Life Direction.

Choosing One

Later, as I began using the Triad in real life, a friend reached out. He was at a crossroads: three job opportunities on the table. All viable. All reasonable. Each had its own long list of pros and cons, but he couldn't move. The more he thought about it, the heavier the decision became, until he was completely stuck.

I didn't give him advice. I just shared with him the Triad. What life did he truly want to create? To decide, he had to reflect on each role and answer three simple questions:

- Which one will have you doing things you love, day in and day out?
- Which one lets you build something that inspires you—something that feels like yours, not just maintaining someone else's machine? Where you enjoy the build?

- And finally, if you built it, would you care about what you created?

He sat back in silence. I could see it, the flicker in his eyes. The model gave him a new way to organize the choices. It stripped away the noise. It let him feel the truth beneath the spreadsheets and salary comparisons. Later, he told me: it was one of the simplest, yet most powerful ways he'd ever been guided through a hard decision. Sometimes the answers aren't out there, waiting to be found. They're already inside you, waiting for the right question.

A Canvas to Fill

The city outside was still, the background noise having long faded as the night stretched toward morning. On my cluttered living room table, in the dim light, something was taking shape.

The pages lay around me, a mosaic of words implying various future possibilities for my life. I leaned forward, the cool surface of the marble table beneath my hands, and began sorting them. Some pages I set aside, those dreams that felt empty, ambitions that belonged to someone else. The ones that aligned best with the Triad, I kept.

I took the final selection and arranged them on the table, each page side by side. I stared at it, unmoving. I could sense a silent constellation forming beneath the lamp's amber light. There it was. The first shape of a new Life Direction. A future was emerging. Unfinished and imperfect, just a draft. But it felt rich. Multidimensional. It wasn't a rigid plan; I could shape and fill it with experiences I wanted to live. With moments that would matter.

And there, in the soft light, I felt it again, the pull. The subtle magnetic pulse rising within me. The excitement for what lay ahead. A life I wasn't just dreaming about anymore but preparing to bring into being. I was ready to begin.

A New Dawn

The world was waking up. And so was I.

I rose early the next morning, the sunlight spilling across the room. Somehow, the air felt different, crisp and alive. Like possibility itself was stirring awake. I stood there for a moment, letting it all sink in, the thrill of starting again. This wasn't just another morning. It was the first step.

The realization from the night before stayed with me. I didn't have to choose. I could live multidimensionally. Still, I knew inspiration alone would not be sufficient. Clarity can flare suddenly, sharp and illuminating, then slip away just as fast. I needed a way to keep that spark alive, to give it shape, and turn it into a path I could walk.

I went back to the half-dreamed visions I had scribbled down the night before, the early shape of a plan. I looked at the pages and started to connect them, letting them take a clearer form. The seven-year horizon was there, captured on paper. Far enough for real transformation, but too distant to guide my daily actions.

So I began to move closer. I asked myself: If that's the horizon, then what needs to be in motion... in three years? What needs to be put in place, already underway? What habits are sustained? What ideas are brought to life? And here again I wrote it all down. I spent time on this, going through each item, getting to the essence of what needed to happen.

And then I narrowed the focus even more to one year out. What are the key things I must change or do this year to ensure I hit what I wanted to achieve at the three-year mark? What bold moves would bring it into being?

Line after line, the details were being etched in ink across once-blank pages. I wasn't just looking at scattered pieces. It was a path. A future with shape and gravity. A direction I could feel. This wasn't a dream anymore. It was a direction. When I stepped back and looked at it all, something struck me. It was no longer abstract. And it was more than goals. It was a system. A rhythm that could carry me forward, not just today, but across the years.

The 7–3–1 Clarity Map

And that's when the full picture took shape, not as a grand master plan, but as a living path forward. I had created a new map that anyone could use. A compass forged from within, one that reminds us who we can become when we stop limiting ourselves.

- 7 Years: What does your fully expressed life look like?
- 3 Years: What must be in motion?
- 1 Year: What bold changes begin now?

The method and steps matter. But it's not about completing a precise list. It's about becoming the kind of person who follows through. And when you begin to move with a clear direction, even slowly, even messily, your whole life starts to reorganize around it. Momentum builds, and you expand beyond the roles you thought defined you.

Then something subtle but real happens. You start to notice opportunities that support your path, where before there was just noise. And this time, you step toward them. A life once pulled apart starts to align. The drift slows. The sense of confinement gives way to possibility. And that's when the transformation gets unlocked. Over time, you become Multidimensional. Fully alive.

There is one caveat. Your dreams are in the future, but their power is only available in the present. So don't wait for the seven-year version of yourself to feel alive. Direction exists to fuel this moment. The now.

A Final Clarity

Fall had settled in. The leaves on the trees along the streets turned into a beautiful palette of deep oranges and reds. Standing at the window, I watched them drift into the air, spinning gently, a reminder that the world is always changing, always unfolding. And so had I.

Over the summer, with the 7-3-1 Clarity Map in hand, I stopped waiting and started moving. I began learning video editing to tell stories that moved people. I built a small streetwear brand with my son, living in the joy of creating and learning together. And I recorded the first clumsy episodes of a YouTube series, real if unpolished.

I poured myself into these projects because they were ignited by what I loved doing. Some weekends, I would wake up early, make coffee, and lose myself in the work, building something tangible, something I genuinely cared about. Before I knew it, the day was gone. No breaks. No pressure. Just pure immersion.

That's when I tasted Flow. Not the fleeting kind, but the kind that arrives only when Love, Build, and Care pull in the same direction.

I knew I didn't have all the answers. I didn't need them. What I had now was stronger. A renewed pull. A clear direction. Not a perfect map, but a signal I could lean into. A kind of magnetic field pulling me toward who I was becoming.

Suddenly, it dawned on me. I had asked the wrong question all along. My life wasn't a problem to fix or a puzzle to solve; it was a canvas to fill. Just waiting for color. And life direction wasn't about having a detailed drawing. It was about gaining clarity on the choices that count.

And that's where the tools came alive. The Creation Triad revealed what truly mattered, while the 7-3-1 Clarity Map took that insight and turned it into a path, a way to move forward. Together, they're not just ideas; they're a way to see your direction clearly and walk toward it.

And your future? Just like the memories of your past, it's malleable. Clay, not stone. And if you shape it with intention, with truth, you'll wake up one day and realize you're living the life you used to dream about. You don't need a perfect plan. You just need a direction worth walking.

As the late afternoon sun was setting, I picked up my notes and stared one last time at all those pages. It wasn't just a list or a plan. It was a silent oath to the person I was becoming. The tools I found were like beacons. Each one illuminated a piece of sky. When I stepped back far enough... I could at last see the full pattern forming.

Yet even with meaning, even with direction, one force remained, the one that can slowly erode it all: beliefs. Because no map can guide you if you believe you're unworthy of the journey. No direction can pull you forward if you're convinced you can't change.

I thought the hardest part was over.

I was wrong.

CHAPTER 24
Beliefs

The Rope and the Flame

The ropes bit into his wrists. Another hour. Another interrogation. The stench of sweat, metal, and blood thick in the humid air. No guarantees he would live through the night. In fact, no guarantees he would ever see the sky without bars again. And yet, somewhere beneath the bruised skin, the fractured ribs,  something stubborn stayed alive, a flame that would not go out. Admiral James Stockdale sat in a North Vietnamese prison camp for eight years. Tortured. Beaten. Left in darkness. He had no idea when, or if, freedom would come.

And still, he told himself one thing: "I will prevail." Not "maybe." Not "if the winds turn." Not "if I'm lucky." Just: I will. It wasn't blind hope. It wasn't naïve optimism. It was something more brutal, more primal. A belief. A truth he chose to hold, even as everything outside of him collapsed. When asked how he survived while so many others broke, he didn't hesitate: "You must never confuse faith that you will prevail in the end, which you can never afford to lose, with the discipline to confront the most brutal facts of your current reality."[83]

That was the difference. The ones who died were the optimists. The ones who kept thinking, we'll be free by Christmas. By Easter. By next year.

And when freedom didn't come, their hearts gave up before their bodies did. Stockdale knew better. He didn't pin his belief to a date; he pinned it to something deeper: the unshakable conviction that the story wasn't over even when he couldn't see how. Even when the world around him said otherwise. Hope is fragile because it depends on the world changing. But belief can be unbreakable because it depends on you.

The Map You Never Drew

We think beliefs are ideas. Thoughts. But they aren't. They are part of the hidden forces that shape our lives. Beliefs influence whether you continue or give up. Whether you reach for the next ledge or stop climbing altogether.

We touched on beliefs earlier: how they form, wire into your brain, and shape how you interpret the world without realizing it. That was the neuroscience view, the mechanics. But now, it's about living them. The challenge is that they're not facts. They're even less true. They're simply fictions we live by. Maps we draw in our minds that we somehow then blindly follow. They're not even ours. They were passed down and absorbed. Mental software we don't know is running.

Don Miguel Ruiz said, "Your whole point of view of your whole reality is based on what you believe you are, but what you believe about yourself is just a concept. It is knowledge, but knowledge does not mean it is the truth. Knowledge only means it is what you know."[84] Unless we change them, our beliefs can silently sabotage everything we are trying to rebuild.

I remembered a study[85] I once read: A group of average students was randomly labeled "gifted." Teachers were told these kids had high potential. By the end of the year? Those students had outperformed everyone else. Not because they were different or smarter. Because they were seen differently. Because someone believed. Belief had rewired the world around them before they even knew it. And then they started to believe it too.

Most of us don't even realize we're carrying them. Old rules. Broken compasses. Stories we picked up so long ago we forgot they were stories. And if you don't stop to rewrite them? They'll keep writing your future for you. It reminds me of something MJ DeMarco wrote in *The Millionaire Fastlane*: "Your belief system acts like a compass that, if errant, can lead you to a lifetime of detours. Fictitious beliefs are lying roadmaps; they escort you down dead-end roads."[86]

Beliefs are like the outer layer of a tree. They protect what's within, guarding the fragile structure from the elements. But when that bark thins, when the stories we live by start to crack, everything beneath is exposed. What once protected us can no longer hold. And when enough people lose that outer layer of faith, when belief itself begins to erode, the whole forest starts to wither.

The New Prisoners

Belief doesn't just die in war. It withers in the unspoken silence. I used to think that kind of collapse only happened under the weight of prison walls or extreme circumstances. But I was wrong.

Today, it happens in bedrooms. In the glow of phone screens. In the classroom, a message flashes under the desk: Shame her. Silence him. Strip someone's worth away, one click at a time. It happens silently. And then, suddenly, belief disappears, and with it, the future. Admiral Stockdale survived because he carried an unshakable belief: I will prevail. Even when the world around him gave him every reason to let go. But what happens when an entire generation grows up without that lifeline to hold onto?

I was lying in bed that evening in the fall. Outside, I could hear the gusts of cold wind, pressing against the window, whispering of winter's approach. The room was dark except for the pale glow of my iPad screen. I was catching up on the news, swiping through the headlines: wars, inflation, scandals. But then one story caught my eye.

It wasn't the first one I'd seen on the topic. In fact, I'd noticed a pattern that appeared with an unsettling frequency: the implosion of young lives. This one was about a girl called B, described by psychologist Jamieson Webster in a *New York Times* essay.[87] A teenager caught in the quiet implosion of it all. She looked around her world and saw no foothold. Climate change. Inequality. Endless medication. Friends self-harming just to feel something. Her own burgeoning future met not with hope, but with dread. The escalator, the one built into the American dream, was broken. Rusted. Going nowhere. Her parents kept telling her it would take her somewhere safe. But she could see it. They didn't even believe in it themselves. They wore the mask, told the story, pushed her toward the same life that they no longer even wanted.

And she was supposed to pretend? Pretend to strive, to smile, to reach for something that felt hollow? "They don't even pretend they want it, really!"[88] she said, the rage and sadness tangled together. So, the belief collapsed. Not just in society. In the self. In the idea that there was anything worth becoming. B didn't want to work, didn't want to chase anything. Instead, she dreamed of disappearing into a small house, far away from it all. Not to build a life, but to escape from one.

When the Flame Falters

The same collapse that Stockdale fought so hard to resist was happening all around us, invisibly. Not with ropes and fists. But with silence. With hopelessness. With the erosion of belief in the future itself. B's collapse wasn't just hers. It was a faint echo of something I felt too, an erosion that unfolded not in a war zone, but during the uncertain days of the pandemic. It was a descent without a single breaking point, a long stairway stretched over time, leading down into darkness.

The danger isn't just in broken systems, it's in broken beliefs. That's what Admiral Stockdale knew, chained in darkness. That's what B showed us, her voice fraying at the edges. When the future becomes a question mark, when the promise of something better disappears, so does the will to reach for it.

I realized it then, sitting with the stories of these young people who stopped believing, reflecting on my own life in the half-light. During the pandemic, it wasn't just the world that had lost faith. I had too.

Inside me, it happened gradually. It was like watching pieces of my life pulling back, little by little, eating away at what lay ahead. I didn't see it at first. I felt it. Dreams that once burned bright began to fade. Plans that once sparked with excitement felt heavy. It wasn't despair. It was something quieter. Colder.

The thoughts were murmurs at first: maybe it's too late. Maybe the best parts are behind me. What if the wide-open sense of possibility I used to feel was a young man's fiction. Dreams had an expiration date, and I had missed it. They worked their way in. Subtle at first. Then suffocating.. A creeping sense that the world was shrinking around me. A new belief settled in, rewriting what I thought was possible. And if I hadn't caught it, I might have mistaken it for truth. Because that's how it happens. Slowly. With a closing in.

The Ember Beneath

And yet, far beneath the surface, an ember still glowed. Fragile, buried, but alive. Without knowing, it kept me going on the darkest days. It was the promise I had made on the edge of the cliff, so faint it was barely there. But despite the storms I faced, it had never gone out.

Suddenly, I saw the promise for what it really was: belief. Belief that somehow, no matter how lost I felt, this wouldn't be the end. That there was a way through. That a life still waited on the other side. And it wouldn't be just some ordinary life. It would be better. The next chapter. One I hadn't imagined yet.

That is when I realized. It was never just a promise to myself. It was a vow to the future. And that belief, battered as it was, still had enough weight to hold me up when everything else was giving way. I didn't draw up some master plan. I did the only thing I could: I held on. First, a breath. Then a step. It showed up through tiny acts of defiance. Quiet rebellions against the voice that said, "Why bother?"

It isn't anchored on certainty or clarity. It's an act of refusal. Refusal to disappear or to go numb. Refusal to let go of the part of you that still believes this life can mean something. Belief isn't built once and carried forever. It's something you defend. Reforge. Reclaim. Every time it tries to slip from your hands. We expect complex solutions for complex problems, but sometimes the most powerful act is simply not letting go.

Lying there in bed, thoughts spiraling in my mind, I finally grasped the full weight of what I'd been through, and how close it was to derailing me. I thought of B. That quiet ache she felt inside, the disillusionment, the silence. I see it differently now. She hadn't lost hope. She lost belief in herself and in the world that awaited her. The ember had gone cold. And when belief dies, the will to live can vanish as well. That's the real danger: not failure, but forgetting that a different life is still possible.

Belief can return, even when it feels gone, even when it barely flickers. It starts small. Silent. The faintest glow in the dark. As long as there's breath, as long as you're alive, the ember remains. And from that… you can rebuild.

In my case, that ember was just enough. Enough to dare to imagine a tomorrow worth living for, to believe the story wasn't over. Even with the data showing that the system was broken, I took one step. Then another.

And now, I wasn't just piecing a life back together; I was rebuilding belief. One choice. One stubborn fragment of hope at a time. And every step became proof that the story wasn't over. I could feel the momentum building.

But belief alone can't carry a life. It must be woven. And in that moment, it felt like it finally was. The time had come to stop reflecting and start building what only I could build. A life that finally felt fully my own.

I thought that was enough. That I had arrived.

But purpose isn't something you find once.

Awareness does not mean integration.

Knowing changes nothing if you don't live it.

CHAPTER 25
Reignite

The Summit and the Silence

I had spent my life mastering systems, breaking things down into equations, frameworks, controllable parts. And for a long time, it worked. It gave me a way to climb out of the dark. Something to lean on when the rest of the world felt uncertain. But the tools I built could not answer the one question that  haunts us when the distractions finally fall away: What is this all for?

At that point, I was wrestling with how to translate the Purpose Formula into something lived, into daily life. Not as a concept, but as a way of being. Alex, my old roommate from St. Louis, reached out and invited me to his place by the ocean, a secluded stretch of coastline nestled between rainforest hills and the gentle curve of the bay.

There are people you meet who leave a deeper imprint on your way of seeing the world. With them, the conversation cuts straight to the marrow, what matters, what hurts, and what might be worth chasing. Alex was one of those people. Over the years, I'd find myself visiting him whenever life got too loud, or the questions too heavy to carry alone. So I went back to Brazil.

The air was warm and heavy, salt mixing with the damp of the jungle. That evening, we walked barefoot along the shore, the sand still warm beneath our feet. The tide was low, the ocean wide and glassy, cradling the last light.

Alex had changed. Not outwardly. He still had that same calm intensity, that quiet gaze that made you feel like he could see right through to the truth of things. But something inside him had shifted. The hunger that once radiated off him, relentless and focused, had softened. Not resignation. But the tension of a man standing at the edge of what used to drive him... unsure of what would come next.

He had sold his company. After decades of building one of Brazil's largest organic food businesses, brick by brick, guided by values he refused to compromise on, he let it go. Nestlé. Pepsi. Unilever had all come knocking. But he didn't pick the highest bidder. He chose the one that aligned with the culture he spent years cultivating. Even if it meant selling for less. "I built this with my soul," he said. "I couldn't just hand it to someone who'd gut it for margin."

We sat on the sand, the sky darkening above us. "I thought I'd feel peace," he said. "But it's strange. When you give everything to something for that long... and then it's gone... the silence feels deafening." He had taken time off, spent it with his family, traveled to faraway places, surfed remote waves, tried to catch up on all the life he'd postponed. But the silence that followed success held an unexpected weight.

"I kept thinking I'd feel... full," he said. "But instead, I started asking myself: What now? What truly matters?" His voice wasn't bitter. Just honest. He had reached the summit and found it beautiful. But also... strangely still. "So many people think that once they make it, that ache inside them will vanish," he said. "But the ache doesn't come from not reaching those heights. It comes from believing the peak you're chasing will finally make you whole. If you can't feel it on the way up, you won't feel it when you arrive."

He looked at me, eyes steady. "Purpose doesn't just arrive." That line felt like being shoved mid-step, my assumptions knocked aside. It echoed something I had only just begun to understand about myself: that life direction isn't a thing you achieve. It's something you continually create. And without it, even paradise feels empty.

Alex didn't rush back into a new title. He turned down private equity offers, advisory boards, and various high-profile roles. He chose instead to pause. To listen. To feel the shape of what came next, not out of ambition, but out of service. "I don't want to chase anymore," he said. "I want to contribute." He had the means to do anything. Yet what he craved... was purpose.

And in that moment, watching the tide roll in, I saw it again, what he had shown me all those years ago on that curb in St. Louis: the ones who are truly successful aren't the ones who have it all. They're the ones who are still connected to why they're doing it.

Chop Wood, Carry Water

The next day, I sat on his porch with a book in hand, enjoying the warmth of the morning sun. Our conversation from the evening before kept circling in my mind. There were moments where giving up didn't just feel tempting, but logical. But something kept me moving. The faint echo of a commitment I made long ago. And if I had stopped and not rebuilt... I don't know where I'd be. Maybe still going through the old motions. One of the millions of people sleepwalking through their own lives, believing they're broken when in truth, they're just adrift. Not seeing that the answer was already there, within reach.

Then a sentence stopped me. A Zen proverb I had never heard before: "Before enlightenment, chop wood, carry water. After enlightenment, chop wood, carry water."[89] I lowered the book, and stayed there, motionless. There is no escaping life. I can't fight the reality of having to feed my family. No path exempts us from the responsibilities of being human. And we can't just live outside of the world; we have to find a way to live within this broken system. No matter who you are or how free you become, you will still wake up, eat, clean, love, contribute, carry your share, and do some form of work. Nobody gets a free pass; even billionaires must pay taxes. No road exempts you from the rhythm of being alive. Enlightenment doesn't free you from the human experience. It anchors you deeper inside it.

Reflecting on my life, I realized it was never the broader societal system. I truly liked my work. I was one of the lucky ones. I had found a path that challenged me, that pushed me to grow. And in the process, I had achieved so much. So no, it wasn't work that held me back. It wasn't even the broken blueprint itself. The fact is, I had abandoned the rest of my life. I stopped showing up to the parts of me that didn't produce, didn't perform, didn't compete. And then I blamed the structure and system for what I had slowly let erode. But that was just part of the story.

Because beneath the excuses and breathless chasing, there was a deep belief that shaped so many of my choices. The belief that I had to choose. I couldn't hold both freedom and responsibility. I couldn't fully integrate the Seeker and the Analyst. And so I learned to conform to the labels, fit into the boxes, and live inside the limiting expectations of who I could be.

Answering the Question

I thought back to François's question that had haunted me for years: "Are we really living... or just running away?" At the time, I laughed it off. Brushed it aside with a drink and a story. We were the adventurers, the free spirits. But in truth, I wasn't ready to face what it really meant. Deep down, he'd hit a nerve, but I could neither see nor name the paradox he exposed, or the long quest that I would embark on to answer that single question.

Back then, I thought there were only two options: escape, or conform. And I lived both. I rode on chicken buses with nothing but a backpack and some books. And I wore suits; I held the prestigious titles. Somehow both, at different times, felt like the truth. And both, at one point, felt like prisons. But in reality, I wasn't running away. I was just searching for a way of living that felt real, a life that could hold all of me. And I didn't find it by escaping the system, or by surrendering to it.

Suddenly, I could see the connection points. Guatemala taught me that freedom without structure collapses into chaos. Entering the System showed me that structure without depth, without spark, decays into numbness. Even understanding the Pillars, the Tools, and reinforcing the Foundation, on their own, without something that unites them, could become an empty scaffolding.

In the end, it was never about choosing one over the other. Guatemala or the big city. Small job or big job. Passion or responsibility. You can master every other part of your life. You can get the house, the accolades, have the beautiful family. You can optimize your habits, your finances, and your body. And still feel hollow.

What mattered was finding a way for these forces to coexist. To be held together. Not on the edges of life, but at its center. But how do you do that?

It all came down to one missing piece. The one that connects it all.

Your *why*.

Not just knowing your why, but forging one that compels you. One that you feel at the deepest level of your being, that pulls you forward when you stumble, and fills your days with meaning.

The Thread That Binds It All

That was the 4th Shift. Not just discovering purpose, but living it, when Meaning, Direction, and Belief stop being separate threads and start functioning as one. They don't emerge by accident. Each one is deliberately forged to support the others. When any one of these is missing, purpose collapses. When all three work together, purpose becomes the integrating force of your life.

Each of the elements I uncovered on this journey—the Lens, the Tools, the Foundation—were powerful on their own, capable of shaping how you live. But without Purpose, they remain fragmented. Purpose, once built and brought to life, is what holds them all together. It gives them coherence. It allows them to move in the same direction.

That's what the 7 Pillars really is. Not a set of ideas, but a life system where the Lens, the Tools, the Foundation, and Purpose finally move together.

And that's when the old conflicts begin to dissolve: the Seeker and the Analyst stop pulling in opposite directions, freedom and responsibility no longer feel incompatible, and the question François asked stops haunting you, because it finally has an embodied answer.

Integration.

When Purpose is lived, it becomes the unifying force, the thread that connects every other part of life.

Rebuilding Purpose

Now the elements finally made sense together. But understanding alone was no longer enough. It had to turn into building. The work, I realized, had already begun months earlier, that summer, when I sat down at the table, pages spread out before me. I had done the hard part, mapping the years ahead, writing the goals, and pressure-testing each one through the same filter.

The answers didn't stay on paper. They showed up in how I spent my days, what I learned, what I built, and what I stopped chasing. It was still the early days, but over time, something had started to take shape. Imperfect, but undeniable.

Sitting there, I could see it clearly for the first time: those weren't isolated experiments. They were the early signs that my internal compass was slowly reorienting.

I hadn't just understood the Shift. I had entered it. And that's the difference. Because the Shift only becomes real when it's truly lived. Stepping all the way through that door means moving from insight to construction.

That does not happen quickly. It takes time, and it demands honesty. When the meetings are over, the kids are asleep, and there is nothing left to distract you, sit with yourself. Not the polished version you show the world. Just you, raw and unfiltered. That's when you ask the hard questions. That's when you go through each of the threads, slowly, one by one. Do the work. Use the tools, go granular. Lay it all out onto paper.

First, start by reviewing the story you've captured. Look back at the key chapters, the struggles, the choices, and the turning points, and ask yourself what they were really trying to teach you. Instead of seeing random chaos, search for the throughline. How your struggles were part of a larger arc. Then do the part most people avoid. Name the Wound, clearly, not poetically. Then Rewrite the Frame, to tell a new story. What happened? What did you decide it meant about you? This takes focus. Don't rush it. Through this process, you rebuild the narrative and bring it back into your life so it no longer feels wasted. This will strengthen Meaning: the thread that gives your past and present depth.

Second, turn to the future. Not to predict it, but to define it. You don't need every step, only the broader aim. See where you want to be in seven years, across each of the Pillars, and then work backward. This is where the 7-3-1 Clarity Map and the Creation Triad come in. They give you structure, helping you translate aspiration into something concrete.

What I hadn't understood before was this: real direction carries two forces at once—expansion and sharpening. It expands who you can be, beyond limiting roles, labels, and single paths, opening you to a version of yourself that once felt out of reach. But Direction sharpens. You begin to narrow your choices around what you love, what you're willing to build, and what you genuinely care about putting into the world.

The result is a multidimensional life, guided by Direction and powered by Love, Build, and Care. In my case, it meant building a life that made room for all of me. The creator. The leader. The writer. The father. The entrepreneur. The boy with the dreams. A bigger life, yes, but one that is clear on what actually matters.

Third, face those hidden scripts you probably don't realize you are following. The limits you've accepted. Some are outdated, others have become walls. Start to question them. Replace them. This is Belief: the thread that holds when motivation fades and pressure rises.

This is the point where the work stops being conceptual. Purpose isn't something you understand and move past. It's something you build and return to when things get hard. And it will be demanding, messy, and uncomfortable. That's not a flaw. This isn't surface-level reflection. It's the slow drafting of real answers to the most important questions of your life. The structure doesn't simplify the journey, it gives you a way to stay oriented when doubts creep in.

But Purpose isn't meant to stand alone. The Pillars show you where your life no longer holds and where you need to strengthen it. The tools—the Equation, the Ascend Wheel, the GearShift—give you ways to keep moving when the ground feels uncertain, while the Foundation reveals what lies beneath. Purpose is what brings it all together. When lived, your goals, your plans, the reason you get up in the morning start pointing in the same direction. You've built something solid enough to guide you forward as the world around you changes.

Where the Spark Begins

I sat in silence on the terrace, gazing out toward the open horizon before me. For once, I had nowhere to go. I let the time stretch and took it all in.

I thought about the years behind me, and everything I'd lived, the spiral, the collapse, and the rebuild. The constant rhythm of breaking things apart, testing them, watching some collapse, keeping others. Systems. Tools. Ideas. All of it seemed random, and yet, now the journey finally made sense. It illuminated where I'd been and gave it meaning.

And in that recognition, I made a decision. One that would redirect the course of my life. It was time to embrace what I saw, lean into it, make it real. To begin my next chapter.

For the first time in a long while, I felt that driving force again. Not just direction, but fire. To be honest, the decision terrified me, because it meant loosening my grip on the familiar rhythms of stability and success I had come to rely on.

But then, something else became clear. It was more than pursuing a path that inspired me. I wanted one that mattered. I decided to give my best to make a difference, to offer what I'd learned, the knowledge and experience that had shaped me, to anyone who could benefit. Maybe it could help just one person face their own dark spiral and find their way out.

The first step, unremarkable on the surface, was the decision to finish this book. To reenter the maze of words and commit to shaping it into work that mattered. Not flawless, just honest and accessible.

Maybe the most important thing we can offer each other... is the truth of how we find our way in life, how we transform for the better. It reminded me of something Jean Houston wrote in *A Mythic Life*: once you answer the call to a larger life, there is no turning back. She asked that we pause and consider where we stand on the arc of our own journey. "Have you heard the call? Have you refused it?"[90] For me, the answer was suddenly clear: I heard the call, and this time, I wasn't going to ignore it.

In the months that followed, after I returned to my life in Paris, I began to see this wasn't just about telling my story. The deeper narrative was still unfolding. The years of collapse, recovery, and reassembly weren't just for me. They were preparing me to see something larger just beginning to rise.

Because when you ignite purpose from the inside out, it doesn't just transform your life, it sends a signal. And that signal spreads.

And that's what rises next. The 5th Shift.

Part 7
THE CONVERGENCE

CHAPTER 26
The Signal

The Point of No Return

I couldn't sleep that night. Not from worry, but from something else that was charged, expansive, alive. What I had uncovered in the months before still echoed inside me. It was no longer theory. It had weight now. Direction. Consequence. It felt like a part of me had been rewired, and now the energy wouldn't settle.

By the time we crossed the ocean, that clarity had already taken hold. My life hadn't just moved forward, it had shifted terrain. With Claudia and her son, I packed up the remnants of that chapter, trading the old streets of Paris for the New York skyline. It wasn't just a move. It was a choice to be nearer to my children after carrying the scars of too much time spent apart. A choice to start again.

And yet, standing there in our Manhattan apartment, I felt it was about more than that. Being here wasn't just about closing that distance and rebuilding a life; it was about expanding and exploring the dimensions I had just begun to uncover within myself. And maybe that was why I couldn't sleep. Uncovering Purpose hadn't just realigned my life; it was widening the field in a way I couldn't yet grasp.

I got out of bed and wandered barefoot into the kitchen. The tiles bit at my feet, cold and grounding. Beyond the window, Manhattan stretched out, a restless tide of motion. The glow of skyscrapers pierced the night, while a streak of red taillights cut across the streets far below. I stood in the dark, feeling the rhythm of the city pulsing through it all. I could see it now: the questions I used to ask were just shadows of something larger. This was never just about me.

The Voice That Refused to Stay Quiet

It was suddenly clear. True purpose doesn't stay confined. What felt like a finish line was just the doorway. A point where everything I'd learned didn't just come together, it broke open. The question was no longer "How do I fix myself?" It was: "How do I take what I uncovered and set something larger alight?"

That voice inside me became ever more pressing. "What if everything you've learned, everything you've struggled through, wasn't just for you?" At first, I resisted that voice. I tried to drown it out, clinging to the new systems and routines I'd built. I told myself that I had enough to deal with. That the world's problems were too big, too far, too complicated. Let me just focus on my own life. That was the deal, wasn't it? But deep down, I knew that was never the deal.

Beneath the pressure, something else began to surface. This was no longer just my story. It was ours. Not just a new chapter, but a shared path. This wasn't just personal. It was collective.

The Illusion of Progress

From that point forward, I stopped looking only at individuals. I began studying broader systems. Societal structures. The hidden forces that shape entire civilizations, unseen currents guiding what we value, how we live, and who we become.[91] But something strange happened. The deeper I looked at the world outside, the clearer I saw my own reflection in it. The hundreds of books I had devoured to understand myself, the years of scribbled notes, weren't just a map of me. They were the hidden codes of the world. The forces I had battled to untangle within myself, the doubts that kept pulling me back, were the same forces shaping entire societies. Inner struggles, multiplied across millions.

It was all converging, two mirrors facing each other. What I had once seen as a personal journey, an excavation of my own soul, was suddenly re-fracted back at me, a thousand times larger. But there was something else. One missing key. A final strand I hadn't yet traced. It would appear in the most unlikely place.

We were in a taxi, inching through the crowded streets of Manhattan, my two teenage boys and my daughter with me. The air conditioner buzzed in the humid air, the faint scent of leather seats mixing with the city's fumes. Outside, skyscrapers stabbed at the gray sky as streams of people rushed beneath the glare of digital billboards. But inside, my mind was even louder, restless, fixed on a realization I couldn't set aside.

How could it be so obvious, yet nobody saw it?

And then, a voice broke through the silence.

"Dad… are you okay?"

CHAPTER 27
The Fictions We Kill For

The Realization

"Dad, did you hear me?" My eldest son's voice broke through the haze. I must've looked wild-eyed, like I'd seen something that profoundly disturbed me. And then, before I could stop myself, I blurted out: "Do you realize... almost everything we build our lives around is just made up?"

"Dad, what are you talking about?"

I took a deep breath. How do you explain this? But I had to try. "Almost everything you've been taught to trust," I said, my voice lower now, "was just invented. A concept created by someone, a story they wrote. And we've all been accepting them as if they were truths."

"Everything," I repeated, gripping the seat. "Think about it. The way we measure time. A week that starts on Monday. A life split between 'work' and 'personal,' as if they were two separate worlds. The idea that you need a degree to be 'successful,' or that owning more makes you more." He stared at me, confused but listening. "We spend years chasing grades, then jobs, then promotions. And we call it progress. But who decided that? Who wrote those rules?" Silence. The moment stretched. He shifted in his seat, unsure if this was a lecture, a joke, or something else altogether.

That realization stayed with me. I wrestled with it, couldn't let it go. Later that evening, I stood by the apartment window, looking out over the city. An endless grid of windows lit up the night, each one a fragment of someone's life. New York, the city of possibilities. But tonight, I saw something different.

The skyline wasn't just a symbol of power, it was a network of silent agreements. A vast, humming machine of routines and rules, unquestioned. A thousand lights flickering in the darkness, each one a life running on a script. But they weren't laws of nature. They were habits: patterns cast so wide they became invisible. Choices made by people who came before us, handed down, inherited, and treated as fixed. But what if, suddenly, we saw them for what they were? Not absolutes, but agreements.

That's when it hit me, and not gently, but like a blade slicing reality open: this world wasn't built to free us. It was designed to keep us asleep. And I had been one of the sleepwalkers. Until now. Because once you wake up, there are only two paths left: pretend you didn't see it or let it change everything. And I knew, with terrifying clarity, that pretending was no longer an option.

The scariest part? It all looked so solid. So permanent. But beneath all the glass and noise, I could finally see it: this place, like the world itself, was a mirage. A maze of unspoken understandings and shared illusions.

Anthony de Mello, a Jesuit priest and psychotherapist who stripped illusions down to their core, once asked: "Can you think of anything more practical than truly loving one another, and being at peace? Yet people call business, politics, and science more practical."[92] His question leaves the illusions exposed. The five-day workweek, why not four? The concept of retirement, why 65? The lie that your worth equals your output. How quickly would it all collapse?

The Invented World

What you think of as "real" in society, including nations, borders, laws, and corporations, none of it actually exists. Not in the way a mountain or the ocean does. These fictions are simply shared agreements embraced so deeply they feel immutable.

Countries? Lines drawn on maps by men who never set foot on the soil they divided. Laws? Rules made up by people no wiser than you or me, then passed down like gospel. Money? Just paper given value only because we've all agreed to treat it like gold. Even identity? Religion, class, and political affiliations are labels we inherit without question.

"It is extremely frightening to doubt the story. For if the story is false, then the entire world as we know it makes no sense," wrote Yuval Noah Harari.[93] And yet we don't just live by these fictions.

We die for them. We kill for them.

The Lies We Were Given

Look at the world today. Wars rage over imaginary lines drawn on a map. Blood spilled over beliefs shaped by geography, not truth. The "us vs. them" narratives crafted to divide and conquer.

Take Rwanda. The genocide in the mid-1990s wasn't an ancient, tribal inevitability. It was manufactured. Labels of "Hutu" and "Tutsi" were reinforced by colonial rulers, codified, and imposed. In reality, these were not two biologically distinct peoples. The line between them was blurred, even arbitrary. Physically, these groups were indistinguishable; only their identity cards set them apart.[94] But once those labels became real in people's minds, the consequences became real too. This incidental classification led to unimaginable horrors: children murdered, women violated. A million lives vanished in a hundred days. Killed not because of who they were, or some inherent difference. But because of what they were called. That's what fictions can do.

And Rwanda is not an anomaly. The pattern repeats across history. One nation against another. One race against another. One faith against another. Yuval Noah Harari, in *Sapiens*, lays it bare: humans exist in two realities. One is tangible: rivers, trees, lions. The other is entirely imagined: gods, nations, corporations. He writes, "None of these things exist outside the stories that people invent and tell one another."[95]

Once you see the machinery behind the curtain, you start to wonder: What else have I believed without question? What else have I fought for, suffered for, sacrificed for, without realizing it was built on air?

The Stories That Divide Us

Neuroscientist Robert Sapolsky takes it even deeper.[96] We're wired to defend these stories, thanks to neurological processes beyond our control. Our brains evolved for tribes. Survival depended on loyalty to a group. That wiring hasn't disappeared. It just wrapped itself in modern fictions.

Anthropologist James C. Scott, in *Seeing Like a State*,[97] demonstrates how entire governments establish order not by seeing people for who they are and what they have in common, but by labeling their differences. Ethnicity. Class. Legal status. Gridlines drawn across human lives, reflecting how systems want to manage people. What is the result? "People find it hard to care about other people beyond their own tribe or country," wrote Edward O. Wilson in *The Meaning of Human Experience*.[98]

Our world is built on fictions we never question. They harden into law, become policies, shape economies and even wars. Over time, they become history. A history built on labels and boxes, not the truth.

And that realization? It can break you or it can free you. Because if we have the power to create these illusions, we also have the power to tear them down. The world as you know it? It's not fixed. It's not final. It can be rewritten. If we can create oppressive hierarchies, we can create uplifting models that bring us together. That's not delusion. That's called design.

Have We Stopped Caring?

There's something I've watched unfold, not in headlines, but in tiny, invisible ways. A quiet dulling of the senses. It's not that people stopped caring overnight. It wasn't sudden. It was slower than that, so slow we barely noticed. A thousand tiny compromises. A thousand shrugged shoulders. Until one day, what used to make us wince... didn't. What once would have horrified us became acceptable. Another headline. Another swipe. Another thing to scroll past on the way to something else. And I can't help but wonder: What happened to us?

I remember it clearly. My son sat across the room, his face aglow with the shifting light of his phone screen. Beyond him, the New York skyline stretched like a jagged horizon. He was grinning at a video on his phone, and I asked what was so funny. He turned it toward me. It was a prank. A monkey was being tricked and terrified by a group of kids. Everyone in the comments thought it was hilarious. But I couldn't laugh. All I could see was the animal's panic. The trembling. The fear in its eyes. And what shook me wasn't just what I was seeing in the video. It was my son's reaction. He didn't even see the cruelty. Not because he's a bad person, but because this is what the world teaches us now. We've turned suffering into content. We've packaged mean pranks as entertainment. Little by little, we've become spectators to things we would have once not accepted. And suddenly, wrong starts to feel ordinary.

I felt something twist in my gut. A flicker of grief, not just for the animal, but for what we're turning into. How did we get here? How did we lose touch with that part of us that once would have said, "This is not okay." We didn't stop caring all at once. We stopped seeing. And once you stop seeing... the rest becomes easier to ignore.

And the question is: Where does it stop?

Losing Our Moral Compass

We're not living in the Dark Ages. We possess more scientific insight, greater awareness of past atrocities, and a deeper psychological understanding than any civilization before us. But look around. Does it feel like we're getting better? I'm not so sure. What scares me most isn't that we're making mistakes, it's that we're repeating them. The signs are there, even if you don't want to admit it. As a species, we are forgetting our own humanity, the ability to choose compassion over indifference.

We like to believe we're above it. But we're not. Our behavior is still shaped, deeply, by the environments we live in. By power structures. By culture. By unseen forces whispering, "This is just the way it is." We've known this for decades. The Stanford Prison Experiment revealed how quickly we can become monsters when given unchecked power.[99] College students were randomly assigned roles of prisoners and guards. Within days, the "guards" began abusing the "prisoners," some with disturbing cruelty. No one told them to. They simply stepped into the role, and the role took over.

The Milgram Experiment revealed something just as chilling.[100] Volunteers were instructed by a scientist to administer electric shocks to a stranger every time they answered a question incorrectly. Most of them obeyed, even when they believed the shocks were causing real pain. Why? Because an authority figure told them to. Ordinary people, hurting others, not out of malice, but out of obedience. These weren't evil men. They were teachers, students, and neighbors. That's the point. Under the right conditions, with the right pressure, almost anyone can become part of something cruel.

And history? It stares at us with such intensity. In every war. Every genocide. Every regime that rose while the masses stayed silent, convinced they had no choice. Cruelty can quickly slip into the mainstream. Suddenly, we've normalized the very things we once swore never to repeat.

But we do have a choice. That's what the world keeps forgetting. The danger now isn't just in the raw violence; it's also in numbness. In resignation. In slowly lowering the bar for what we allow. What we accept. What we stop noticing.

If we're not careful, it will happen again. Because human nature hasn't changed, but the systems that guide us, the moral guardrails that once held us back? They're rusting. Fading. Some are already gone. And in their place, we've built algorithms of distraction. Empires of convenience. And a kind of moral amnesia that makes nearly anything forgivable, as long as it entertains us.

If we don't wake up, truly wake up, we won't just lose our way. We'll lose something far more precious. We'll lose our ability to care. The alternative is a world where we keep slipping, one small compromise at a time. And that is a future we must refuse to accept.

That question stayed with me. Long after the city slipped past the windows of the taxi. I kept turning it over, wondering where these rules came from, and why we accept them so easily.

The Debate They Buried

We've been told a story. So often, so convincingly, we stopped realizing it was a story at all. It goes like this: Power is the natural order, because without hierarchy, without rigid control, humanity would collapse into chaos. That before civilization, before kings, before empires, people lived in a constant state of war. Violent. Brutish. Primitive. It's a convincing story. Reassuring for those in charge. Because if some form of domination is the only thing that keeps the world from falling apart, then this power structure becomes necessary. Even noble.

But what if the story isn't true? What if hierarchy isn't the default setting for humanity, but a choice? What if there is another path we walked, one that was erased, buried, forgotten? It isn't just an idea. It happened. In real societies, between real people, in periods of history where two worlds collided. In *The Dawn of Everything*, anthropologist David Graeber and archaeologist David Wengrow recount a moment that should have changed the model by which societies are built.[101]

Picture this: A cold autumn night in 1690. A group of men sat in a dimly lit French fort on the edge of what is now Canada. The fire crackled. Outside, the wind howled through the trees. Inside, two men, their breath visible in the air, their voices rising in heated debate. On one side, Baron de Lahontan, a French aristocrat, soldier, and explorer. On the other, Kondiaronk, an Indigenous Huron-Wendat leader, one of the sharpest minds of his time, known for being unafraid to speak the truth. They faced each other, wine on the table, a battle of ideas unfolding between them.

Lahontan, like any European noble, believed in the divine order of kings, the necessity of law, and that society needed structure. He argued that without rulers, without enforcement, civilization could not stand. Without control, there would be nothing but violence and ruin.

Kondiaronk laughed. Not out of disrespect, but with the calm clarity of someone who has seen another way. To him, the entire premise was absurd. "You Frenchmen," he said, "are like slaves to your own system. You talk of liberty, but you spend your entire lives obeying laws you had no say in. You call us 'savages,' yet we live without masters. No man among us has the right to command another. No one starves while another feasts. We do not hoard wealth while others suffer. And yet—you call us uncivilized?"[102] Lahontan was stunned. How did one counter such a stark, clear argument? You didn't. You ignored it. And made sure no one else heard it either.

The Civilization Model They Erased

Kondiaronk wasn't an anomaly. He was part of a culture, a vast network of Indigenous societies across the Americas, where power was often decentralized, where leaders led by persuasion rather than force, where cooperation, not domination, was the foundation of society.

That moment, those conversations, should have sparked a revolution of thought. They should have made Europe stop and ask: If another society can live without domination, what does that mean for ours? But they didn't. Why? Because the ideas were too dangerous, too threatening to the order of things. That wasn't the story Europe's elites wanted to hear. Because to acknowledge these ideas meant admitting that another way was possible. That hierarchy wasn't natural. That exploitation wasn't inevitable.

And so, the idea that Indigenous nations could offer an alternative to European power structures? Buried. Not forgotten entirely, but erased from the story we were told about progress. About what it means to be human. And what we must sacrifice for civilization. We were left with a myth, a story crafted not to reveal truth, but to justify control. The idea that civilization only moves one way: from disorder to order, from chaos to control, from "primitive" to "advanced."

But the truth remains, smoldering beneath the official version of history. There was a different way. And it wasn't a fantasy. It was lived, practiced, protected. Until it was crushed. If we look closely, every society, every civilization, organized itself around distinct models. Two of them have shaped human history and still shape the world today.

And maybe now, for the first time in generations, we're not just ready to see it. We're ready to stand up for a different model altogether. The fictions won't fall on their own. Someone has to name them. Dismantle them. Build something better. That someone… might be you. Or maybe, it already is.

Because the moment you start questioning the story, the moment you stop nodding along, you're already more awake than most.

And from that moment on, your life isn't just your own.

It's part of the rewrite.

CHAPTER 28
Domination Versus Care

The Competing Models of Civilization

When the weight of the city began to settle and New York's streets filled with last-minute holiday shoppers, I slipped away to Sedona with my children. A quiet escape from the city's pulse. Sedona had become my refuge: a place where the world slows, where noise falls away beneath the vast, unyielding sky.

New York was all momentum: a city pulsing with ambition, a world where everything felt like it was always just within reach. Sedona was the counterweight. Not fast, but deep, where the constant pressure eased.

I have seen the importance of where you live on how you feel, just one of the many lessons from the Pillars. Some places expand you, wake something buried. Sedona did that for me. Edward Abbey captured it best in *Desert Solitaire*: "This is the most beautiful place on earth. There are many such places... Every man, every woman, carries in heart and mind the image of the ideal place, the right place, the one true home, known or unknown, actual or visionary."[103] It anchored me back to childhood hikes with my father: sunlight filtering through canyon walls, stories and tales of wild, sacred places. It was a balancing force: my yin to New York's yang.

Years had passed since my first visit, since that quiet session with Elizabeth dismantled a wall I hadn't known I'd built. The canyons still held their vastness, the kind that doesn't answer your questions but somehow dissolves the noise.

Winter there is different: crisp air under a blinding blue sky, sunlight warm against red rock. We wandered with my children along the canyon's edge, the trails sinking into shadow, and for a moment, it felt like everything in the world was silent. And then my daughter's voice broke through the quiet, clear and unguarded.

"Dad... why do adults always have to be right, even when they're wrong?"

I smiled, the reflexive, soft smile parents give when they don't have an answer. I muttered something, half reassurance, half dismissal, about how sometimes people get caught up in their own opinions. But even as I spoke, I felt an emptiness in my words. They didn't answer her question. Not really. Because deep down, I knew she had touched something raw, an uncomfortable truth.

That night, after she fell asleep, I stood by the wide window of the living room, the desert stars suspended like faint signals in the dark. I pulled out my journal, opened to a blank page, and wrote her question at the top: *"Why do adults always have to be right?"*

Beneath it, I wrote quick, instinctive lines:

"What kind of world will she inherit if being right matters more than being kind? If strength means control, and progress means conquest? Is this the legacy we're handing down, a world where winning is everything, and connection is just an afterthought?"

The silence pressed in. But it wasn't just her question. It was a shadow I'd felt for years, the unseen force pushing people not just to win, but to dominate. Even here, in the stillness of Sedona, I could sense it. That relentless drive to prove. To conquer. To win. And I couldn't shake the question: What would that other way look like?

The next day, we wandered through one of Sedona's hidden sanctuaries, a bookstore tucked beside Oak Creek, where the air smelled of cedar and sage, and the light filtered through stained glass. Rows of books spoke of mysticism, healing, and ancient wisdom. They didn't just rest on the shelves; each one seemed to carry its own quiet pull, subtle as the vortex currents that shape the land around them.

I wasn't searching for anything in particular. My fingers brushed across the spines: alchemy, meditation, the nature of the soul. And then a title caught my eye: *The Power of Partnership*. A simple cover. A name I didn't know: Riane Eisler.[104]

I pulled it from the shelf and opened it. The words seemed to speak directly to the questions I had been asking but hadn't yet been able to articulate. She didn't just describe the world we inherited, she revealed the one we forgot. A buried blueprint. A lost possibility.

The Domination Model

Riane Eisler, in her groundbreaking research, proposed that human history has followed two competing models of civilization.[105] The first, the Domination model, is the one we were born into, so deeply embedded in the world around us that most people never stop to question it. From childhood, we're taught life is competition. Power is something you chase. Control isn't optional; it's expected. The strong rise. The weak fall.

In this system, wealth is concentrated at the top and kept there. Power isn't shared, it's protected. It moves in tight circles, handed from one gatekeeper to the next. Violence becomes part of the structure, sometimes visible in war and oppression, other times hidden in laws, systems, and economic rules designed not to serve, but to maintain control and order.

It's a world where your value is measured by how much you own, not who you are. Where winning matters more than fairness, and the goal is always more: more growth, more profit, more control, more domination. It's the system that built empires. That fueled colonialism. That justified slavery.[106] That turned human lives into commodities, nations into corporations, and war into business.

And worst of all? We've been conditioned to believe that this is human nature. That is just how the world works. That there's no other way. But that's a lie. Because there is another model. There has always been another model.

The Partnership Model

There is another way, a quieter path, one that has existed all along, even if it's been overshadowed, dismissed, or erased.

The Partnership Model is built on connection. It recognizes others not as threats, but as allies.[107] In this world, power isn't something you hoard, it's something you share. This isn't softness. It reflects an understanding that real strength comes from collaboration, not conquest.

In these systems, success is measured by collective well-being. Winning fades in importance. Empathy is viewed as wisdom. It's the ability to listen, adapt, to build with others rather than against them. Leadership isn't forced through fear but earned through trust. And violence? It's the last resort, not the first instinct.

This isn't about some variation of socialism, or some utopian dream where no one works and everyone expects a reward. In these societies, contribution matters. Everyone has a role. There is no free ride. You are expected to show up for your group, for the whole. This isn't about replacing one domination system with another disguised as benevolence. It isn't about control in softer clothing. It is about mutual responsibility. Shared effort. And shared benefit.

Because real partnership doesn't mean no structure. It means not pretending that central power is acting "for the people" while draining them behind the scenes. That's just domination in a different outfit.

These models have existed, in communities that valued balance over dominance, in cultures where generosity was a strength,[108] and status came not from what you took, but from what you gave, how you contributed.

This model, real partnership, isn't perfect. No system is. But it proves this: domination is not destiny. It's a choice.

Why We Rarely See It in Action

Why haven't we heard more about it? Why aren't we taught about these systems in school? There were glimpses, brief periods when societies functioned on cooperation rather than conquest. Cultures that prioritized balance. But the Domination Model doesn't just exist, it defends itself. It invades, absorbs, erases. Not just people or places, but ideas. Until we forget that other ways are even possible.

That's why the Partnership Model is so rare, not because it doesn't work, but because it gets buried. It threatens the very logic of control. If people saw another path, if they knew this way had existed, and worked, then maybe they'd stop obeying. They might stop playing the game and start building something new.

But the erasure is never complete. Traces remain in small societies organized around balance rather than power. Places where leadership means serving the broader community, the greater good, not superiority. They've been pushed to the margins. Because domination cannot tolerate alternatives. But this time, what was pushed aside is pushing back.

Crossing the Line

That evening in Sedona, after the day's momentum had subsided, the house shifted to a slower pace. I stood by the window, the silhouette of the Twin Buttes cutting into the darkening sky. Outside, the desert had settled into its night rhythms. Yet my mind refused to rest.

What had once felt like half-formed observations had sharpened. I had carried them through the days, wrestling with what was surfacing.

Standing there, I felt it clearly: a line had been crossed. We had to make different choices. We had to begin again, not from fear, but from vision. Not with more noise, but with a new clarity. The kind of clarity that doesn't just suggest, "Something's wrong." But declares, "Something else is possible."

The invitation wasn't just personal. It was collective.

And it began with a question: Would we continue to revive the machinery that drained us, or choose a different future before it was chosen for us?

CHAPTER 29
The Paradigm Shift

The Breaking Point Is Here

Sometimes, change arrives in small increments, barely noticed until it's already reshaping everything. But not this time. This is not the slow kind of change. This is a rupture. One moment, everything seems intact. The next, something snaps. Not just within us but around us. When reality no longer matches the story we've been told, and the illusions we clung to begin to give way, what we  called "the way things are" reveals itself for what it truly is: just a version. And one that no longer fits.

Philosopher Thomas Kuhn, who coined the term "paradigm shift," showed that major changes, whether in science or civilization, don't happen when people slowly update their beliefs.[109] They happen when the contradictions pile up so high that they collapse the old worldview under their own weight. Not through agreement. Through implosion.

And when that moment arrives, we have two choices: cling to the old model, sealing the fault lines and pretending the foundations still hold, or we begin again and build something new.

The pandemic was one of those breaking points. It didn't just stop the world. It shook it violently.[110] It forced billions into introspection, into existential questioning. And in that stillness, something was exposed. People saw, really saw, that the systems we've built aren't just fragile. They aren't fulfilling. People began to say it out loud:

"I'm not okay." "This can't be it."

They started asking: "Who wrote this story? And why does it hurt so much to live in it?"

And despite the chaos, despite the conflicts, despite the confusion, something deeper has been unlocked.

A shift in consciousness.

A recognition that *this*—this way of living, this endless cycle of work and consumption, this constant state of division—isn't *inevitable*. There is another way. But it will only happen if enough people choose to step forward.

And for the first time in modern history, many aren't just adapting to the system—they're walking away from it. As if a threshold had been crossed, people began making drastic choices. Some left six-figure careers to live in cabins, to wake up to the sound of birds instead of inboxes. Others packed their lives into vans, chasing beautiful vistas instead of promotions. Some moved halfway across the world to cheaper countries, not to escape, but to finally breathe and live a simpler life. These aren't breakdowns. They are breakaways.

We are even starting to see, in some groups, a rejection of tribalism, of being divided by politics, race, ideology. It's not just exhausting. It's destroying us as a civilization.

More and more people are tired of being used, of being pitted against each other, of living inside inherited stories that quietly govern their choices. They reject being reduced to sides in a battle no one truly wins.

They're searching for something real.

The Point of No Return

That's when it became clear what was actually happening. This wasn't just a wave of personal awakenings or individual change. It was something deeper.

For centuries, we organized our lives, our institutions, and our sense of success around domination: control, competition, accumulation. That logic built the world we inherited. But it is no longer holding. Not because we dismantled it, but because it's collapsing under its own weight. It doesn't inspire. It doesn't fulfill. It leaves people empty. And we feel it every day. The old logic is failing, structurally, visibly, irreversibly. And when it fails, something else begins to rise in its place.

This marks a transition toward a different organizing principle, rooted in shared responsibility. Not personal, but collective. It changes how value is measured, how power is exercised, and what kinds of systems can endure.

Everything that follows is determined by the choices we make in the years ahead. Because if the new system isn't designed with intention, the old one will reassert itself in different forms.

When Enough Voices Rise Up

Those who benefit from the old system will not let it go quietly.[111] They hold the reins. They write the laws. They are the dominant forces driving the agenda of countries. Their survival depends on people staying asleep. Systems built on fear always resist awakening. But the world is waking up.

There is this growing worry that perhaps we are trapped in old habits, that humanity might repeat the same damaging patterns no matter how much we learn. I don't believe that's the whole story. I see signs of hope everywhere. People who know that life cannot be reduced to winners and losers. They feel another way is possible, even if they don't yet have the words to describe it. They're searching for a path that hasn't been mapped. Waiting for a compass. A guide.

When enough people awaken, something begins to shift, not just individually, but collectively. At first it's imperceptible. A ripple. Then it grows. And as voices turn into action, even those clinging hardest to the old model will be forced to listen.

That's how every paradigm shift has happened in history. The resistance tries to hold the walls. Yet no wall can stop a rising tide. For all its posturing, power is fragile. Leaders, no matter how forceful they appear, depend on those beneath them to go along. No regime, no ideology, can stand if the people stop playing their part.

We don't need revolution through blood. We need revolution through vision. Through presence. This isn't a single act. It's a million quiet revolutions. A mother raising her voice, a leader stepping down with grace, or a child asking why things must be this way.

The old model used fear to maintain control. The new one will be built through care, compassion, and love—one of the few forces strong enough to bend the arc of history.[112] It's written in every sacred text. But we stopped reading and left it buried in the pages.

That's what this moment calls for. To remember the most human truth of all: that we are one. But this moment isn't asking us to agree on everything. It's asking us to take responsibility for what we design next. Because every system we live inside—economic, social, cultural—began as a story, hardened into logic, and eventually became structure.

And if the old story is breaking, then the work ahead is not to protest it forever, but to design what comes next.

I believe it has already begun.

CHAPTER 30
The New Blueprint

The New Story Begins

The world is fracturing. The model we relied on is no longer holding. Yet something is emerging in its place.

All the contradictions, the opposing forces, even the broken parts, are circling toward the same center. The forces within, and those in the world around us. The individual and the collective. The old paradigm and the new. What we once saw as separate is converging, forming a larger truth that is only now coming into focus.

Every system, every society, is built around organizing principles. A set of rules and assumptions that shape what we reward, what we fear, and what we call success. For centuries, that logic has been domination, control, and accumulation. When that logic breaks, the paradigm shifts. The belief in the old system collapses. And what follows is not an instant replacement, but a slower process of rebuilding as life begins to reorganize itself.

What comes next doesn't begin in policies or politics, but in a change in what we value, in how we see each other, and in the story we choose to believe about what it means to be human. It isn't imposed from above or engineered by force. It rises from within, through millions of individual choices that begin to align.

And that is when the bars of the old order start to bend. Not all at once. Priorities shift. Incentives change. And what once felt normal starts to feel hollow. The old structure begins to give way. Not to a new set of rules, but to early signals—operating principles that point in a different direction.

They are taking shape through the choices of builders, thinkers, and quiet creators whose purpose has stretched beyond the self. Not a finished design, nor a single path. But a different way of living, emerging as we move from the old logic and fictions we inherited toward a new Blueprint beginning to take shape.

From Fear-Based Work → To Choice-Driven Living

From a system organized by fear, where insecurity and scarcity shape how people work, to one organized around choice, where people decide what they build and how they contribute. In this logic, work adds value, supports long-term independence, and wealth expands beyond money into how time is spent and what meaning is created.

From Passive Consumption → To Active Creation

Scrolling. Watching. Numbing. It's the trap that keeps people asleep. The new model? You create more than you consume. Whether it's businesses, relationships, or impact, you move from being a spectator to being the architect of your life.

From Isolation → To True Community

We were never meant to do this alone. The old world made self-worth a solo battle. But the shift ahead is about communities that lift each other, built on meaning, not status, where we choose how we build together.

From Achievement Addiction → To Purposeful Work

The system taught us that success is about more: more titles, more promotions, more accolades. But purposeful work is about depth. About whether what you do aligns with who you are becoming, and whether your effort contributes to something larger than status or reward.

From Domination → To Care

The old model relied on domination and control to maintain order. In the new, power shifts from those who take to those who enable, who elevate. Leaders who design systems rooted in trust, compassion, and care, meant to serve the whole.

Each of these changes alone is powerful. But combined, they signal something bigger. More than isolated adjustments, they point to a fundamental reorientation in how we live together. A new structure taking form through how we work, relate, and build. This is the moment when opposing forces begin to align—when the noise of the old system fades, inherited stories loosen their grip, and people begin moving together toward a common purpose.

Convergence

This is where Purpose expands beyond the individual into a broader responsibility. Where *me* and *we* stop being separate. The work is no longer confined to the self. It extends into the world you help shape, where human life and the planet are no longer competing interests.

The old rules get rewritten, not as a new doctrine to obey, but as a direction to choose. Control and domination no longer organize how we work, lead, or build. A different set of operating principles takes their place— guided by care, responsibility, and long-term thinking, and expressed through everyday decisions, shared systems, and collective effort.

This is the 5th Shift.

And when enough people choose these principles, when enough lives, communities, and efforts begin moving in the same direction, a new structure forms, shaped by what we repeatedly choose to value and build together.

The Time Has Come to Decide

It starts with the decision to step away from the old rules. To reject the story you were handed and write your own.

This is the moment when the illusion breaks and something true cuts through, so clearly you know you'll never see the world the same way again. Awareness demands action. It pulls you forward toward a world not yet built.

But we can't fight the old world by becoming it. If we build the new with the same weapons, control, fear, and domination, we repeat the very cycle we're trying to escape. The real revolution isn't in tearing it all down. It's in building something with humanity, guided by new principles.

Imperfect, yes, but shaped by our choices.

Maybe you're one of the builders.

Maybe what comes next isn't out there, waiting to be discovered, but waiting to be created.

The choices you make next may shape not just your own life, but the world you live in... and the one we leave behind.

CHAPTER 31
Back to the Cliff

Closing the Circle

There I was again, back at the Corsican cliff where it all began. Years had passed, the signs of time now etched onto my face. Yet, there was a spark in my eyes, a lightness in my body. I stood overlooking the sea that stretched out toward the silhouette of Sardinia. I remembered the emptiness I had felt, the sense of loss, the feeling of my life unraveling before me.

I followed the narrow path down the cliffside. The sun was setting, and I felt the warm breeze gently gliding over my face. My stride was light, my senses sharpened. I walked toward the large boulder jutting out over the sea. I had sat there once, my heart aching. The rock was still there, unchanged. But the broken man who once sat there was gone.

As I lingered, the sea opening before me, I remembered the poster that once hung in my childhood room. A man diving off a cliff, fearless, suspended between sky and sea. Beneath him, a single line: "You only live once, but if you live right, once is enough."[113] I hadn't understood it then. But now, I knew. It wasn't about chasing adrenaline or escaping pain. It was about steady, daily courage. Choosing a direction you can claim as your own instead of the one handed to you. Living right is shaping a life so honest, so fully yours, that even in the mess and mystery of it you can look yourself in the mirror and say, "This is the life I choose."

I closed my eyes and drew in a slow, steady breath as the world around me began to dissolve. I could hear the waves crashing into the cliffs far below, just as they had years earlier, when I spoke those words into the void.

Time softened. And in that hush, the memories returned. Images flickered, brief scenes projected across my mind's inner screen. Somehow... through it all, I endured. That promise became a silver thread, steadying me through the downward spirals and guiding me forward as I rebuilt my life. Maybe that was the lesson: our struggles, our grief, even the darkness, are not detours. They become the catalysts that show us we're alive. The fall doesn't have to break us. It can open us, teaching us how to rise.

In that moment, I felt an energy rise inside me. What had been caught in my body, bound by the edges of my own skin, began to release. I felt one with the ground below me and the air around me. I sensed how much life still had to offer: to love, to share, to create, to grow. I saw the invisible links between all things. How we are not just shaped by the world, but actively shaping it. Not someday. Right now.

I opened my eyes and sat in silence. The sky had deepened; a few stars sparkled faintly above. And then a memory stirred. I reached into my pack and pulled out my old notebook. There they were, constellations sketched across the pages. Drawn under Icelandic skies, on windswept cliffs in Patagonia, beneath Sedona's desert sky, carried with me for years.

As I sat there, one truth shimmered in the night. We've always searched the skies. Not because the stars tell us who we are, but because we need something to reach for when the story below breaks apart. And now, when I look up, I don't just see stars. I see the thread I've traced through my life, stretched across time. A reminder: I chose this path. I walked it. I rose.

Then... it all came together. The pieces that once felt scattered fell into place, as if the entire system was assembling itself before my eyes.

The journey had unlocked the Five Doors. Not just ideas, but thresholds, points of no return. Each time I stepped through, a new world waited on the other side, where everything was different. Five Shifts, simple yet powerful. They didn't just change how I lived; they changed what I could see. And these doors were never meant for me alone.

The map was finally complete. The compass ready. Suddenly, I could see it everywhere, in everything around me. I exhaled slowly, letting the realization settle within me. Then, from somewhere deep inside, an image began to rise. I reached for my pen and drew. A form slowly emerged. A tree.

Beneath it, the foundation was alive, a hidden web running through soil, holding memory and code, interconnected to the forest itself. From it rose the roots, the Pillars, grounding the whole structure and feeding its rise, seven vantage points shaping how we see ourselves, others, and the world. The trunk followed, Purpose taking shape through its layers: the rings that hold the past and present, the upward force that reaches toward the light, and the bark that protects while it grows. Above, the branches mirrored the roots below, the tree's outer expression in the world. Within it all flowed a single rhythm, the pulse of life rising like sap, linking roots to the farthest leaves. For a long moment, I just sat with it, letting the vision expand within me.

Then I closed the notebook, my hands resting on the worn cover. A gentle breeze moved along the cliffs. I stood up, left the boulder, and stepped back onto the narrow path, stones settling beneath my feet. The stars above kept glowing, witnesses to what was unfolding. I walked in silence, the moonlight tracing a path before me.

And that's when I felt it. This guide wasn't something I invented.

It had been there all along. Waiting. Forgotten truths, lost beneath the noise. Now reclaimed.

And now... yours too.

EPILOGUE
Beyond the Shore

With morning breaking, I tasted the salt on my lips as I leaned forward into the wind, eyes locked on the pale outline of land rising in the distance. The sun struck the water in fractured golden shards.

Behind me, the cliffs of Bonifacio shrank into the soft morning haze. I didn't look back. Not because I wasn't grateful, but because I finally understood: the past is a place we pass through, not a place we live.

The small vessel cut through the last dark folds of sea. As the dock came into view, something stirred. A knowing. This was the moment I stepped away from the world I once called stable. The structures that had held me: titles, expectations, the illusion of control. Something distant, unknown, was calling me forward. This was not a detour. It was the path.

I exhaled slowly as I stepped off in Santa Teresa Gallura on the northern coast of Sardinia. My eyes scanned the winding streets, whitewashed walls lined with turquoise shutters, open to the morning sun. I turned a corner and saw her: an old woman sitting at a chipped blue table set against a stone wall. Her eyes, pale green, nearly translucent, caught mine before I could speak. Her skin looked like sun-scorched parchment, creased and alive. There was a hint of a knowing smile on her lips.

She lifted her hand, a small flick of the wrist, not a wave, more a summoning. I felt a stir of childhood curiosity cutting through the hum of my mind. I stepped toward her without thinking. A young girl appeared from the doorway behind her, maybe 12, her hair loose and dark, her eyes the color of chestnuts. She wore a white cotton dress that moved gently in the wind. She looked at me with a grin too wide for her face, as if she had already guessed my story.

The old woman pushed a stack of yellowed cards across the table. The girl pointed to a paper and said, with a strong Italian accent, "Your birth date, please." I wrote the numbers with growing curiosity, and somehow sensing this small act was important. The old woman scribbled quickly on a piece of paper, adding the numbers, then shuffled through the cards with slow precision. Finally, she pulled one card free and set it on the table between us. A bold, uneven 7 at the top, the ink slightly faded.

The girl leaned forward, translating as her grandmother's fingers traced the words on the card. "Seven... the Seeker of Truth," she said. "The one who dives beneath surface appearances, forever drawn to deeper meaning. Philosophical. Intuitive. A deep analytical mind that longs to unlock life's mysteries, and a light for others even when walking through shadow." Pointing to the page, she said: "Three plus four plus one plus nine plus seven plus one. You cannot fake it; you cannot change it. In the end, this is the only number you were born to carry."

The old woman touched the card lightly, her eyes bright and unwavering. Then she tapped her fingers against my chest, as though pointing to truths hidden within me. "This is your Life Path Number," the young girl translated, with a secretive smile.

I started to step back, but the lady raised a finger. The girl's eyes danced as she asked, "What is your full name?" "Nathan Erik Moris," I said, the words landing heavier than I expected. The old woman scribbled rapidly, her fingers blackened by years of ink. She counted each letter, her lips moving silently as if reciting an invisible code. Then she slid out a second card marked with a simple symbol, sketched in deep ink: a small structure rising from rough ground, lines radiating outward like beams. The girl looked at it, her voice turning soft: "The Builder. In numerology, this is the one who turns hidden truths into structures and shapes systems from chaos." The girl read from the card again, her voice now a soft echo: "It represents the architect of new worlds."

The old woman slid both cards toward me, her hands trembling but her gaze steady. There was a brief shimmer in her eyes, and in that instant, I felt a strange certainty that she had been waiting to hand me this single, silent confirmation. Her words echoed in my mind: *A light for others.* The day on the cliff, the promise spoken into the dark, the long journey that followed. Years of seeking. Of building. Of becoming. Of lighting a path. Until finally, I had crossed over, and now, I was here. I looked down at the two cards. A Seeker. A Builder. I laughed, not because I finally understood, but because I couldn't believe how often life places these signals in plain sight.

I climbed the narrow street, the wind moving around me like a gentle hymn, and stepped into a small square above the village. For a while, I just stood there. The view stretched in every direction. Not just sea and stone before me, but something broader. My mind carried me outward, beyond the horizon.

Looking out over the expanse of water, I could feel them. Others standing at their own edge. Breath held, heart pounding. Facing their own cliff. The same choice I had faced. To step back into what was known, or forward into what called them. The life they would choose to build.

The wind quieted. The village fell away behind me.

Ahead, only water and sky.

This isn't the end. It never was. This is the crossing.

The page is blank. The pen is in your hands.

Write the life that only you can live.

For yourself. For others.

For what comes next.

ACKNOWLEDGMENTS

To my family—my wife, Claudia, and my children—thank you. Your love and support carried me through everything, the highs and especially the lows. You believed in me when I wanted to give up. Your strength kept me going.

To the friends and mentors who walked beside me during the worst of it, who reminded me this work mattered even when I couldn't see it anymore, thank you. You might not realize the role you played. But you did. You kept me standing.

If something in these pages speaks to you, if you find even one idea worth holding onto, the best way to support this work is by leaving a review online. It seems small but it matters more than you know. Every word shared helps this reach someone else who might need it.

Thank you for reading. Thank you for being here.

ABOUT THE AUTHOR

Nathan Moris has spent three decades searching for answers. A Swiss and U.S. citizen, he studied international relations in Geneva, Switzerland, and climbed the corporate ladder across 10 cities and three continents. He became one of the youngest general managers in the European operations of a Fortune 500 company, managing large teams. He speaks four languages. He checked every box of success.

But something was missing. Standing on the cliffs of Corsica, watching his marriage and carefully constructed life come apart, he realized the conventional blueprint was broken. He spent the next decade rebuilding everything from the inside out, immersing himself in behavioral science, neuroscience, and the psychology of transformation.

The 7 Pillars emerged from that collapse and reconstruction. It's built for people who've followed the rules, chased their goals, and still feel something is off. Nathan chose to leave the stability of his senior position to pursue a more intentional path, supporting others through their own transformations and contributing on a larger scale. He now lives what he calls a multidimensional life—one where purpose, growth, and impact replace the old metrics of success.

This is his first book. His work continues at the intersection of inner exploration and building a life that is truly lived.

Follow his journey at www.the7pillars.com

HOW THIS BOOK CAME
TO BE

I started writing this over ten years ago. Back then, it was just journals, scattered thoughts I was trying to make sense of. Over the years, those fragments became essays, and the essays became chapters. I rewrote them again and again. I worked with three different professional editors at different stages, each one helping me see what the book was trying to become while keeping my voice intact. There were late nights, early mornings, moments when I almost gave up. This is the hardest thing I've ever done.

During the final stretch, I also used large language models (LLMs) and digital editing tools for consistency, phrasing, and readability. I used them the way you'd use a skilled editor or a very good thesaurus. They helped with polish and flow, and sometimes with filling gaps I couldn't quite bridge on my own. Every core story here, every concept, every moment that matters, comes from my own life and research. I reviewed everything, rewrote what needed rewriting, made the final call on every word.

Some names, identifying details, timelines, and locations have been changed or combined for narrative flow. While inspired by true events, certain conversations and moments have been reconstructed to convey the emotional truth of what I lived through.

The illustrations were developed under my creative direction, in collaboration with freelance designers, and supported by digital design tools and AI-assisted software. All visual content was created specifically for this book.

AN INVITATION

Now, it's in your hands.

Whatever your cliff is, whether it's buried pain, truth you've delayed, or a piece of yourself you left behind, you can cross each threshold. Pick up the thread. The 7 Pillars and the full transformation system are now yours.

Your life need not remain as it has been. It can be reimagined. Renewed. Expanded. The time has come to choose your path. Because the life you long for is possible.

Sometimes, all it takes is a single promise, spoken into the dark, to become the light that leads you toward the life that's genuinely yours. Beneath the surface, the roots are already reaching, quietly steadying what's beginning to grow.

And when the storms come, and they always do, let that promise carry you. Not away from who you were, but toward everything you are choosing to become. In the end, only you are the builder of your life.

Not just the one you inherited, but the one you choose to create.

Continue the Journey

If something in these pages stayed with you, the work continues beyond this book.

You can find additional tools, exercises, and resources that expand on the content at www.the7pillars.com. Ongoing reflections and conversations are available on Instagram and TikTok at @the7pillars, as well as on YouTube at youtube.com/@the7pillars.

Thank you for walking this path with me.

REFLECTIONS & NOTES

The page is blank.
The pen is still in your hands.
For what surfaces.
For what you're ready to see.
For the life you're choosing to build.

REFERENCES

[1] Julianne Holt-Lunstad, "The Potential Public Health Relevance of Social Isolation and Loneliness: Prevalence, Epidemiology, and Risk Factors," *Public Policy & Aging Report* 27, no. 4 (2017): 127–130.

[2] U.S. Department of Health and Human Services, *Our Epidemic of Loneliness and Isolation: The U.S. Surgeon General's Advisory* (U.S. Public Health Service, 2023).

[3] U.S. Department of Health and Human Services, *Our Epidemic of Loneliness and Isolation*

[4] Centers for Disease Control and Prevention, *Youth Risk Behavior Survey Data Summary & Trends Report: 2011–2021* (CDC, 2023).

[5] Rumi, *The Essential Rumi*, trans. Coleman Barks (HarperOne, 1995), 3.

[6] James Hillman, *The Soul's Code: In Search of Character and Calling* (Random House, 1996), 5.

[7] Mae West, *Every Day's a Holiday* (Paramount Pictures, 1938).

[8] Antoine de Saint-Exupéry, *The Little Prince*, trans. Katherine Woods (Harcourt, Brace & World, 1943), 63.

[9] Jaak Panksepp and Lucy Biven, *The Archaeology of Mind: Neuroevolutionary Origins of Human Emotions* (W.W. Norton & Company, 2012), 95–96.

[10] Don Miguel Ruiz, *The Four Agreements* (Amber-Allen Publishing, 2000), 155–156.

[11] Edward Abbey, *Desert Solitaire: A Season in the Wilderness* (Ballantine Books, 1968), xiv.

[12] Robert Louis Stevenson, *Travels with a Donkey in the Cevennes* (Kegan Paul, 1879), 91.

[13] M. Scott Peck, *The Road Less Traveled: A New Psychology of Love, Traditional Values and Spiritual Growth* (Simon & Schuster, 1978), 15.

[14] Rolf Potts, *Vagabonding: An Uncommon Guide to the Art of Long-Term World Travel* (Random House Trade Paperbacks, 2003), 35.

[15] See Chapter 5, "Entering the System," for original scene with François; the question recurs here as a thematic echo of freedom versus conformity.

[16] Hermann Hesse, *Siddhartha* (New Directions Publishing, 1951), 76.

[17] Pierre Béarn, *Couleurs d'usine* (Éditions du Scorpion, 1949).

[18] Paulo Coelho, *Manuscript Found in Accra* (Alfred A. Knopf, 2013), 37.

[19] Hermann Hesse, *Steppenwolf* (Henry Holt and Company, 1990), 27.

[20] Blaise Pascal, *Pensées*, no. 139, trans. Roger Ariew (Hackett Publishing, 2005), 44.

[21] Sadhguru, *Inner Engineering* (Penguin Ananda, 2016), 35.

[22] Claude François, Jacques Revaux, and Gilles Thibaut, *"Comme d'habitude,"* recorded 1967, Disc AZ OS 129.

[23] U.S. Department of Health and Human Services, *Our Epidemic of Loneliness and Isolation: The U.S. Surgeon General's Advisory*.

[24] CDC, *Youth Risk Behavior Survey Data Summary & Trends Report: 2011–2021*; World Health Organization, *Burn-out an "Occupational Phenomenon": International Classification of Diseases Update* (WHO, 2019); Gallup, *State of the Global Workplace 2023 Report* (Gallup, 2023).

[25] Panksepp and Biven, *The Archaeology of Mind*, 123–135.

[26] Jalāl al-Dīn Rūmī, *The Essential Rumi*, trans. Coleman Barks (HarperOne, 1995), 34.

[27] Iris B. Mauss et al., "Can Seeking Happiness Make People Unhappy? Paradoxical Effects of Valuing Happiness," *Emotion* 11 (2011): 807–815.

[28] Victor Webster, *This Is the Way of the Spirit* (Spiritus Press, 2019), 17.

[29] *Dhammapada*, verse 1, trans. Acharya Buddharakkhita (BPS, 1985).

[30] Will Durant, *The Story of Philosophy* (Simon & Schuster, 1926), 76.

[31] Brett Q. Ford, Iris B. Mauss et al., "Getting Happier Takes Work: The Paradoxical Effects of Pursuing Positive Emotion," *Emotion* 14, no. 5 (2014): 908–919.

[32] Eric Hoffer, *The True Believer: Thoughts on the Nature of Mass Movements* (Harper & Row, 1951), 91.

[33] Daniel Kahneman, *Thinking, Fast and Slow* (Farrar, Straus and Giroux, 2011), 417.

[34] *The Economist*, "Suicide is born of despair. Suicide prevention is from hopeless," June 16, 2018, 24

[35] Daniel Goleman, *Emotional Intelligence: Why It Can Matter More Than IQ* (Bantam Books, 1995), 60.

[36] Michelangelo Buonarroti, *The Notebooks of Michelangelo*, ed. Valerie Shrimplin (Thames & Hudson, 2005), 112.

[37] Jordan Peterson, "2 Hours for the NEXT 20 Years of Your LIFE," *Jordan Peterson Motivation* (YouTube video), November 30, 2023, https://www.youtube.com/watch?v=La_o-buk_tM.

[38] Plato, *Apology*, 38a, trans. Benjamin Jowett (Oxford University Press, 1892).

[39] Tara Brach, *Radical Acceptance: Embracing Your Life with the Heart of a Buddha* (Bantam Books, 2003), 57.

[40] Ralph Waldo Emerson, *The Essays of Ralph Waldo Emerson*, vol. 2 (Houghton Mifflin, 1904), 182.

[41] Thomas Jefferson, letter to Peter Carr, August 19, 1785, in *The Papers of Thomas Jefferson*, vol. 8 (Princeton University Press, 1953), 406.

[42] Johann Wolfgang von Goethe, *Maxims and Reflections*, no. 283 (John Murray, 1906).

[43] Ruiz, *The Four Agreements*, 81.

[44] James Clear, *Atomic Habits: An Easy & Proven Way to Build Good Habits and Break Bad Ones* (Avery, 2018), 38.

[45] Sir Dave Brailsford, "The Aggregation of Marginal Gains," *The Guardian*, August 3, 2012.

[46] Attributed to Archimedes, quoted in *The Works of Archimedes*, trans. T. L. Heath (Cambridge University Press, 1897), 127.

[47] Steve Jobs, quoted in *The Wall Street Journal*, "Steve Jobs: The Lost Interview," 1995.

[48] Tony Robbins, *Unlimited Power: The New Science of Personal Achievement* (Free Press, 1986), 34.

[49] Cal Newport, *Deep Work: Rules for Focused Success in a Distracted World* (Grand Central Publishing, 2016).

[50] Aristotle, quoted in *Protrepticus*, fragment 13, in *The Works of Aristotle*, ed. W.D. Ross (Oxford University Press, 1924).

[51] Robert Collier, *The Secret of the Ages* (Harper & Brothers, 1926), 85.

[52] Kahneman, *Thinking, Fast and Slow*; Amos Tversky and Daniel Kahneman, "Judgment Under Uncertainty: Heuristics and Biases," *Science* 185 (1974): 1124–1131.

[53] Lisa Feldman Barrett, *How Emotions Are Made: The Secret Life of the Brain* (Houghton Mifflin Harcourt, 2017).

[54] Jonathan Haidt, *The Happiness Hypothesis: Finding Modern Truth in Ancient Wisdom* (Basic Books, 2006), 4–7.

[55] Epictetus, *The Enchiridion*, trans. Elizabeth Carter (Thomas Nelson, 1900), §5.

[56] James S. Nairne, Sarah R. Thompson, and Joséfa N. Pandeirada, "Adaptive Memory: Survival Processing Enhances Retention," *Journal of Experimental Psychology: Learning, Memory, and Cognition* 33, no. 2 (2007): 263–273.

[57] Robert Plomin, *Blueprint: How DNA Makes Us Who We Are* (MIT Press, 2018); Jason M. Fletcher and Dalton Conley, *The Genome Factor: What the Social Genomics Revolution Reveals About Ourselves, Our History, and the Future* (Princeton University Press, 2017).

[58] Joseph LeDoux, *The Emotional Brain: The Mysterious Underpinnings of Emotional Life* (Simon & Schuster, 1996).

[59] Karl Friston, "The Free-Energy Principle: A Unified Brain Theory?," *Nature Reviews Neuroscience* 11 (2010): 127–138.

[60] Ruiz, *The Four Agreements*, 22.

[61] John Krakauer, *Into the Wild* (Anchor Books, 1997), 137.

[62] Caroline Myss, *Why People Don't Heal and How They Can* (Harmony Books, 1997), 69–72.

[63] Jeffrey Pfeffer and Robert I. Sutton, *The Knowing-Doing Gap: How Smart Companies Turn Knowledge into Action* (Harvard Business School Press, 2000).

[64] John Barth, *The End of the Road* (Doubleday, 1958), p. 203.

[65] For representative foundational works, see Martin E.P. Seligman & Mihaly Csikszentmihalyi, "Positive Psychology: An Introduction," *American Psychologist* 55 (2000): 5–14; Richard M. Ryan and Edward L. Deci, "Self-Determination Theory and the Facilitation of Intrinsic Motivation," *American Psychologist* 55 (2000): 68–78; and B. F. Skinner et al., *The Behavioral Design Approach* (Cambridge University Press, 1997).

[66] Dan Cable, "The Three Secrets of Resilient People," talk presented at London Business Forum, 2018; see also Dan Cable, *Alive at Work: The Neuroscience of Helping People Love What They Do* (Harvard Business Review Press, 2018).

[67] Paolo Morrison (pseudonym), conversation with the author, Todos Santos, Mexico, 2015.

[68] U.S. Bureau of Labor Statistics, *Job Openings and Labor Turnover Summary*, January 2022 release (covering 2021 data).

[69] Patrick L. Hill and Nicholas A. Turiano, "Purpose in Life as a Predictor of Mortality Across Adulthood," *Psychological Science* 25, no. 7 (2014): 1482–1486; see also P.A. Boyle, L.L. Barnes, A.S. Buchman, and D.A. Bennett, "Purpose in Life Is Associated with Mortality Among Community-Dwelling Older Persons," *Psychosomatic Medicine* 71, no. 5 (2009): 574–579, https://doi.org/10.1097/PSY .0b013e3181a5a7c0.

[70] Dan Buettner, *The Blue Zones: Lessons for Living Longer from the People Who've Lived the Longest* (National Geographic Society, 2008).

[71] Dan Buettner, *The Blue Zones of Happiness: Lessons from the World's Happiest People* (National Geographic Society, 2017), 52–55.

[72] James C. Crumbaugh and Leonard T. Maholick, "An Experimental Study in Existentialism: The Psychometric Approach to Frankl's Concept of Noogenic Neurosis," *Journal of Clinical Psychology* 20, no. 2 (1964): 200–207.

[73] Michael F. Steger, Patricia Frazier, Shigehiro Oishi, and Matthew Kaler, "The Meaning in Life Questionnaire: Assessing the Presence of and Search for Meaning in Life," *Journal of Counseling Psychology* 53 (2006): 80–93; Michael F. Scheier et al., "The Life Engagement Test," *Journal of Behavioral Medicine* 29 (2006): 291–298; Carol D. Ryff and Corey L.M. Keyes, "The Structure of Psychological Well-Being Revisited," *Journal of Personality and Social Psychology* 69, no. 4 (1995): 719–727.

[74] Ryff and Keyes, "The Structure of Psychological Well-Being Revisited," 719–727.

[75] Steger et al., "The Meaning in Life Questionnaire," 80–93.

[76] Clayton R. Critcher and David Dunning, "Purpose as a Self-Regulatory Structure: Integrating the Cognitive and Motivational Functions of Meaning," *Review of General Psychology* 19, no. 3 (2015): 298–308.

[77] Julie Beck, "Life's Stories," *The Atlantic*, December 2015. https://www.theatlantic.com/health/archive/2015/08/lifes-stories/400796/.

[78] James J. Gross, "Emotion Regulation: Conceptual Foundations," in *Handbook of Emotion Regulation*, ed. J.J. Gross (Guilford Press, 2007), 3–24.

79 Viktor E. Frankl, *Man's Search for Meaning* (Beacon Press, 2006 [orig. 1946]).

80 Kevin S. LaBar and Elizabeth A. Phelps, "Reinstatement of Conditioned Fear in Humans Is Context Dependent and Develops over Time," *Learning & Memory* 12 (2005): 302–309; see also Y. Schiller et al., "Preventing the Return of Fear in Humans Using Reconsolidation Update Mechanisms," *Nature* 463 (2010): 49–53.

81 Alan Watts, *What Is Zen?* (Vintage Books, 1973), 45.

82 Philip G. Zimbardo and John N. Boyd, *The Time Paradox: The New Psychology of Time That Will Change Your Life* (Free Press, 2008).

83 Jim Collins, *Good to Great: Why Some Companies Make the Leap… and Others Don't* (Harper Business, 2001), 86–87.

84 Ruiz, *The Four Agreements*, 156.

85 Robert Rosenthal and Lenore Jacobson, *Pygmalion in the Classroom: Teacher Expectation and Pupils' Intellectual Development* (Holt, Rinehart and Winston, 1968).

86 MJ DeMarco, *The Millionaire Fastlane* (Viperion Publishing Corporation, 2011), 27.

87 Jamieson Webster, "Teenagers Are Telling Us That Something Is Wrong with America," *The New York Times*, October 11, 2022, https://www.nytimes.com/2022/10/11/opinion/teenagers-mental-health-america.html.

88 Webster, "Teenagers Are Telling Us That Something Is Wrong with America."

89 Traditional Zen proverb, popularized in Shunryu Suzuki, *Zen Mind, Beginner's Mind* (Weatherhill, 1970), 41.

90 Houston, *A Mythic Life*, 92–93.

91 See Thomas S. Kuhn, *The Structure of Scientific Revolutions* (University of Chicago Press, 1962); Michel Foucault, *The Order of Things* (Vintage Books, 1970).

92 Anthony De Mello, *Awareness* (Zondervan, Michigan, 1990), 11.

[93] Yuval Noah Harari, *Sapiens: A Brief History of Humankind* (Harper, 2015), 115.

[94] Mahmood Mamdani, *When Victims Become Killers: Colonialism, Nativism, and the Genocide in Rwanda* (Princeton University Press, 2001).

[95] Harari, *Sapiens*, p. 33.

[96] Robert M. Sapolsky, *Behave: The Biology of Humans at Our Best and Worst* (Penguin Press, 2017).

[97] James C. Scott, *Seeing Like a State: How Certain Schemes to Improve the Human Condition Have Failed* (Yale University Press, 1998).

[98] Edward O. Wilson, *The Meaning of Human Existence* (Liveright Publishing Corporation, 2014), 177.

[99] Philip G. Zimbardo, Craig Haney, W. Curtis Banks, and David Jaffe, "The Stanford Prison Experiment: A Simulation Study of the Psychology of Imprisonment," *Naval Research Reviews* 30 (1973): 4–17.

[100] Stanley Milgram, *Obedience to Authority: An Experimental View* (Harper & Row, 1974).

[101] David Graeber and David Wengrow, *The Dawn of Everything: A New History of Humanity* (Farrar, Straus and Giroux, 2021), chapter 2.

[102] Louis-Armand de Lom d'Arce, Baron de Lahontan, *Dialogues with a Savage Named Adario* (1703), in Graeber and Wengrow, *The Dawn of Everything*, 61–63.

[103] Abbey, *Desert Solitaire*, xv.

[104] Riane Eisler, *The Power of Partnership: Seven Relationships That Will Change Your Life* (New World Library, 2002).

[105] Riane Eisler, *The Chalice and the Blade: Our History, Our Future* (Harper & Row, 1987).

[106] Eisler, *The Chalice and the Blade*, 41–47.

[107] Eisler, *The Power of Partnership*, 14–18.

[108] Riane Eisler and Douglas P. Fry, "The Systemic Nature of Domination and Partnership Societies," *World Futures* 67, no. 4–5 (2011): 285–296.

[109] Kuhn, *The Structure of Scientific Revolutions*, 66–76.

[110] Arundhati Roy, "The Pandemic Is a Portal," *Financial Times*, April 3, 2020.

[111] Naomi Klein, *The Shock Doctrine: The Rise of Disaster Capitalism* (Metropolitan Books, 2007), 17.

[112] Martin Luther King Jr., "The Moral Arc of the Universe," speech at Temple Israel of Hollywood, Los Angeles, February 26, 1965.

[113] Mae West, *The Wit and Wisdom of Mae West*, ed. Joseph Weintraub (G.P. Putnam, 1967).

www.ingramcontent.com/pod-product-compliance
Lightning Source LLC
Chambersburg PA
CBHW071630140626

46555CB00022B/2046